The Econometrics of Individual Risk

The Econometrics of Individual Risk

Credit, Insurance, and Marketing

Christian Gourieroux

Joann Jasiak

Princeton University Press

Princeton and Oxford

ISBN-13: 978-0-691-12066-9 (alk. paper)
ISBN-10: 0-691-12066-8 (alk. paper)

Library of Congress Control Number: 2006933832

A catalogue record for this book is available from the British Library

This book has been composed in Times

Typeset by T&T Productions Ltd, London

Printed on acid-free paper ⊗

pup.princeton.edu

Printed in the United States of America

10 9 8 7 6 5 4 3 2 1

To Manon

Contents

Preface

This book is an introduction to the analysis of individual risks as a newly emerging field of econometrics. We believe that there is a sufficient body of literature and a critical mass of outstanding contributions to explore this field. The aim of this monograph is to convince the reader that the econometrics of individual risks is self-contained, fascinating, and rapidly growing.

The content of the book is a course in econometric theory of individual risks illustrated using selected empirical examples. While many practical issues are discussed in the text, the goal is to establish a clear and systematic structure of theoretical findings. As with most econometric textbooks, this one is organized around various econometric models and their estimation techniques. The text examines three main domains of applications: credit, insurance, and marketing. Despite the variety of practical purposes the models presented in the text can serve, this is not a "hands-on" type of textbook that provides solutions to problems concerning the pricing of loans, bonds, and insurance policies. It is also not an overview of probabilistic modelling of risk by random variables. Monographs that provide excellent coverage of these topics already exist (for example, *Probability for Risk Management* by Hassett and Stewart and *Loss Models: From Data to Decisions* by Klugman, Panjer, and Willmot). Instead, we focus on econometric models, which involve score functions and are applicable to cross-section and panel data. Our purpose is to put together an inventory of relevant results on individual risks that are currently scattered throughout different strands of literature, and to reshape it into a coherent system of econometric methods. We hope that, as a result, this book conveys a fair and clear picture of the new discipline—a picture which students, researchers, and practitioners will be willing to contemplate.

The text covers a wide range of econometric methods. At one end of the spectrum, the reader will find very simple statistical methods, such as linear regression and the ordinary least squares estimator; at the other end are some state-of-the-art techniques, such as the latent variable polytomous probit model for serially correlated panel data and the simulated method of moments estimator. While we have strived to keep the technical part of the text as comprehensible as possible, we are obviously unable to explain all concepts from scratch, given the limited space. Therefore, we expect the reader to be familiar with the basics of mathematical statistics, and to have some background in econometrics. We encourage readers who do not satisfy these prerequisites to keep a textbook in introductory econometrics or intermediate mathematical statistics to hand. More proficient readers should consult the original publications listed among the references at the end of each chapter.

To keep a balance between the theoretical and practical content, each chapter provides at least one empirical example, based on real life data. These examples are not intended to teach rigorous econometric analysis but rather to inform the reader about the technical progress of financial institutions and insurance companies, and to point out interesting directions for applied research. Several empirical illustrations were extracted from larger projects that are beyond the scope of this book. We apologize for examples sometimes presented with only partial information. We hope that the empirical content of the book is rich enough to attract the attention of practitioners and to inspire academics. Unfortunately, in most cases, the data sources are not disclosed for confidentiality reasons, and the data sets cannot be provided by the authors. Also, the names of the companies and individuals used in the text are purely fictional.

Acknowledgments

The authors thank the editor Richard Baggaley for encouragement and support. We also thank three anonymous referees for helpful comments and Sam Clark and Ruth Knechtel for excellent assistance. Very special thanks go to Manon, the bright-eyed source of ultimate inspiration for completing this monograph.

The Econometrics of Individual Risk

1

Introduction

1.1 Market Risk and Individual Risk

People and businesses operate in uncertain environments and bear a variety of risks. As the service sector of the economy grows rapidly, the risk exposure of financial institutions, insurers, and marketers becomes more and more substantial. The risks grow and diversify in parallel with the offering of market and retail financial products, insurances, and marketing techniques. Private businesses adapt to the increasingly risky environment by implementing quite sophisticated, and often costly, systems of risk management and control. Recent corporate history has proven, however, that these are far from flawless and that financial losses can be devastating.

The risk can be viewed from four perspectives. The first concerns the occurrence of a loss event. One can think of it as an answer to the question, Did a loss event occur or not? The answer is either yes or no.[1] The second is about the frequency or count of loss events in a period of time. It answers the question, How many losses were recorded in a year? The answer is zero or any positive integer. The third refers to timing. It is about determining when a loss event has occurred. The answer is an interval of time, usually measured with reference to a fixed point of origin, such as the beginning of a contract, for example. The last is the severity. It tells us how much money is spent to cover the losses caused by a risk event. The answer is measured in currency units, such as dollars.

From all four perspectives, risk is quantifiable. Therefore, it is easy to imagine that risk can be formalized using statistical methodology. The elementary approach consists of determining what type of random variable would match the four aspects of risk listed in the last paragraph. Accordingly, the occurrence can be modeled by a qualitative dichotomous variable, the frequency by a count variable, the timing by a duration variable, and the severity by any continuous, positive variable.

The econometric analysis concerns modeling, estimation, and inference on random variables. In order to proceed to risk assessment we need to first establish the assumptions about the mechanism that generates the risk. The concept that acts as a guideline for this book is the notion that any risk is associated with an individual who is either bearing the risk or is perceived as risky by another individual. At this

---

[1] For clarity, the answer "uncertain" is not admissible.

point, an individual can be a person, a company, an insurance policy, or a credit agreement. It is crucial that it is an entity that can be depicted by some individual characteristics, which, like risk, can be quantified and recorded in a data set. The individual characteristics are an essential part of any model for individual risk assessment. Their statistical summary is called a score.

Among the approaches to risk modeling it is important to distinguish between the parametric and nonparametric methods. The parametric methods consist in choosing a model based on a specific distribution, characterized by a set of parameters to be estimated. The nonparametric approach is to some extent model free and relies on generic parameters, such as means, variances, covariances, and quantiles. The semiparametric methods bridge the gap and share some features of the pure parametric and nonparametric approaches.

In the remainder of this chapter we elaborate more on the four types of risk variable and the score. In the final part, we discuss the organization of the book.

1.2   Risk Variable

Any loss event, such as a road accident or default on a corporate loan, can be viewed as the outcome of a random phenomenon generating economic uncertainty. An event associated with a random phenomenon that has more than one possible outcome is said to be contingent or random.

Let us consider an individual car owner whose car is insured for the period January–December 2000. After this period, the realization of a random risk variable is known. According to the classification given earlier one can consider the following risk variables.

(i) **Dichotomous qualitative variable.** The dichotomous qualitative variable indicates if any road accidents were reported to the insurance agency, or equivalently if any claims on the automobile insurance were filed in the given year. To quantify the two possible outcomes, "yes" and "no," the dummies 1 and 0 are assigned to each of them respectively.

(ii) **Count variable.** The count variable gives the number of claims filed on the automobile insurance in the year 2000.

(iii) **Duration variable.** The duration variable can represent the time beginning with the issuing of the insurance policy and ending with the first incidence of a claim. It can also be the time from the incidence of a claim to the time of its report to the insurer, or else the time from the reporting of a claim to its settlement.

(iv) **Continuous variable.** The continuous positive variable can represent the amount of money paid by the insurer to settle each claim, or the total cost of all claims filed in the year 2000.

Let us consider a series of loss events recorded sequentially in time, along with a characteristic, such as the severity. This sequence of observations associated with

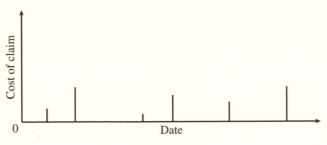

Figure 1.1. A claim history.

specific points in time forms the so-called *marked-point process*. A marked-point process can model, for example, the individual risk history of a car owner, represented by a sequence of timed road accidents. A trajectory of a marked-point process[2] is shown in Figure 1.1.

Each event is indicated by a vertical bar. The height of each bar is used to distinguish between accidents of greater or lesser severity. The bars are irregularly spaced in time because the time intervals between subsequent accidents are not of equal length.

1.3 Scores

The score is a quantified measure of individual risk based on individual characteristics. The dependence between the probability of default and individual characteristics was established for the first time by Fitzpatrick (1932) for corporate credit, and by Durand (1941) for consumer credit. Nevertheless, it took about 30 years to develop a technique that would allow the quantification of the individual propensity to cause financial losses. In 1964, Smith computed a risk index, defined as the sum of default probabilities associated with various individual characteristics. Even though this measure was strongly biased (since it disregards the fact that individual characteristics may be interrelated), it had the merit of defining risk as a scalar function of covariates that represent various individual characteristics. It was called the *score* and became the first tool that allowed for ranking the individuals in a sample. Scores are currently determined by more sophisticated methods, based on models such as the linear discriminant, or the logit. In particular, scores are used in credit and insurance to distinguish between low-risk (good-risk) and high-risk (bad-risk) individuals. This procedure is called *segmentation*. In marketing, segmentation is used to distinguish the potential buyers of new products or to build mailing lists for advertising by direct mail.

---

[2] This a selected trajectory among many possible ones.

1.4   Organization of the Book

The book contains eleven chapters. Chapters 2–6 present models associated with various types of risk variable. The risk models based on (1) a dichotomous qualitative variable appear in Chapter 2, (2) a count variable appear in Chapter 4, and (3) a duration variable appear in Chapter 6. Basic estimators and simple sample-based modeling techniques are given in Chapter 3. Up to Chapter 6 the methodology relies on the assumption of independent and identically distributed (i.i.d.) variables. Chapters 7 and 8 cover departures from the i.i.d. assumption and full observability of variables. Chapter 9 discusses multiple scores. Chapters 10 and 11, on panel data and the "Value-at-Risk" (VaR), respectively, can be seen as smorgasbords of selected topics, as comprehensive coverage of these subjects is beyond the scope of this text.

Chapters 2–7 can be taught to graduate students at either the master's or doctorate levels. At the master's level, the sections on technically advanced methods can be left out. The material covered in the first seven chapters can be taught in a course on risk management offered in an MBA program or in an M.A. program in Mathematical Finance, Financial Engineering, Business and Economics, and Economics. The text in its entirety can be used as required reading at the Ph.D. level in a course on topics in advanced econometrics or advanced risk management.[3] The text can also be used as suggested reading in a variety of economic and financial courses.

A detailed description of the book follows.

Chapter 2 considers a dichotomous qualitative risk variable. The links between this variable and individual covariates can be examined by comparing the distribution of the characteristics of individuals who defaulted on a loan with the characteristics of those who repaid the debt. Econometric models introduced in this chapter include the discriminant analysis and the logit model.

Chapter 3 presents the maximum likelihood estimation methods, their implementation and related tests.

In practice, a quality of a score may deteriorate over time and regular updating may be required to preserve its quality. Chapter 4 introduces statistical methods that allow for monitoring the score performance.

The models for count variables of risk are introduced in Chapter 5. These include the Poisson and the negative-binomial regression models, the latter accommodating unobserved heterogeneity. This chapter describes their application to automobile insurance for determination and updating of risk premiums.

Chapter 6 examines the timing of default, with the focus on the analysis of durations. We describe the basic exponential model, and study the effect of unobservable

---

[3] The first draft of the book was taught in the Advanced Econometrics class at the University of Toronto, attended by Ph.D. and M.A. students in Economics and Finance, including a group of students from the Rotman School of Management. The last five chapters were taught in Ph.D. courses on credit risk in Paris, Geneva, and Lausanne.

heterogeneity. We also discuss semi-parametric models with accelerated and proportional hazards. Applications include the design of pension funds and the pricing of corporate bonds.

Chapter 7 covers the problems related to endogenous selection of samples of individuals for risk modeling. Endogenous selection can result in biased score, wrong segmentation, and unfair pricing. Various examples of endogenous selection and the associated correction techniques are presented.

Chapter 8 introduces the transition models for dynamic analysis of individual risks. These models are used to predict risk on a portfolio of individual contracts with different termination dates.

In the presence of multiple risks, the total risk exposure has to be summarized by several scores (ratings). Examples of the use of multiple scores are given in Chapter 9. In this framework, profit maximization is discussed, and the approach for selecting the minimal number of necessary scores is outlined.

Chapter 10 examines serial dependence in longitudinal data. The Poisson and the compound Poisson models, the nonlinear autoregressive models, and models with time-dependent heterogeneity are presented.

The econometric models for credit quality rating transitions and management of credit portfolios are discussed in Chapter 11. As in Chapter 10, the content is limited to selected topics as comprehensive coverage is beyond the scope of this text.

References

Durand, D. 1941. *Risk Elements in Consumer Installment Lending*. Studies in Consumer Installment Financing, Volume 8. New York: National Bureau of Economic Research.

Fabozzi, F. 1992. *The Handbook of Mortgage Backed Securities*. Chicago, IL: Probus.

Fabozzi, F., and F. Modigliani. 1992. *Mortgage and Mortgage Backed Securities*. Harvard, MA: Harvard Business School Press.

Fitzpatrick, P. 1932. A comparison of ratios of successful industrial enterprises with those of failed firms. *Certified Public Accountant* 12:598–605, 659–62, 721–31.

Frachot, A., and C. Gourieroux. 1995. *Titrisation et Remboursements Anticipés*. Paris: Economica.

Hassett, M., and D. Stewart. 1999. *Probability for Risk Management*. Winsted, CT: Actex.

Klugman, S., H. Panjer, and G. Willmot. 2004. *Loss Models: From Data to Decisions*. Wiley.

Sandhusen, R. 2000. *Marketing*. Hauppauge, NY: Barron's.

Smith, P. 1964. Measuring risk installment credit. *Management Science* November:327–40.

2

Dichotomous Risk

The probability of the occurrence of a loss event is measured on a scale from zero to one. This chapter presents simple models for assessing the probability of a loss event represented by a dichotomous qualitative random variable.

Formally, let the loss event be denoted by A and consider the following random variable defined as the indicator of event A:

$$\mathbf{1}_A = \begin{cases} 1 & \text{if } A \text{ occurs,} \\ 0 & \text{if } A \text{ does not occur.} \end{cases}$$

It is clear that $Y = 1 - \mathbf{1}_A$ is a random variable that takes the value 0 if A occurs and 1 otherwise. Both variables $\mathbf{1}_A$ and Y take only two values, and are therefore called dichotomous qualitative variables. They are both good candidates to represent the risk of a loss. Y, however, provides a more convenient setup for risk analysis, as it allows for defining the score as a decreasing function of risk. Accordingly, to assess the probability of a loss event in a fixed period of time, we need to find the probability that Y will be equal to 0, or, equivalently, we need to predict this outcome. From now on, Y will be called the risk variable, and the probability that Y takes a given value 0 or 1 will be called the risk prediction.

In the first part of the chapter we study prediction of the dichotomous risk variable for a single individual, and introduce some key concepts such as the conditional density, conditional expectation, and conditional variance. Next we consider a group of individuals. Given the outcome of risk prediction for each individual in a population (such as the population of automobile insurance holders, for example), we can distinguish the individuals for whom outcome 1 is more likely than outcome 0, and those for whom outcome 0 is more likely than outcome 1. This procedure is called segmentation and yields two categories of individuals labeled as (expected) "good" and "bad" risks, respectively. Segmentation is discussed in the second part of the chapter. The last part of the chapter covers the more technically advanced methods of risk prediction and segmentation, based on the *linear discriminant model* and the *logit model*.

2.1 Risk Prediction and Segmentation

Let us consider individual risk and introduce risk variable Y_i, where subscript i indicates the individual. Suppose that Y_i is equal to 1 if individual i is involved in a road accident and to 0 if no accident occurs. For individual i, the occurrence of an accident can be predicted by finding the probability of $Y_i = 1$, or by finding the expected value of Y_i. The accuracy of the latter prediction will be assessed by the variance of the prediction error.

Accurate risk prediction has to be based on individual characteristics. These can include personal demographic and behavioral characteristics of individual i, such as age, gender, and occupation, as well as characteristics of the car driven by i and the environment. Risk prediction that takes account of individual characteristics is called conditional prediction of risk.

The individual characteristics may be quantitative, such as age, or qualitative, such as gender. To avoid technical difficulties in numerical calculations, the qualitative variables are frequently replaced by dummy variables, which are various types of indicator. For example, marital status can be represented by an indicator that takes the value 1 for individuals from the category "married," and 0 otherwise. By definition, indicators belong to discrete variables that take values from a finite set of admissible values. Variables that admit a continuum of values, i.e., can take on any positive or any real value, for example, are called continuous. The set of admissible values of a continuous variable can be divided into distinct categories. Then, a continuously valued individual characteristic can be replaced by the set of associated i indicator variables, which take value 1 if the individual belongs to the category and value 0 otherwise. Accordingly, age can be replaced by an indicator variable that takes the value 1 for one among the following four categories "less than 25," "25 to 30," "30 to 40," "more than 40," and the value 0 for the remaining categories. Suppose that the individual characteristics of i are quantified and written in the form of vector x_i. From now on, x_i will be referred to as an individual covariate.

2.1.1   Risk Prediction

Let us focus on one individual, and drop index i for clarity of exposition. To assess the risk associated with the individual, we consider the joint distribution of (Y, X), where Y is the dichotomous risk variable and X is the vector of individual covariates.

2.1.1.1   Conditional Probability

The first approach to individual risk prediction is based on computing the conditional probability of a loss event. For any discrete variable the conditional (respectively, marginal) probabilities of all outcomes form a conditional (respectively, marginal) probability function. The conditional probability function of the dichotomous risk variable Y given X has two components. The first is the probability that a loss event will occur, given the covariates, and the second is the probability that a loss event will not occur, given the covariates. Hence, individual risk prediction is obtained by computing the conditional probability of $Y = 0$ given X or of $Y = 1$ given X, since they sum to one.

The marginal probability function of Y consists of the probabilities that a loss event will or will not occur, regardless of individual covariates. We will see later in the text that, on average, the conditional probability is expected to provide better risk prediction than the marginal probability, which disregards the information on individual covariates.

Since Y takes only two values, 0 and 1, the conditional and marginal probabilities are easy to compute. The conditional probability function of Y given $X = x$ is denoted by

$$P[Y = 1 \mid X = x] = p_1(x), \qquad P[Y = 0 \mid X = x] = p_0(x) = 1 - p_1(x), \tag{2.1}$$

and the marginal distribution function of risk variable Y is denoted by

$$P[Y = 1] = p_1, \qquad P[Y = 0] = p_0. \tag{2.2}$$

For continuous variables, the equivalent of the conditional (respectively, marginal) probability function is the conditional (respectively, marginal) probability density function (p.d.f.).[1] Let us assume that the covariates representing individual characteristics are continuous variables with marginal multivariate density $f(x)$. The conditional probability densities of interest are the p.d.f. of X given $Y = 1$ and the p.d.f. of X given $Y = 0$, denoted

$$f_1(x) \quad \text{and} \quad f_0(x), \tag{2.3}$$

respectively. The marginal and conditional probabilities introduced so far satisfy the following relationships:

$$f(x) = p_1 f_1(x) + p_0 f_0(x), \tag{2.4}$$

$$p_1 = \int p_1(x) f(x) \, dx, \qquad p_0 = \int p_0(x) f(x) \, dx. \tag{2.5}$$

Using the Bayes formula we find the following conditional probabilities of both outcomes of Y:

$$p_1(x) = p_1 \frac{f_1(x)}{f(x)}, \qquad p_0(x) = p_0 \frac{f_0(x)}{f(x)}, \tag{2.6}$$

expressed as the marginal probability of Y times the ratio of the conditional and marginal densities of covariates. The Bayes formula shows the difference between the conditional and the marginal probabilities, and emphasizes the importance of information on individual characteristics. *A priori*, i.e., without any knowledge of X, the best possible prediction that a loss event will not occur is the marginal probability p_1. Once the information about the individual characteristics becomes available, in other words, *a posteriori*, the risk assessment can be refined so that the

---

[1] The value of a marginal univariate (respectively, multivariate) density evaluated at a given point (respectively, vector) provides the probability that the random variable takes a value (respectively, a vector of values) from the neighborhood of that point (respectively, vector).

conditional probability $p_1(x)$ can be computed. In statistics, the terms "*a priori*" and "*a posteriori*" emphasize the updating based on new or additional information on individual characteristics. At the end of the observational period, we know whether a loss event has occurred or not. Then the final updating yields

$$P[Y = 1 \mid Y, X] = \begin{cases} 1 & \text{if } Y = 1, \\ 0 & \text{otherwise,} \end{cases}$$

or, equivalently, $P[Y = 1 \mid Y, X] = Y$.

The probability updating can be summarized as follows:

p_1	$\longrightarrow$	$p_1(x)$	$\longrightarrow$	y
no information		information on X		information on X and Y
a priori		*a posteriori*		*ex post*

2.1.1.2 *Conditional Expectation*

An equivalent risk prediction is provided by the expected value of Y. If information about the covariates is not available, or is disregarded for some reason, the marginal expected value can be calculated. In contrast, if the covariate values are taken into account, the conditional expected value, that is, the expected value of Y conditional on the covariate values of a given individual, is obtained. In particular, for Y, which takes only the values 0 and 1, the conditional (respectively, marginal) expectation of Y is equal to the conditional (respectively, marginal) probability that the individual will be a "good" risk:

$$EY = P[Y = 1] = p_1, \qquad E(Y \mid X = x) = P[Y = 1 \mid X = x] = p_1(x).$$

The relationship between the marginal probability and marginal expectation on the one hand and the conditional probability and conditional expectation on the other is formalized in the property of iterated expectations. Using the iterated expectation theorem, we can rewrite the integrals in (2.5) as follows:

$$p_1 = \int p_1(x) f(x) \, dx \iff EY = EE(Y \mid X).$$

The theorem of iterated expectations tells us that for any random variable, the marginal expectation is equal to the expectation of the conditional expectation.

2.1.1.3 *Conditional Variance*

The marginal (respectively, conditional) expectation defines the mean of the marginal (respectively, conditional) probability density function of any random variable. The marginal (respectively, conditional) variance provides a measure of dispersion of a random variable about the marginal (respectively, conditional) mean.

The marginal and the conditional variances of risk variable Y, given individual covariates, are, respectively:

$$VY = E(Y - EY)^2 = p_1(1 - p_1), \tag{2.7}$$

$$V(Y \mid X = x) = E[(Y - E(Y \mid X))^2 \mid X = x] = p_1(x)[1 - p_1(x)]. \tag{2.8}$$

Note that the terms $Y - EY$ and $Y - E(Y \mid X)$ define the differences between the true Y and the predicted value of Y, which is either the marginal or the conditional expectation, depending on the available information. These two terms define the marginal and conditional prediction errors, respectively. In addition, the same expressions of variances of Y given in (2.7), (2.8) also define the variances of prediction errors. The variance of a prediction error is a measure of accuracy of the prediction.

At the beginning of this chapter, we wrote that risk prediction is better when it is based on some information about individual characteristics. Let us now provide a formal argument stating that, on average, the conditional expectation provides a better and more accurate prediction of Y than the marginal expectation. This argument can be proven by showing that the expected value of conditional variance is less than or, at most, equal to the marginal variance. To show the difference, we consider the following marginal *variance decomposition* formula:

$$VY = VE(Y \mid X) + EV(Y \mid X), \tag{2.9}$$

which implies that $VY \geqslant EV(Y \mid X)$.

On average, in a large number of repeated experiments, the variance of the conditional prediction error is less than or, at most, equal to the variance of the marginal prediction error. Since lower variance means higher accuracy, we conclude that, on average, in a very large number of repeated experiments, the conditional expectation provides a better prediction of risk than the marginal expectation, which disregards the information on individual characteristics.[2]

2.1.2 Segmentation

The prediction of individual risk from the joint distribution of risk variable Y_i and covariates X_i can be carried out in a group of individuals, such as the population of automobile policyholders insured at a given insurance company or the population of applicants for a consumer loan at a given bank. The outcome of risk prediction will be a partition of the population (sample) into two categories of "good" and "bad" expected risks, depending on whether or not the predicted probability of outcome 1 (respectively, 0) is sufficiently high (respectively, low). This operation is called segmentation.

---

[2] The fact that the conditional prediction is more accurate on average does not exclude the possibility that in a small number of trials the marginal prediction outperforms the conditional one in terms of the variance of the prediction error.

The following example illustrates the segmentation in a population of applicants for a consumer loan. Most consumers obtain credit from conventional sources such as banks, credit cards, department stores, finance companies, and so on. In standard consumer lending practices, the lenders use information on various individual characteristics, elicited in credit application forms. Typical questions include age, marital status, annual income, number of years in the current job, whether the applicant rents or owns a home, age of their car, balances on all bank accounts, amount of existing debt, type and amount of investment owned, whether the applicant has declared bankruptcy in the past, and so on. The information available to the lender also includes the features of the contract, such as the principal, the term, and the amount of monthly installments. Suppose that the credit institution has to decide whether to accept or reject an application for a personal loan, given the type of contract requested by the applicant and the available set of covariates representing her personal characteristics. The decision on credit granting is a dichotomous variable defined as follows: A denotes a subset of the set $\mathcal{X}$ of all possible covariate values. The decision-making process is

$$\text{the credit application is} \begin{cases} \text{accepted} & \text{if } X \in A, \\ \text{rejected} & \text{if } X \notin A. \end{cases}$$

The lender needs to determine the partition A, $\bar{A} = \mathcal{X} - A$ in order to maximize the expected gain, or equivalently to minimize the expected loss. The selection of applicants may induce two types of error. The lender can either "accept the application $[X \in A]$ of a 'bad' risk individual $[Y = 0]$," or "reject the application $[X \notin A]$ of a 'good' risk individual $[Y = 1]$."

In practice, these two errors imply different losses: the loan will either never be repaid, or a trustworthy customer will be denied. To formalize this problem, let the associated losses be denoted by c_0, c_1 and the gain on credit granted to a "good" risk by γ. The losses c_0, c_1 and gain γ depend on the characteristics of the contract. Let us introduce indicator function $\mathbf{1}_A$ such that

$$\mathbf{1}_A(X) = 1 \iff X \in A.$$

The expected individual gain is

$$G(A) = \gamma P[X \in A, \ Y = 1] - c_0 P[X \in A, \ Y = 0] - c_1 P[X \notin A, \ Y = 1], \tag{2.10}$$

and the *optimal credit-granting strategy* consists of selecting A in order to maximize the expected gain:

$$A^* = \arg \max_A G(A). \tag{2.11}$$

To find the solution of (2.11) we need an expression of expected gain in which the indicator variable appears explicitly. We have

$$
\begin{aligned}
G(A) &= \gamma P[Y = 1] P[X \in A \mid Y = 1] - c_0 P[Y = 0] P[X \in A \mid Y = 0] \\
&\quad - c_1 (P[Y = 1] - P[Y = 1] P[X \in A \mid Y = 1]) \\
&= \gamma P[Y = 1] E[\mathbf{1}_A(X) \mid Y = 1] - c_0 P[Y = 0] E[\mathbf{1}_A(X) \mid Y = 0] \\
&\quad - c_1 P[Y = 1] + c_1 P[Y = 1] E[\mathbf{1}_A(X) \mid Y = 1] \\
&= -c_1 P[Y = 1] + \int \mathbf{1}_A(x) [(\gamma + c_1) p_1 f_1(x) - c_0 p_0 f_0(x)] \, dx.
\end{aligned}
$$

Since the indicator function takes the values 0 and 1, the maximum is reached for the indicator function equal to 1 when $(\gamma + c_1) p_1 f_1(x) - c_0 p_0 f_0(x)$ is positive, and 0 otherwise. We obtain the following optimal credit-granting strategy:

$$
A^* = \{x : (\gamma + c_1) p_1 f_1(x) - c_0 p_0 f_0(x) > 0\}. \tag{2.12}
$$

The strategy depends on the joint distribution of (Y, X) and the relative sizes of gains and losses. The lender can optimize its credit-granting strategy by using one of the two following approaches to decision making.

(1) Under the first approach, the decision is based on the *discriminant ratio* (or *likelihood ratio*) $f_1(x)/f_0(x)$. The credit is granted when

$$
x \in A^* \iff \frac{f_1(x)}{f_0(x)} > \frac{c_0 p_0}{(\gamma + c_1) p_1}, \tag{2.13}
$$

that is, when the alternative "good risk" is more likely than the alternative "bad risk."

From the Bayes formula we get

$$
\frac{p_1 f_1(x)}{p_0 f_0(x)} = \frac{p_1(x)}{p_0(x)} = \frac{p_1(x)}{1 - p_1(x)}.
$$

Thus the discriminant ratio is an increasing function of risk prediction $p_1(x)$.

(2) Under the second approach, the credit application is accepted when

$$
x \in A^* \iff p_1(x) \geqslant \frac{c_0}{c_0 + c_1 + \gamma}, \tag{2.14}
$$

that is, when the conditional probability of "good" risk is sufficiently high.

Our discussion suggests that segmentation can be viewed either as a procedure for discriminating between the bad and good risks, which consists in testing the null hypothesis $H_0 = \{$ the individual belongs in the subpopulation of "good" risks $\}$ against the alternative $H_1 = \{$ the individual does not belong in "good" risks $\}$, or as a risk-prediction problem. While in the first case the focus is on the conditional distribution of individual covariates given risk, in the second case we are concerned about the conditional distribution of risk given the covariates. This duality in risk assessment will be explored further in Section 2.2 below.

The ratio $f_1(x)/f_0(x)$ and $p_1(x)$ are interrelated risk measures which are increasing functions of one another. They can be used to rank individuals in a sample according to the following rule: the higher the rank, the better the (expected) risk. Such a ranking would be based on a *scoring* (or *rating*) function, which associates a quantitative *score* to a given covariate value. In practice, lenders use a predetermined scoring system to make credit decisions by adding or deducting points for various individual characteristics; an applicant is accepted if the score is high enough. Generally, the absolute value of a score has no direct interpretation. The relative value of a score assigned to an individual is meaningful only when it is compared with scores of other individuals. Thus, the score is a purely comparative tool for individual ranking. It is easy to set a convenient scoring function that takes values between 0 and 1 (or 0 and 100) by transforming some other scoring function in an appropriate manner. However, it is essential that the initial and the transformed scores remain increasing functions of one another. It is important to note that $p_1(x)$ is a scoring function that is easy to interpret and lies necessarily between 0 and 1. It is called the *canonical scoring* function or the *canonical rating* function.

2.2   Econometric Models

Due to the duality in risk assessment methods, a scoring function needs to be determined either from the conditional distribution of covariates given risk, by performing so-called *discriminant analysis*, or from the conditional distribution of risk given covariates, by using the *dichotomous qualitative model*. The approach may be either parametric or nonparametric. In the remainder of this section, we consider different parametric methods including the *linear discriminant analysis* and the *logit model* (see Efron 1975; McFadden 1976; Press and Wilson 1978; Amemiya and Powell 1982).

2.2.1   Discriminant Analysis

Discriminant analysis is based on a parametric model of the conditional distributions of X given Y:

$$\left.\begin{array}{l} f_1(x) = f_1(x; \alpha), \\ f_0(x) = f_0(x; \alpha), \end{array}\right\} \qquad (2.15)$$

where $f_1(\cdot\,; \alpha)$ and $f_0(\cdot\,; \alpha)$, α varying, define two parametric families of densities of X given $Y = 1$ and $Y = 0$, respectively. The true value of parameter α in (2.15) is unknown and has to be estimated from the data (see Chapter 3).

The parametric specification of the scoring function is derived from the likelihood ratio $f_1(x; \alpha)/f_0(x; \alpha)$. After replacing parameter α by estimator $\hat{\alpha}$, we get an estimated scoring function (defined up to a multiplicative factor, which means that its value is a relative and not an absolute measure).

In practice, the number of individual covariates that lenders check is quite large (20–30). As mentioned earlier, some covariates are quantitative, while others are dichotomous or polytomous qualitative. The fact that the set of covariates includes variables of different types makes it difficult to choose an appropriate parametric specification of the conditional distribution of individual covariates. For example, we describe below the approach available for handling quantitative and conditionally normally distributed covariates.

Example 2.1 (linear discriminant analysis). Suppose that the conditional distributions of X given $Y = 1$ and $Y = 0$, respectively, are (multivariate) normal with different (vector) means m_0 and m_1, respectively, and the same variance–covariance matrix Σ:

$$f_1(x; \alpha) = \frac{1}{(2\pi)^{L/2}} \frac{1}{\sqrt{\det \Sigma}} \exp(-\tfrac{1}{2}(x - m_1)' \Sigma^{-1}(x - m_1)),$$

$$f_0(x; \alpha) = \frac{1}{(2\pi)^{L/2}} \frac{1}{\sqrt{\det \Sigma}} \exp(-\tfrac{1}{2}(x - m_0)' \Sigma^{-1}(x - m_0)),$$

where L is the number of covariates, $\alpha = (m_0, m_1, \Sigma)$, and the prime denotes the transpose.

The *discriminant ratio* is an increasing function of $(x - m_0)' \Sigma^{-1}(x - m_0) - (x - m_1)' \Sigma^{-1}(x - m_1)$, or equivalently of the scoring function:

$$S_{\mathrm{LDA}}(x) = (m_1 - m_0)' \Sigma^{-1} x.$$

Under the normality assumption, the ranking of individuals can be based on a scoring function which is linear in the covariates. This explains why the approach is called the *linear discriminant analysis*. For instance, if $\Sigma = \mathrm{Id}$, where Id denotes the identity matrix, the score becomes $S_{\mathrm{LDA}}(x) = (m_1 - m_0)' x$. The individuals have identical scores if and only if the values of their covariates lie on a line orthogonal to the line that passes through the means m_0 and m_1 (see Figure 2.1).

In the special case of only one covariate, we can set $S_{\mathrm{LDA}}(x) = x$, that is, we can use the covariate value as a scoring function.

Example 2.2 (quadratic discriminant analysis). When the conditional distributions are multivariate normal, with different variance–covariance matrices Σ_0, Σ_1 (say), the discriminant ratio is still an increasing function of $(x - m_0)' \Sigma_0^{-1}(x - m_0) - (x - m_1)' \Sigma_1^{-1}(x - m_1)$. However, this cumbersome expression cannot be simplified. We end up with a scoring function that is defined as a quadratic function of the covariates.

2.2.2 Dichotomous Qualitative Models

Banks, finance companies, and other lenders make choices about whose credit application should be accepted and under what conditions. The choices are discrete in nature and involve "either–or" situations, in which one alternative or another must be

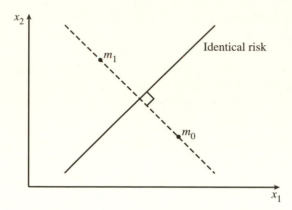

Figure 2.1. Linear discriminant analysis.

chosen. According to the assumptions made earlier in this chapter, the lender must choose between two alternatives and either accept or reject a given credit application. There exist statistical models in which the dependent variable Y is a dummy variable that takes the value 1 for one choice and 0 for the other. These models for explaining discrete outcomes assume the following parametric expression for probability of acceptance $p_1(x)$:

$$p_1(x) = g(x; \theta), \tag{2.16}$$

where g is a given function that takes values between 0 and 1, and θ is an unknown parameter. Recall that predicting Y, given the covariates of a credit applicant, is equivalent to finding the conditional probability $p_1(x)$ that the person will be "good risk" given the covariates.

There exist two standard functional forms of g under which the model is known as the logit or the probit. Some preliminary transformations of individual covariates are necessary to take into account various nonlinearities and cross-effects of basic covariates. The set of transformations of individual covariates is denoted by $z_1 = g_1(x), \ldots, z_K = g_K(x)$.

Example 2.3 (logit model).

$$p_1(x) = \frac{1}{1 + \exp(-z'\theta)} = \frac{1}{1 + \exp(-\sum_{k=1}^{K} z_k \theta_k)} = \text{logit}(z'\theta),$$

where $\text{logit}(z) = (1 + \exp(-z))^{-1}$ denotes the logistic cumulative distribution function (c.d.f.) (see Appendix 2.5 for standard properties of the logistic distribution). If parameter θ were known, then by inserting its value along with the values of the covariate transforms for a given credit applicant on the right-hand side of the last expression would yield $p_1(x)$, that is, the probability that the applicant will be trustworthy.

Example 2.4 (probit model).

$$p_1(x) = \Phi(z'\theta),$$

where Φ is the c.d.f. of the standard normal. Again, if parameter θ were known, then by inserting its value along with the values of the covariate transforms for a given credit applicant on the right-hand side of this expression would yield $p_1(x)$, that is, the probability that the applicant will be trustworthy.

In practice, the parameter values are unknown and need to be estimated from a sample of credit applications that have been previously accepted and rejected. The performance of the two models is close and the choice between the probit and logit specifications often depends on the technical skills of the analyst and the purpose of study. The next chapter outlines the details concerning estimation and inference.

It is important to note that the logit and probit models suggest the following admissible scoring function: $S(x) = z'\theta$. The score is a linear function of variables z, which are nonlinear transformations of basic covariates by $g_1, \ldots, g_K$.

More generally, risk prediction $p_1(x)$ can be written as $p_1(x) = F(z'\theta)$, where F is a given c.d.f., not necessarily of a logistic or normal distribution. This functional form has the following interpretation. Let us assume that a consumer loan has been granted, and is supposed to be repaid in monthly installments with a constant monthly payment M_0 (say). It is natural to introduce the *reservation level of a monthly payment M_i*, defined as the maximum monthly payment that the borrower can afford. It is clear that a monthly installment in excess of M_i would lead to default on the loan. Formally, default does not occur as long as the monthly payment is less than the reservation level:

$$Y_i = 1 \iff M_i > M_0.$$

According to this statement, the risk of default is a function of an unobservable (latent) quantitative variable M_i. It follows that the distribution of risk is determined by the distribution of M_i. Let us assume that

$$\log M_i = z_i'\theta + u_i,$$

where u_i has a symmetric distribution F. We have

$$
\begin{aligned}
P[Y_i = 1 \mid X] &= P[M_i > M_0 \mid X] \\
&= P[\log M_i > \log M_0 \mid X] \\
&= P[u_i + z_i'\theta > \log M_0 \mid X] \\
&= P[u_i > -z_i'\theta + \log M_0 \mid X] \\
&= F[z_i'\theta - \log M_0].
\end{aligned}
$$

As expected, the probability of no default (good risk) is an increasing function of variables z. It increases with the reservation level of a monthly payment, and decreases with the amount of monthly installments.

The unobserved reservation level of a monthly payment can be predicted. When θ and F are known, the prediction interval for M_i is

$$(\exp[z_i'\theta + F_{2.5\%}], \exp[z_i'\theta + F_{97.5\%}]),$$

where $F_{\alpha\%}$ is the α-percentile of distribution F. This prediction interval can be used to fix the budget line of an open account. For instance, $M_{0i} = \exp(z_i'\theta + F_{2.5\%})$ is the maximal budget line compatible with a default probability of 2.5%. Note that these "optimal" levels of budget line are individual dependent. In the last chapter of the book we outline more details about the structural model of default risk developed by Merton (1974).

2.2.3 Comparison of Discriminant and Logit Models

The discriminant analysis and the logit model both provide risk prediction $p_1(x)$ for a credit applicant with covariates x. It is interesting to note that the two risk representations are interrelated.

The discriminant analysis involves the conditional distribution of covariates given risk: $f_1(x) = f_1(x; \alpha)$ and $f_0(x) = f_0(x; \alpha)$, and the marginal distribution of risk

$$P[Y = 1] = p_1, \qquad P[Y = 0] = p_0.$$

It is a fully parametric model with $K + 1$ parameters that consist of vector α and scalar p_1.

The dichotomous qualitative model relies on a parametric specification of the conditional distribution $p_1(x) = g(x; \theta)$, while the marginal distribution of covariates is not constrained to be of a given parametric form. Thus, this is a semi-parametric model, with a p-dimensional parameter θ and a functional parameter f.

We see that the discriminant model is specified in greater detail, and is subject to more constraints than the dichotomous qualitative model. In general, a more constrained model (i.e., the discriminant model in our study) can be derived from a less constrained one (i.e., the dichotomous qualitative model). Indeed, the conditional probability of default computed from the discriminant model is

$$p_1(x; \alpha, p_1) = \frac{f_1(x; \alpha)p_1}{f_1(x; \alpha)p_1 + f_0(x; \alpha)(1 - p_1)}, \tag{2.17}$$

by the Bayes formula. It follows that the two types of model are compatible if for any θ (respectively, α, p_1) the system of equations given below has a solution in α, p_1 (respectively, θ):

$$g(x; \theta) = \frac{f_1(x; \alpha)p_1}{f_1(x; \alpha)p_1 + f_0(x; \alpha)(1 - p_1)}. \tag{2.18}$$

It is interesting to derive the compatibility condition for the linear discriminant model. We obtain

$$g(x; \theta)$$

$$= \left(1 + \frac{1-p_1}{p_1} \frac{f_0(x; \alpha)}{f_1(x; \alpha)}\right)^{-1}$$

$$= \left(1 + \frac{1-p_1}{p_1} \exp -\frac{1}{2}\{(x-m_0)' \Sigma^{-1}(x-m_0) - (x-m_1)' \Sigma^{-1}(x-m_1)\}\right)^{-1}$$

$$= \left(1 + \exp -\left\{(m_1 - m_0)' \Sigma^{-1} x - \log \frac{1-p_1}{p_1} - \frac{1}{2}m_0' \Sigma^{-1}m_0 + \frac{1}{2}m_1' \Sigma^{-1}m_1\right\}\right)^{-1}.$$

This leads to a logit model with a constant term $\theta_0 + x'\theta$, where

$$\theta_0 = -\log \frac{1-p_1}{p_1} - \frac{1}{2}m_0' \Sigma^{-1}m_0 + \frac{1}{2}m_1' \Sigma^{-1}m_1,$$

$$\theta = \Sigma^{-1}(m_1 - m_0).$$

The results above can be summarized as follows (see Amemiya and Powell 1982).

Proposition 2.5. *The linear discriminant model implies a logit specification of the conditional probability of a loss. In this logit specification the scoring function may be written as a linear affine function of the basic covariates.*

We conclude that the linear discriminant model is a special case of a dichotomous logit model, with the scoring function written as a linear function of basic covariates. In practice, it is preferable to use the less constrained model, that is, the logit model. This is done to avoid misspecification of the relationship between individual covariates and risk, which could entail wrong decisions about credit granting.

2.3 Risk Heterogeneity

All risk-prediction methods discussed so far perform well in practice, provided that the population of individuals (the sample) in the study is sufficiently heterogeneous, and provided that this heterogeneity can be adequately captured by the observable covariates. The role of observable heterogeneity is illustrated in Table 2.1 by data from an automobile insurance company in Canada.

The insurance holders are divided into twelve categories with respect to age and type of car use (column 1). Column 2 shows the claim frequency for each category in a given year. Column 3 presents the average cost per claim settlement for each category. We see that each class of risk has different values of claim frequency and different average costs of claim settlement. The coefficient of variation (which is the standard deviation divided by the mean) is 48.2% for claim frequency and 81.2% for average cost of settlement. Moreover, we observe that the ranking of risk categories with respect to increasing claim frequency and increasing average cost are not identical. Thus, it is not possible to measure the two different risks (which are risks associated with claim occurrence and severity) by a single score.

Table 2.1. Claim frequency and average cost of settlement.

Class	Claim frequency (%)	Average cost ($)
1	5.0	87
2	5.5	100
3	5.1	103
4	7.9	192
5	9.6	167
6	19.0	559
7	7.8	113
8	7.7	194
9	18.4	652
10	9.2	184
11	9.6	205
12	10.0	149

2.4 Concluding Remarks

In this chapter, risk associated with an individual is represented by a dichotomous qualitative variable that takes the values 0 and 1 depending on the occurrence or nonoccurrence of default. Two important topics were discussed: the optimal credit-granting strategy, and the definition of a scoring function.

We have shown that the optimal credit-granting strategy requires segmentation of the population of customers, which can be determined from a discriminant ratio or a risk-prediction model. In practice, risk prediction is more robust and outperforms linear discriminant analysis. Both approaches emphasize the importance of the scoring (rating) function, which is used to rank individuals with respect to risk. Interested readers are referred to Anderson (1958), Anderson and Bahadur (1962), Krzanowski (1975), Lachenbruch (1975), Lachenbruch et al. (1973), and Ripley (1994) for further readings in discriminant analysis and to Boyes et al. (1989), Hand and Henley (1997), Rosenberg and Gleit (1994), and Wigington (1980) for readings on consumer credit behavior.

2.5 Appendix: The Logistic Distribution

The logistic c.d.f. is $F(x) = 1/(1 + \exp(-x))$. This c.d.f. is symmetric with respect to the point $[0, \frac{1}{2}]$. The associated p.d.f. is easy to express as a function of F. Indeed we have

$$f(x) = \frac{\mathrm{d}F(x)}{\mathrm{d}x} = \frac{\exp(-x)}{(1 + \exp(-x))^2} = F(x)[1 - F(x)].$$

This density function is symmetric, and has mean zero. The variance is equal to $\frac{1}{3}\pi^2$ and the standardized logistic distribution with c.d.f., $F(\pi x/\sqrt{3})$, provides an accurate approximation of the standard normal distribution, except for the tails. This explains why the logit and probit models provide similar results for scoring.

References

Amemiya, T., and J. Powell. 1982. A comparison of the logit model and normal discriminant analysis, when the independent variables are binary. In *Studies in Econometrics, Time Series and Multivariate Statistics* (ed. S. Karlin, T. Amemiya, and L. Goodman). Academic Press.

Anderson, T. 1958. *An Introduction to Multivariate Statistical Analysis*. Wiley.

Anderson, T., and R. Bahadur. 1962. Classification into two multivariate normal distributions with different covariance matrices. *Annals of Mathematical Statistics* 33:420–31.

Ball, C., and A. Tscheogl. 1982. The decision to establish a foreign branch bank or subsidiary: an application of binary classification procedures. *Journal of Financial and Quantitative Analysis* 17:411–24.

Boyes, W., L. Hoffman, and S. Low. 1989. An econometric analysis of the bank credit scoring problem. *Journal of Econometrics* 40:3–14.

Cox, D. 1970. *Analysis of Binary Data*. London: Methuen.

Efron, B. 1975. The efficiency of the logistic regression compared to normal discriminant analysis. *Journal of the American Statistical Association* 70:892–98.

Granger, C. 1979. Outline of forecast theory using generalized cost functions. *Spanish Economic Review* March:161–74.

Hand, D. J., and W. E. Henley. 1997. Statistical classification methods in consumer credit scoring: a review. *Journal of the Royal Statistical Society* A 160:523–41.

Hastie, T., R. Tibshirani, and A. Buja. 1994. Flexible discriminant analysis by optimal scoring. *Journal of the American Statistical Association* 89:1255–70.

Krzanowski, W. 1975. Discrimination and classification using both binary and continuous variables. *Journal of the American Statistical Association* 70:782–90.

Lachenbruch, P. 1975. *Discriminant Analysis*. New York: Hafner.

Lachenbruch, P., C. Sneeringer, and L. Revo. 1973. Robustness of the linear and quadratic discriminant function to certain types of non normality. *Journal of the American Statistical Association* 68:176–79.

McFadden, D. 1973. Conditional logit analysis of qualitative choice behavior. In *Frontiers in Econometrics* (ed. P. Zarembka). Academic Press.

McFadden, D. 1976. A comment on discriminant analysis versus logit analysis. *Annals of Economic and Social Measurement* 5:511–24.

Merton, R. 1974. On the pricing of corporate debt: the risk structure of interest rates. *Journal of Finance* 29:449–70.

O'Neil, T. 1980. The general distribution of the error rate of a classification procedure with application to logistic regression discrimination. *Journal of the American Statistical Association* 75:154–60.

Press, S., and S. Wilson. 1978. Choosing between logistic regression and discriminant analysis. *Journal of the American Statistical Association* 73:699–705.

Ripley, E. 1994. Neural networks and related methods for classification. *Journal of the Royal Statistical Society* B 56:409–56.

Rosenberg, E., and A. Gleit. 1994. Quantitative methods in credit management: a survey. *Operations Research* 42:589–613.

Walker, S., and D. Duncan. 1967. Estimation of the probability of an event as a function of several independent variables. *Biometrika* 1:167–79.

Wiginton, J. C. 1980. A note on the comparison of the logit and discriminant models of consumer credit behaviour. *Journal of Financial Quantitative Analysis* 15:757–70.

3

Estimation

There are a variety of statistical data-based methods for computation and analysis of scores. In this chapter, we assume that a set of data on risk and individual covariates is available, and that we also have access to statistical software for numerical implementations. Formally, the data on both risk and individual covariates are required to be i.i.d., that is, to contain observations which are independently and identically distributed. This assumption is satisfied when the sample of observed individuals is random, that is, when each observation is drawn independently with identical probability from the same population. It becomes violated whenever unequal weights are attributed to individuals, or when these are endogenously selected (see Chapter 7). The i.i.d. assumption is a standard assumption, very often encountered in statistical literature on individual data. It is compatible with risk heterogeneity, that is, with the fact that individual risk depends on the covariates. Also, from a technical point of view, it allows us to avoid unnecessary difficulties in discussing the estimation procedures for linear discriminant and logit models, and their extensions.

3.1 Estimation Methods

3.1.1 The Maximum Likelihood Approach

Let us consider i.i.d. observations (Y_i, X_i), $i = 1, \ldots, n$, on risk and individual covariates with a distribution of a known form $f(y, x; \theta_0)$, which depends on an unknown parameter. This is a parametric model, since the family of distributions $\theta \rightarrow f(y, x; \theta)$ is known, while the true value θ_0 of the K-dimensional parameter is unknown. Our objective is to approximate, as accurately as possible, the unknown value θ_0 by a function of observations called an *estimator*. The *maximum likelihood estimator* (ML estimator) is defined as the solution

$$\hat{\theta}_n = \arg\max_{\theta} \sum_{i=1}^{n} \log f(y_i, x_i; \theta), \tag{3.1}$$

where the maximization is performed over the set of all admissible values of θ. The objective function is called the *log-likelihood function* and is denoted by $L(y, x; \theta) = \log l(y, x; \theta)$.

If the parameters are not subject to any particular equality or inequality constraints (suggested by the theory, for example), and the log-likelihood function is

differentiable with respect to the parameter, the ML estimator satisfies the system
of first-order conditions (FOCs):

$$\frac{\partial \log l}{\partial \theta}(y, x; \hat{\theta}_n) = \sum_{i=1}^{n} \frac{\partial \log f}{\partial \theta}(y_i, x_i; \hat{\theta}_n) = 0, \tag{3.2}$$

where $\partial \log l / \partial \theta$ is the vector of K partial derivatives of the log-likelihood function.

The ML estimator has good statistical properties, provided that the model is
well-specified and the number of observations is sufficiently large. Under standard
regularity conditions, which generally hold in applications of interest to us, the
following statements hold.

(i) The ML estimator is consistent, that is $\hat{\theta}_n$ tends to the unknown true value θ_0,
when the sample size n tends to infinity.

(ii) The ML estimator follows asymptotically (that is, for large n) a multivariate
normal distribution. Let us recall that a K-variate normal distribution with
mean m and covariance matrix Σ is a continuous distribution with probability
density function

$$f(y; m, \Sigma) = \frac{1}{(2\pi)^{K/2}(\det \Sigma)^{1/2}} \exp(-\tfrac{1}{2}(y - m)' \Sigma^{-1}(y - m)).$$

We write

$$\hat{\theta}_n \sim N\left[\theta_0, \frac{1}{n} I(\theta_0)^{-1}\right], \tag{3.3}$$

where the variance–covariance matrix is proportional to the inverse of the
Fisher information matrix:

$$\begin{aligned}
I(\theta_0) &= \underset{\theta_0}{E}\left[-\frac{\partial^2 \log f(Y, X; \theta_0)}{\partial \theta \partial \theta'} \right] \\
&= \underset{\theta_0}{E}\left[\frac{\partial \log f(Y, X; \theta_0)}{\partial \theta} \frac{\partial \log f(Y, X; \theta_0)}{\partial \theta'} \right].
\end{aligned} \tag{3.4}$$

In formula (3.4) the expectation taken with respect to the true distribution of
(Y, X) is denoted by $\underset{\theta_0}{E}$.

(iii) The ML estimator is asymptotically unbiased:

$$\underset{\theta_0}{E}\hat{\theta}_n \simeq \theta_0.$$

This means that, on average, the estimator hits the target in a large number
of replicated estimations. It is also asymptotically efficient, which means
that it has the lowest asymptotic variance among all asymptotically unbiased
estimators.

Since the variance of the ML estimator depends on the unknown true value θ_0, it has to be estimated by replacing the true parameter value with an estimated one. Specifically, the asymptotic variance can be consistently estimated from the information matrix in (3.4) by computing either

$$\frac{1}{n}\hat{I}_n^{-1} = \frac{1}{n}\left[\frac{1}{n}\sum_{i=1}^{n}\frac{\partial \log f}{\partial \theta}(y_i, x_i; \hat{\theta}_n)\frac{\partial \log f}{\partial \theta'}(y_i, x_i; \hat{\theta}_n)\right]^{-1}, \qquad (3.5)$$

or

$$\frac{1}{n}\hat{J}_n^{-1} = \frac{1}{n}\left[-\frac{1}{n}\sum_{i=1}^{n}\frac{\partial^2 \log f}{\partial \theta \partial \theta'}(y_i, x_i; \hat{\theta}_n)\right]^{-1}, \qquad (3.6)$$

or

$$\hat{V}_n = \frac{1}{n}[I(\hat{\theta}_n)]^{-1} = \frac{1}{n}E_{\hat{\theta}_n}\left[\frac{\partial^2 \log f}{\partial \theta \partial \theta'}(y_i, x_i; \hat{\theta}_n)\right]^{-1}. \qquad (3.7)$$

The estimators of asymptotic variance are asymptotically equivalent:

$$\hat{V}_n \approx \frac{1}{n}\hat{I}_n^{-1} \approx \frac{1}{n}\hat{J}_n^{-1}.$$

Remark 3.1. The ML approach can be applied to a model in which only the conditional distribution of Y_i given X_i is specified, and depends on some unknown parameters. For the family of conditional distributions $f(y \mid x; \theta)$ and the true value of the parameter θ_0, the *conditional ML estimator* is given by

$$\hat{\theta}_n = \arg\max_{\theta}\sum_{i=1}^{n}\log f(y_i \mid x_i; \theta) = \arg\max_{\theta}\log l(y \mid x; \theta).$$

The properties of the conditional ML estimator are similar to the properties of the ML estimator. The formulas given above remain valid upon replacing the joint p.d.f. $f(y, x; \theta)$ with the conditional density $f(y \mid x; \theta_0)$.

3.1.2 Maximum Likelihood Estimation of a Logit Model

A logit model represents the conditional distribution of dichotomous risk given the covariates. The conditional probability of $Y_i = 1$ (good risk) is

$$p_1(x_i) = \frac{1}{1 + \exp(-z_i'\theta)} = \text{logit}(z_i'\theta), \qquad (3.8)$$

where the z_i variables are transformations of basic covariates x_i. The endogenous variable in the model to be estimated is Y. The observations on Y consist of zeros and ones for all individuals in the sample of size n, depending on whether or not individual i has defaulted in a given fixed period of time. The conditional p.d.f. is a

Bernoulli density function:

$$f(y_i \mid x_i; \theta) = \left[\frac{1}{1 + \exp(-z_i'\theta)}\right]^{y_i} \left[\frac{\exp(-z_i'\theta)}{1 + \exp(-z_i'\theta)}\right]^{1-y_i}$$

$$= \begin{cases} \dfrac{1}{1 + \exp(-z_i'\theta)} = \text{logit}(z_i'\theta) & \text{if } y_i = 1, \\[3mm] \dfrac{\exp(-z_i'\theta)}{1 + \exp(-z_i'\theta)} = 1 - \text{logit}(z_i'\theta) & \text{if } y_i = 0. \end{cases} \tag{3.9}$$

The conditional log-likelihood function is given by

$$\log l(y \mid x; \theta) = \sum_{i=1}^{n} \left\{ y_i \log\left(\frac{1}{1 + \exp(-z_i'\theta)}\right) + (1 - y_i) \log\left(\frac{\exp(-z_i'\theta)}{1 + \exp(-z_i'\theta)}\right) \right\}$$

$$= \sum_{i=1}^{n} \{-\log[1 + \exp(-z_i'\theta)] - (1 - y_i)z_i'\theta\}.$$

The FOCs are

$$\frac{\partial \log l(y \mid x; \hat{\theta}_n)}{\partial \theta} = 0 \iff \sum_{i=1}^{n} z_i \left[y_i - \frac{1}{1 + \exp(-z_i'\hat{\theta}_n)} \right] = 0$$

$$\iff \sum_{i=1}^{n} z_i \left[y_i - \text{logit}(z_i'\hat{\theta}_n) \right] = 0. \tag{3.10}$$

The first-order conditions in (3.10) resemble the orthogonality conditions for residuals and explanatory variables in a standard linear regression model. Let us define the residuals of a logit model:

$$\hat{u}_i = y_i - \text{logit}(z_i'\hat{\theta}_n), \quad i = 1, \ldots, n. \tag{3.11}$$

These residuals measure the discrepancy between the endogenous variable y_i and its fitted value obtained from the model. In our case the residual defines the difference between the true risk y_i associated with an individual and its approximation by the canonical score $\hat{p}_1(x_i) = \text{logit}(z_i'\hat{\theta}_n)$. In this context, the first-order conditions simply become the orthogonality conditions for variables $z_{i,k}$ and the residuals

$$\sum_{i=1}^{n} z_{i,k}\hat{u}_i = 0, \quad k = 1, \ldots, K.$$

The asymptotic variance of the estimator can be approximated by formula (3.6). Since

$$\frac{\partial^2 \log l(y \mid x; \theta)}{\partial \theta \partial \theta'} = -\sum_{i=1}^{n} z_i' z_i \, \text{logit}(z_i'\theta)[1 - \text{logit}(z_i'\theta)],$$

we find the estimated asymptotic variance expression

$$\hat{V}(\hat{\theta}_n) \simeq \left\{ \sum_{i=1}^{n} z_i' z_i \operatorname{logit}(z_i'\hat{\theta}_n)[1 - \operatorname{logit}(z_i'\hat{\theta}_n)] \right\}^{-1}. \qquad (3.12)$$

The asymptotic variance is a matrix that resembles the variance of a weighted least squares estimator.

3.1.3 Maximum Likelihood Estimation in Linear Discriminant Analysis

In the linear discriminant model, the joint distribution of (Y_i, X_i) depends on the following unknowns: (1) the conditional expectations (means) m_0, m_1 of the covariates given $Y = 1$ and $Y = 0$, respectively; (2) the common conditional variance–covariance matrix of the covariates Σ; and (3) the marginal probability of good risk p_1. The joint log-likelihood function can be written as the following sum of marginal and conditional log-likelihoods:

$$\log l(y, x; m_0, m_1, \Sigma, p_1)$$
$$= \log l(y; p_1) + \log l(x \mid y; m_0, m_1, \Sigma)$$
$$= \sum_{i=1}^{n} [y_i \log p_1 + (1 - y_i) \log(1 - p_1)]$$
$$+ \sum_{i=1}^{n} \{ y_i [-\tfrac{1}{2} L \log 2\pi - \tfrac{1}{2} \log \det \Sigma - \tfrac{1}{2}(x_i - m_1)' \Sigma^{-1}(x_i - m_1)]$$
$$+ (1 - y_i)[-\tfrac{1}{2} L \log 2\pi - \tfrac{1}{2} \log \det \Sigma - \tfrac{1}{2}(x_i - m_0)' \Sigma^{-1}(x_i - m_0)] \}.$$

Due to the additive form of the log-likelihood function, maximization can be performed in two steps, that is, first with respect to p_1 and next with respect to (m_0, m_1, Σ). Analytically, this procedure provides closed-form expressions of the ML estimators for all parameters in the model.

The risk probability is estimated by computing the fraction of individuals without default in the whole sample of size n:

$$\hat{p}_1 = \frac{1}{n} \sum_{i=1}^{n} y_i = \bar{y} \quad \text{(say)}. \qquad (3.13)$$

The parameters of the conditional normal distributions of covariates are estimated by the following sample means and sample variance matrix:

$$\hat{m}_1 = \bar{x}_1 = \frac{\sum_{i=1}^{n} y_i x_i}{\sum_{i=1}^{n} y_i}, \qquad \hat{m}_0 = \bar{x}_0 = \frac{\sum_{i=1}^{n} (1 - y_i) x_i}{\sum_{i=1}^{n} (1 - y_i)}, \qquad (3.14)$$

$$\hat{\Sigma} = \frac{1}{n} \left[\sum_{i=1}^{n} y_i (x_i - \bar{x}_1)(x_i - \bar{x}_1)' + \sum_{i=1}^{n} (1 - y_i)(x_i - \bar{x}_0)(x_i - \bar{x}_0)' \right]. \qquad (3.15)$$

$\hat{m}_1$ (respectively, $\hat{m}_0$) is the average covariate value computed from the subsample of nonrisky individuals, that is, from the data on individuals i for whom $y_i = 1$ (respectively, risky individuals are $y_i = 0$).

$$\hat{\Sigma} = \frac{n_1}{n}\hat{\Sigma}_1 + \frac{n_0}{n}\hat{\Sigma}_0$$

is a weighted average of sample variance matrices computed from the two subsamples.

For a well-specified linear discriminant model, the asymptotic properties of ML estimators are identical to the general properties outlined in Section 3.1.1. We do not provide the analytical expressions of asymptotic variances of these estimators. Their estimated values are provided among standard outputs of any statistical software used for linear discriminant analysis. Let us mention that ML estimators $\hat{p}_1$ and $(\hat{m}_0, \hat{m}_1, \hat{\Sigma})$ are asymptotically independent due to the additive form of the log-likelihood function.

3.1.4 *Test of the Linear Discriminant Hypothesis*

In Chapter 2 we explained that the linear discriminant model is compatible with a logit model with a constant, and with basic covariates among the explanatory variables:

$$p(x_i) = \text{logit}(\theta_0 + x_i'\theta). \tag{3.16}$$

Moreover, the parameters of the logit model are related to the parameters of the linear discriminant model as follows:

$$\theta_0 = \log\frac{1-p_1}{p_1} - \tfrac{1}{2}m_0'\Sigma^{-1}m_0 + \tfrac{1}{2}m_1'\Sigma^{-1}m_1,$$

$$\theta = \Sigma^{-1}(m_1 - m_0).$$

Let us now compare the two types of estimators of θ_0, θ, which are (1) the estimators $\hat{\theta}_0$, $\hat{\theta}$, derived by maximizing the conditional likelihood based on the logit model (3.16) (see Section 3.1.2), and (2) the estimators obtained from the linear discriminant approach:

$$\tilde{\theta}_0 = -\log\frac{1-\hat{p}_1}{\hat{p}_1} - \tfrac{1}{2}\hat{m}_0'\hat{\Sigma}^{-1}\hat{m}_0 + \tfrac{1}{2}\hat{m}_1'\hat{\Sigma}^{-1}\hat{m}_1,$$

$$\tilde{\theta} = \hat{\Sigma}^{-1}(\hat{m}_1 - \hat{m}_0).$$

Two cases have to be distinguished.

(i) When the linear discriminant model is well-specified, the logit model is also well-specified. Both estimators

$$\begin{pmatrix}\hat{\theta}_0\\\hat{\theta}\end{pmatrix} \quad\text{and}\quad \begin{pmatrix}\tilde{\theta}_0\\\tilde{\theta}\end{pmatrix}$$

are consistent, with asymptotic variance–covariance matrices $\hat{V}_\infty$ and $\tilde{V}_\infty$, respectively. Since the logit model takes into account only information contained in the conditional distribution, the resulting estimators are less efficient: $\hat{V}_\infty \gg \tilde{V}_\infty$, where "$\gg$" is a symbol used for standard ordering of symmetric matrices (two symmetric matrices A, B both of dimension (n, n) are such that $A \gg B$ if and only if $u'Au \gg u'Bu$ for any vector u of n elements).

(ii) It is possible that the logit model is well-specified, while the linear discriminant model is not. In this case,

$$\begin{pmatrix} \hat{\theta}_0 \\ \hat{\theta} \end{pmatrix}$$

is consistent, whereas

$$\begin{pmatrix} \tilde{\theta}_0 \\ \tilde{\theta} \end{pmatrix}$$

is generally inconsistent.

The comparison of the two types of estimator provides a convenient framework for hypotheses testing. In particular, we can perform a specification test proposed by Hausman (1982). Let us consider the following measure of discrepancy between estimators:

$$\xi = \left[\begin{pmatrix} \hat{\theta}_0 \\ \hat{\theta} \end{pmatrix} - \begin{pmatrix} \tilde{\theta}_0 \\ \tilde{\theta} \end{pmatrix} \right]' [\hat{V}_\infty - \tilde{V}_\infty]^- \left[\begin{pmatrix} \hat{\theta}_0 \\ \hat{\theta} \end{pmatrix} - \begin{pmatrix} \tilde{\theta}_0 \\ \tilde{\theta} \end{pmatrix} \right], \qquad (3.17)$$

where $[\cdot]^-$ denotes a generalized inverse. Under the null hypothesis of correct specification of the linear discriminant model, this statistic is asymptotically chi-squared distributed, with $r = \text{rank}[\hat{V}_\infty - \tilde{V}_\infty]$ degrees of freedom, whereas under the alternative it tends to infinity.

The testing procedure initially developed by Lo (1986) consists of

$$\begin{cases} \text{rejecting the linear discriminant hypothesis} & \text{if } \xi > \chi^2_{95\%}(r), \\ \text{accepting it} & \text{otherwise,} \end{cases}$$

where $\chi^2_{95\%}(r)$ is the 95% quantile of the $\chi^2(r)$ distribution.

3.2 Significance Tests

The ML estimators of unknown parameters can be used for testing various hypotheses. In this section, we consider the tests of significance for a single explanatory variable or a subset of explanatory variables in a score. Before we proceed to testing hypotheses related to the logit model, let us first recall the main testing procedures.

3.2.1 *Likelihood-Based Testing Procedures*

The basic principles of likelihood-based tests can be discussed in the framework of a conditional parametric model defined in Remark 3.1. The vector of parameters θ is partitioned into two subvectors $\theta' = (\alpha', \beta')$, of sizes $K - r$ and r, respectively. The (conditional) log-likelihood function is

$$\log l(y \mid x; \alpha, \beta) = \sum_{i=1}^{n} \log f(y_i \mid x_i; \alpha, \beta).$$

In the remainder of this section, we are interested in testing the null hypothesis, $H_0 = \{\beta = 0\}$, that the last r components of the parameter vector are zeros. For testing this null hypothesis we can consider methods based on either the unconstrained ML estimators of α and β given above, or on the ML estimators computed under the constraint $\beta = 0$.

Let us introduce

(1) the unconstrained ML estimators $\hat\alpha$, $\hat\beta$, which maximize $\log l(y \mid x; \alpha, \beta)$,

(2) the constrained ML estimators $\hat\alpha_0$, 0, which maximize $\log l(y \mid x; \alpha, 0)$.

3.2.1.1 *Wald Test*

The test procedure consists in rejecting the null hypothesis H_0 when the unconstrained estimator $\hat\beta$ is sufficiently different from zero. We consider the following measure of distance between $\hat\beta$ and 0:

$$\xi_W = \hat\beta'(\hat V \hat\beta)^{-1}\hat\beta, \qquad (3.18)$$

where $\hat V \hat\beta$ is a consistent estimator of the asymptotic variance–covariance matrix of $\hat\beta$. Under the null hypothesis, the statistic ξ_W asymptotically follows a chi-squared distribution with r degrees of freedom. The degree of freedom is equal to the number of conditions imposed by the null hypothesis, that is, the number r of parameters supposed to be equal to zero under H_0. We consider the 95% quantile $\chi^2_{95\%}(r)$ of this distribution and perform the test as follows:

$$\begin{cases} \text{accept } H_0 : \{\beta = 0\} & \text{if } \xi_W < \chi^2_{95\%}(r), \\ \text{reject } H_0 : \{\beta = 0\} & \text{if } \xi_W > \chi^2_{95\%}(r). \end{cases}$$

3.2.1.2 *The Likelihood Ratio (LR) Test*

The idea is to compare the maximum values of the constrained and unconstrained log-likelihood functions, which are the log-likelihoods computed from the constrained and unconstrained models. The LR statistic is

$$\xi_{LR} = 2[\log l(y \mid x; \hat\alpha, \hat\beta) - \log l(y \mid x; \hat\alpha_0, 0)]. \qquad (3.19)$$

Under the null hypothesis this statistic asymptotically follows a chi-squared distribution with r degrees of freedom.

The testing procedure consists in

$$\begin{cases} \text{accepting } H_0 : \{\beta = 0\} & \text{if } \xi_{LR} < \chi^2_{95\%}(r), \\ \text{rejecting } H_0 : \{\beta = 0\} & \text{otherwise.} \end{cases}$$

3.2.1.3 The Lagrange Multiplier (LM) Test

The test statistic measures how close to zero the partial derivatives of the log-likelihood function are with respect to β at the constrained maximum. The test statistic is given by

$$\xi_{LM} = \frac{\partial \log l(y \mid x; \hat{\alpha}_0, 0)}{\partial \beta'} \hat{V}\hat{\beta} \frac{\partial \log l(y \mid x; \hat{\alpha}_0, 0)}{\partial \beta}. \tag{3.20}$$

It asymptotically follows a $\chi^2(r)$ distribution, which implies the following testing procedure:

$$\begin{cases} \text{accept } H_0 : \{\beta = 0\} & \text{if } \xi_{LM} < \chi^2_{95\%}(r), \\ \text{reject } H_0 & \text{otherwise.} \end{cases}$$

It can be verified that the Wald, LR, and LM tests provide similar outcomes when the number of observations is large and the hypothesis $H_0 : \{\beta = 0\}$ is satisfied.

3.2.1.4 A Drawback of the Test Theory

It is important to comment on the limitation of the test theory in very large data samples, such as those used in our empirical applications. Let us consider, for example, a Wald statistic (3.18) with a single parameter to be tested: $\xi = n\hat{\beta}^2 I_{\beta\beta}$, where $I_{\beta\beta}$ denotes information. A large number of observations n increases the value of the test statistic. In the limiting case $n \to \infty$, the test statistic tends to infinity. As a consequence, the test at the 5% level will reject the null hypothesis "β is zero," even if the estimated value of β is numerically very close to zero. Indeed, it would be preferable to change the standard practice of testing by adjusting the level of the test with respect to the increasing number of observations; for example, by replacing level 5% by level 1%. Technically, this adjustment is difficult. Therefore, below we will focus more on comparing the test statistics, rather than interpreting their values.

3.2.2 Application of the LM Test to the Logit Model

Let us consider the logit model, with explanatory variables z_i partitioned into two subsets z_{i1} and z_{i2}:

$$p(x_i) = \frac{1}{1 - \exp(-z_i'\theta)} = \frac{1}{1 + \exp(-z_{i1}'\alpha - z_{i2}'\beta)} \quad \text{(say)}.$$

When $\beta = 0$, variables z_2 are not relevant and the score can be computed given variables z_1 only. The constrained and unconstrained ML estimators do not have closed-form expressions. Hence, in practice, their values have to be determined numerically. Let us discuss in detail the LM test procedure, which is easy to interpret. The derivative of the log-likelihood function is

$$\frac{\partial \log l(y \mid x; \alpha, \beta)}{\partial \beta} = \sum_{i=1}^{n} z_{i2}[y_i - \text{logit}(z'_{i1}\alpha + z'_{i2}\beta)].$$

Let us introduce the residuals of the logit model computed under the null hypothesis:

$$\hat{u}_{i,0} = y_i - \text{logit}(z'_{i1}\hat{\alpha}_0), \quad i = 1, \ldots, n.$$

The LM test statistic measures the distance between zero and

$$\frac{\partial \log l(y \mid x; \hat{\alpha}_0, 0)}{\partial \beta} = \sum_{i=1}^{n} z_{i2}\hat{u}_{i,0},$$

which is the sum of the constrained residuals multiplied by the variables in z_2. The variables in z_2 are considered irrelevant if they are found to be almost uncorrelated with the residuals. This interpretation is the same as in the linear regression model.

The expression of the LM statistic generally involves the variables z_1 that appear in the estimated variance of $\hat{\beta}$. The test statistic, ξ_{LM}, is given by

$$\left(\sum_{i=1}^{n} z_{i2}\hat{u}_{i,0}\right)' \left[\sum_{i=1}^{n} z_{i2}z'_{i2}\hat{u}^2_{i,0}\right.$$
$$\left. - \sum_{i=1}^{n} z_{i2}z'_{i1}\hat{u}^2_{i,0}\left(\sum_{i=1}^{n} z_{i1}z'_{i1}\hat{u}^2_{i,0}\right)^{-1}\sum_{i=1}^{n} z_{i1}z'_{i2}\hat{u}^2_{i,0}\right]^{-1} \sum_{i=1}^{n} z_{i2}\hat{u}_{i,0}.$$

The presence of z_1 in this expression matters if and only if these variables are not orthogonal to z_2. Note that the orthogonality condition requires very specific weights, equal to the squares of constrained residuals:

$$\sum_{i=1}^{n} z_{i,1}z'_{i,2}\hat{u}^2_{i,0} = 0.$$

3.3   Implementation

Since the mid 1980s, the use of discriminant and logit models for prediction of qualitative risks has became a standard routine. In spite of this, it is hard to find a comprehensive and detailed description of the procedure of risk prediction used in practice by banks and other financial institutions. The reason for such a lack is that risk-prediction formulas are also used by banks for determining various conditions of credit agreements, such as credit line limits, interest rates (see Section 6.4.2), and so on. Therefore, some details about the scoring system have to remain confidential to protect banks from competition. These include the transformations z of basic characteristics x and the values of coefficients. Publicly available information about the score is provided, for example, by the Federal Reserve Bank of New York.

Under a bank monitoring program, the Federal Reserve Bank of New York has created a nationwide database of twenty-five financial ratios. The financial institutions under supervision are required to keep the values of these ratios updated regularly. This requirement is a direct incentive for lenders to partly control their own risk exposure.

3.3.1 Development of Score Methodology

The scoring system for the prediction of corporate failures has developed gradually over the last century. In recent financial and macroeconomic literature, the prediction of corporate failures has received considerable attention (see the list of references) because of the interdependence between corporate bond prices and corporate-failure rates, which in turn have a direct impact on unemployment.

In the past, the prediction of corporate failures was determined by the univariate ratio analysis. Under this approach, the means of a given set of financial ratios are computed separately from a population of firms that went out of business and from a population of firms that survived. Next, the two population means are compared (Fitzpatrick 1932). A variety of ratio formulas has emerged in the literature. They were compared by Beaver (1967, 1968a,b), who established which among them were the most discriminatory. Altman (1968) was among the first researchers to use several ratios in the discriminant analysis. He noticed that, due to the joint effect, the method based on multiple ratios outperformed the single-ratio approach. The so-called multiple-discriminant approach has later become popular among other authors (see, for example, Deakin 1972; Blum 1974; Pinches and Trieschman 1977).

Although the multiple-ratio analysis dominated the single-ratio approach, it had its own drawbacks. The prediction accuracy was poor, the scores were time varying, and the assumptions underlying the linear discriminant analysis were contradicted by empirical evidence. Let us first focus on the last deficiency.

The linear discriminant analysis assumes the normality of the joint distribution of covariates. However, financial ratios do not satisfy this condition, even under logarithmic or square root transformations (see Deakin 1976; Eisenbeis 1977; Barnes 1982; Bedingfield et al. 1985). As an illustration, we consider the financial ratios listed in Table 3.1. Table 3.2 reports their standardized-sample third- and fourth-order moments (skewness and kurtosis, respectively) computed for firms in the U.S. manufacturing sector in 1979. We observe that these financial ratios are not marginally normal, since their skewnesses are far from zero and their kurtosis are far from three (skewness equal to zero and kurtosis equal to three are the benchmark characteristics of the normal distribution). Earlier in the text, we argued that a remedy to this problem would consist in replacing the discriminant analysis by a more robust model such as the logit. To our knowledge, the first logit-based analysis of corporate failures was carried out by Martin (1977) (see also Zavgren (1985) and Gentry et al. (1987) for related studies).

Table 3.1. List of financial ratios (Deakin 1976; So 1987).

Ratio	Abbreviation
Asset turnover ratios	
Current assets/sales	CA/S
Quick assets/sales	QA/S
Working capital/sales	WC/S
Liquid asset ratios	
Current assets/current liabilities	CA/CL
Quick assets/current liabilities	QA/CL
Current assets/total assets	CA/TA
Quick assets/total assets	QA/TA
Working capital/total assets	WC/TA
Profitability ratios	
Cash flow/total debt	CF/TD
Net income/total assets	NI/TA
Debt/equity ratio	
Total debt/total assets	TD/TA

Table 3.2. Skewness and kurtosis of financial ratios (So 1987).

Ratio	Skewness	Kurtosis
CA/S	1.38	4.2
QA/S	2.48	12.2
WC/S	1.58	7.13
CA/CL	2.20	9.67
QA/CL	4.97	42.76
CA/TA	−0.36	0.53
QA/TA	0.92	1.78
WC/TA	0.18	0.62
CF/TD	4.95	38.62
NI/TA	1.66	6.58
TD/TA	0.12	1.20

The two other deficiencies mentioned earlier, i.e., the lack of accuracy and variation of predictions in time, can be eliminated by appropriate nonlinear transformations of financial ratios, and by incorporating some cross-effects of covariates or additional variables. A substantial improvement can be achieved by purging past dependence from the covariates, if these are serially correlated. For this reason, and also because the change of a ratio is often more informative than its level, both current and lagged values of financial ratios need to be considered. In addition, variables reflecting the fund flow of corporates should be included in the analysis. Indeed, the differences between firms that succeeded in business and those who are close to failure become clear when the corporate cash inflows and outflows are examined. In this spirit, Gentry et al. (1987) included among the explanatory variables the measures of evolution of fund flow components from the balance sheet. Empirical evidence on the link between risk and the variation of financial ratios in time was provided by Betts and Belhoul (1987). They studied the standard deviations of financial ratios computed over a sequence of fixed periods of time. They found that the larger the observed variability of a financial ratio, the greater the risk of failure. This means that higher volatility implies higher risk of bankruptcy.

To seek further improvement of corporate-failure prediction, one can consider adding explanatory dummy variables to the set of covariates. In particular, qualitative variables such as the indicators of industrial sector, seasonal or cyclical effects, management type and structure, and so on can be relevant for the assessment of corporate risk.

3.3.2 Mortgage Score

There exists a variety of scores for consumption credit, depending on the type of credit (open account credit, credit card, home mortgage) and on information about the borrower. While for a new customer the information is typically limited to the individual characteristics elicited in the credit application form, for an established customer the information on payment history is also available.

Access to individual information and the procedure of individual rating varies from country to country. In Canada, lenders routinely perform a credit check on anyone who applies for a credit card, a loan, a mortgage, or any form of financing at the credit reporting agency. The credit reporting agencies keep files on all individuals who have applied or used any form of credit in the past. They provide different kinds of credit information to lenders for a fee. The credit reporting agencies do not evaluate the credit file. Their job is to record all relevant information in the customer's file and make the information available to banks, mortgage companies, trust companies, insurance companies, and other lenders and issuers of credit. In France, the banks hold their own databases and use their internal models for individual scoring.

3.3.2.1 Quick-Scoring Methods

A commonly used quick-scoring method for loan applications is the debt service ratio, used as a single covariate. The advantage is that it is readily available, but at the cost of low accuracy. The two popular debt service ratios are the Gross Debt Service (GDS) ratio (annual mortgage payments plus property taxes divided by gross family income) and the Total Debt Service (TDS) ratio (annual mortgage payments plus property taxes plus other debt payments divided by gross family income). The two benchmarks for credit granting are a GDS ratio of not over 30% and a TDS ratio of not over 40%. These ratios and benchmarks were developed by analysing a large number of previous credit files for which the payment histories were known.

They may be useful for financial institutions that require a quick-scoring method to process a large number of loan applications. However, they are especially inaccurate for households with extremely high or low incomes. Also, the TDS and GDS ratios do not account for tax effects or the size of the household, and, most importantly, they fail to account for risk of income variation in time (Ho and Robinson 2000). Hence, the debt service ratio is not reliable and should be used only in conjunction with more sophisticated scoring methods.

To make final credit decisions, lenders use advanced scoring systems, which require processing a large amount of data. If the number of customers is about 100 000, a financial institution has to handle several hundred transformed explanatory variables z. One has to keep in mind that the observed individual characteristics are often qualitative with a finite set of admissible values. However, if we consider three basic covariates x_1, x_2, x_3 (say), divided respectively into 10, 20, and 10 categories, and want to take into account all possible cross-effects, we end up with $10 \times 20 \times 10 = 2000$ indicator variables z. Therefore, it may not be feasible to account for all cross-effects in a large sample.

3.3.2.2   *Example of Home Mortgage Scoring*

To illustrate, let us describe score estimation from a sample of 10 000 Spanish home mortgage contracts. The observed variables are risk ($Y_i = 0$ if default on mortgage has occurred in the sampling period, $Y_i = 1$ otherwise) and various characteristics of each borrower provided in the mortgage application form. We show in Table 3.3 the logit estimates of score coefficients.

The score is based on twelve variables in vector x. These variables consist of the characteristics of borrowers and of mortgage contracts (such as the term, interest rate, and principal), as well as of the characteristics of the lender (for example, the variable "Location of bank agency" is an indirect way of auditing the agencies of a bank).[1] The variables are of different types, quantitative and qualitative. Each quantitative or polytomous qualitative variable in x is transformed into indicators. For this purpose, we introduce a partition of the set of admissible values of that variable, and assign the values 0 or 1 for each class. For example, we divide the variable "age" into five categories, "20–30," "30–40," "40–60," "greater than 60," and "unknown," and transform age into a matrix of five columns and n rows, where n is the number of individuals under study. Then, in every row corresponding to each individual, the value 1 will be marked in the column associated with the age group to which the individual belongs, and zeros will appear in all other columns. Since all relevant alternatives of a variable are disjoint and cover all admissible classes, the values of indicator functions associated with a given variable in x sum up to one across the columns. To avoid collinearity among the explanatory variables z, it is necessary to omit one alternative in each variable x prior to estimation. The omitted alternatives

---

[1] Such a score is a mixed measure of risks due to the borrower, lender, and type of contract.

in our example are given in Table 3.3 with the corresponding coefficients (computed from the estimated constant term and the sum of other estimated coefficients) without standard errors. For example, for age, the omitted category is "unknown."

Table 3.3 also shows various cross-effects included in the analysis; in particular, the cross-effects related to the family structure. Other cross-effects are monthly income and age, and mortgage term and age.

The score is designed so that high ratings indicate good risks, and low ratings indicate bad risks. Therefore, the ranking of customers who apply for a mortgage increases with the values of coefficients in the score. For instance, individual risk diminishes with the duration of a customer–bank relationship and seniority in the current job. Withholding any personal information on an application form (by marking the alternative "unknown") sends a highly unfavorable signal about the customer, and is therefore highly informative.

Using the data in Table 3.3 and logit formula (3.8) it is easy to calculate the score for mortgage applicants. Let us compare the chances of getting a mortgage for two individuals. The first applicant is Pedro, a young farmer who is 25 years old and lives in the region of Catalogna. He is getting married, and needs to buy a bigger house for his future family. Pedro inherited the farm two years ago and his last annual income was 55 000 pesetas. He wants to buy a house worth 7 000 000 pesetas and considers a downpayment of 5%. He plans to repay the debt in 20 years. The set of coefficient values for Pedro, in the same order as the variables appear in Table 3.3, is

$$\theta = [0.65, 0.52, -0.43, -0.87, -0.003, -0.08, 1.58, -0.30,$$
$$- 0.10, 0.16, 0.42, -0.37].$$

Recall that the canonical score is $1/(1 + \exp(-\sum_i \theta_i))$. Inserting the sum of coefficients plus the constant yields 0.43. Pedro's score is low and he has no chance of getting a mortgage.

The second applicant is Don Diego, a grocery store manager from Madrid. Don Diego is 35 years old, and has established a long (12 years) and impeccable credit history. Don Diego has been employed at the store for 10 years and earns 200 000 pesetas. His wife earns 220 000, which adds up to an annual income of 420 000 for his family of three. Don Diego needs a mortgage to buy a small house worth 5 500 000 pesetas with a downpayment of 35% to be repaid in 16 years. The set of coefficient for Don Diego is

$$\theta = [0.38, 0.51, 0.43, 0.35, 0.12, 1.58, 0.60, 0.27, 1.58, 0.40, 0.07].$$

Inserting the sum of coefficients plus the constant in the logit formula yields 0.99. Don Diego is predicted to be a good risk, and will get a mortgage.

The bank will probably also consider other facts about Pedro and Don Diego before making the final decision. While the score value is against Pedro's application,

Table 3.3. Estimated score.

Variable	Alternative	Estimated coefficient	Standard error
Family structure	Single		
	– Zero dependents	0.65	0.10
	– At least one dependent	−0.17	0.23
	Married		
	– Zero or one dependent	0.16	0.09
	– At least two dependents	−0.13	0.12
	Other		
	– Zero or one dependent	−0.12	0.12
	– At least two dependents	−0.38	—
Age	20–30	0.52	0.17
	30–40	0.51	0.17
	40–60	0.36	0.17
	⩾ 60	−1.28	0.40
	Unknown	−0.11	—
Monthly income	< 50 000	−0.35	0.18
(pesetas)	50 000 ⩽ ⋯ < 70 000	−0.43	0.15
	70 000 ⩽ ⋯ < 100 000	−0.14	0.08
	100 000 ⩽ ⋯ < 175 000	0.28	0.07
	175 000 ⩽ ⋯ < 250 000	0.43	0.09
	⩾ 250 000	0.21	—
Occupation	Employee	0.35	0.12
	Executive	0.54	0.15
	Artisan, business oriented	−0.28	0.14
	Worker	0.23	0.14
	Farmer	−0.87	0.55
	Retired	0.03	—
Customer of the	< 2	−0.003	0.07
bank for (years)	2 ⩽ ⋯ < 6	−0.05	0.07
	6 ⩽ ⋯ < 15	0.12	0.07
	⩾ 15	0.07	0.10
	Unknown	−0.14	—
Professional	< 3	−0.08	0.06
seniority (years)	3 ⩽ ⋯ < 5	0.18	0.07
	5 ⩽ ⋯ < 10	0.32	0.08
	⩾ 10	0.18	0.08
	Unknown	−0.60	—

his solvency, that is, his long-run ability to pay the debt, will improve in time, while the solvency of Don Diego can deteriorate. This, and other factors that are unaccounted for in score computation, remain at the discretion of credit managers.

Table 3.3. (*Continued.*)

Variable	Alternative	Estimated coefficient	Standard error
Debt/income	< 50%	1.58	0.07
ratio	50% ⩽ · · · < 60%	0.87	0.07
	60% ⩽ · · · < 70%	−0.55	0.10
	70% ⩽ · · · < 80%	−0.92	0.13
	⩾ 80%	−0.97	—
Monthly income	No co-borrower	−0.30	0.09
of the co-borrower	< 5000	−0.47	0.08
	50 000 ⩽ · · · < 200 000	0.18	0.08
	⩾ 200 000	0.60	—
Amortization	< 10	−0.62	—
(years)	10 ⩽ · · · < 12	0.28	0.10
	12 ⩽ · · · < 15	0.17	0.15
	15 ⩽ · · · < 17	0.27	0.07
	⩾ 17	−0.10	0.07
Principal	< 6 000 000	0.38	0.06
	6 000 000 ⩽ · · · < 9 000 000	0.16	0.05
	⩾ 9 000 000	−0.55	—
Location of the	Catalogna, Aragon, Valencia	0.42	0.08
the bank agency	Basque region, Navarre	−0.12	0.15
	Galicia, Asturia	0.09	0.12
	Andalousia	0.19	0.09
	Madrid	0.40	0.09
	Estramadure	−0.60	0.32
	Other	−0.39	—
Downpayment	< 20%	−0.37	0.10
	20% ⩽ · · · < 30%	−0.16	0.06
	30% ⩽ · · · < 40%	0.07	0.05
	⩾ 40%	0.46	—
Constant		−1.45	0.24

3.4 Concluding Remarks

In this chapter we provided an overview of estimation and testing procedures for the logit and linear discriminant models. The key estimation method is called the maximum likelihood (ML) estimator and consists in maximizing a log-likelihood function, whose form depends on the (conditional) density and on a set of parameters. The ML estimators are asymptotically unbiased and efficient, that is, in a large sample the estimated value of a parameter is close to the true parameter value, and the variance of the estimator is almost as small as possible in the class of consistent estimators.

We discussed three asymptotically valid and equivalent test procedures: the Wald, likelihood ratio, and Lagrange multiplier tests. Under the null hypothesis, the associated test statistics follow the chi-squared distribution asymptotically. The tests consist in rejecting the null hypothesis when the value of the test statistic computed from the data exceeds the critical value from a chi-squared distribution at a given level α (equal to 0.05 in most cases), and accepting it otherwise.

In the last part of the chapter we turned our attention to practical implementations. We provided evidence against the normality of financial ratios that are, by definition, assumed to be normally distributed for linear discriminant analysis. This suggests that, in practice, the linear discriminant analysis may not be accurate. We also illustrated the logit-based computation of a score from a sample of home buyers whose mortgage was provided by a Spanish bank.

The list of references for this chapter includes a comprehensive set of papers on applications to credit risk. Software for the logit model is, for instance, available from SAS. Further reading on maximum likelihood and related tests for qualitative models can be found in Maddala (1983), Cox and Snell (1989), and Gourieroux (1989).

References

Aharony, J., C. Jones, and I. Swary. 1980. An analysis of risk and return characteristics of corporate bankruptcy using capital market data. *Journal of Finance* 35:1001–16.

Altman, E. 1968. Financial ratios, discriminant analysis and prediction of corporate bankruptcy. *Journal of Finance* 23:589–609.

Altman, E., and M. Brenner. 1981. Information effects and stock market response to firm deterioration. *Journal of Financial and Quantitative Analysis* March:35–51.

Altman, E., R. Haldeman, and P. Narayanan. 1977. Zeta analysis: a new model to identify bankruptcy risk of corporations. *Journal of Banking and Finance* 1:29–54.

Barnes, P. 1982. Methodological implications of non-normally distributed financial ratios. *Journal of Business Finance and Accounting* Summer:51–62.

Beaver, W. 1966. Financial ratios as predictors of failure. *Empirical Research in Accounting Selected Studies (Supplement to Journal of Accounting Research)* 4:35–51.

Beaver, W. 1968a. Market prices, financial ratios and the prediction of failure. *Journal of Accounting Research* Autumn:79–92.

Beaver, W. 1968b. Alternative financial ratios as prediction of failure. *Accounting Review* 12:1–25.

Bedingfield, J., P. Reckers, and J. Stagliano. 1985. Distributions of financial ratios in the commercial banking industry. *Journal of Financial Research* Spring:77–81.

Betts, J., and D. Belhoul. 1987. The effectiveness of incorporating stability measures in company failure models. *Journal of Business Finance and Accounting* 14:323–35.

Bird, R., and A. McHugh. 1977. Financial ratios: an empirical study. *Journal of Business Finance and Accounting* 4:29–45.

Blum, M. 1974. Failing company discriminant analysis. *Journal of Accounting Research* 12:1–25.

Bougen, P., and J. Drury. 1980. UK statistical distributions of financial ratios, 1975. *Journal of Business Finance and Accounting* 7:39–47.

Chesser, D. 1974. Predicting loan noncompliance. *Journal of Commercial Bank Lending* August:28–38.

Collins, R. 1980. An empirical comparison of bankruptcy prediction models. *Financial Management* 9:51–57.

Cox, D., and E. Snell. 1989. *The Analysis of Binary Data*. London: Chapman & Hall.

Dambolena, I., and S. Khoury. 1980. Ratios stability and corporate failure. *Journal of Finance* 35:1017–26.

Deakin, E. 1972. A discriminant analysis of predictors of business failure. *Journal of Accounting Research* 10:167–79.

Deakin, E. 1976. Distributions of financial accounting ratios: some empirical evidence. *Accounting Review* January:90–96.

Dopuch, N., R. Holthausen, and R. Leftwich. 1987. Predicting audit qualifications with financial and market variables. *Accounting Review* 62:431–54.

Ederington, L. 1985. Classification models and bond ratings. *Financial Review* 20:237–62.

Eisenbeis, R. 1977. Pitfalls in the application of discriminant analysis in business, finance and economics. *Journal of Finance* 32:875–900.

Epley, D., T. Cronan, and L. Perry. 1985. A research note on discrimination in mortgage lending. *Journal of the American Real Estate and Urban Economics Association* 13:446–51.

Fitzpatrick, P. 1932. A comparison of ratios of successful industrial enterprises with those of failed firms. *Certified Public Accountant* 12:598–605, 659–62, 721–31.

Frecka, T., and W. Hopwood. 1983. The effects of outliers on the cross-sectional properties of financial ratios. *Journal of Accounting Research* January:115–28.

Freidman, J., T. Hastie, and R. Tibshirani. 1999. Additive logistic regression: a statistical view of bootstrapping. Working Paper, Stanford University.

Galitz, L. 1983. Consumer credit analysis. *Managerial Finance* 9:27–33.

Gentry, J., P. Newbold, and D. Whitford. 1987. Funds flow components, financial ratios and bankruptcy. *Journal of Business Finance and Accounting* 14:595–606.

Gourieroux, C. 1989. *Econométrie des Variables Qualitatives*, 2nd edn, Chapters 1 and 3. Paris: Economica. (English version, 2000: *Econometrics of Qualitative Dependent Variables*. Cambridge University Press.)

Hausman, J. 1982. Specification tests in econometrics. *Econometrica* 50:749–59.

Ho, K., and C. Robinson. 2000. *Personal Financial Planning*. Toronto: Captus.

Horrigan, J. 1965. Some empirical bases of financial ratios analysis. *Journal of Accounting Research* July:558–68.

Johnson, C. 1970. Ratio analysis and the prediction of firm failure. *Journal of Finance* 25:1166–68.

Joy, M., and J. Tollefson. 1975. On the financial applications of discriminant analysis. *Journal of Financial and Quantitative Analysis* December:723–38.

Karel, G., and A. Prakash. 1987. Multivariate normality and forecasting of business bankruptcy. *Journal of Business Finance and Accounting* Winter:573–92.

Lev, B., and S. Sunder. 1979. Methodological issues in the use of financial ratios. *Journal of Accounting and Economics* December:187–210.

Lo, A. 1986. Logit versus discriminant analysis. *Journal of Econometrics* 31:151–78.

McDonald, B., and M. Morris. 1984. The statistical validity of the ratio method in financial analysis: an empirical examination. *Journal of Business Finance and Accounting* Spring:89–98.

McLeay, S. 1986a. The ratio of means and the mean of ratios and other benchmarks: an examination of characteristic financial ratios in the french corporate sector. *Finance* 7:75–93.

McLeay, S. 1986b. Student's *t* and the distribution of financial ratios. *Journal of Business Finance and Accounting* Summer:209–21.

Maddala, G. S. 1983. *Limited dependent and qualitative variables in econometrics*, Chapters 2 and 4. Cambridge University Press.

Maddala, G. S. 1991. A perspective in the use of limited dependent and qualitative variables in accounting research. *Accounting Review* 66:788–807.

Martin, D. 1977. Early warning of bank failure: a logit regression approach. *Journal of Banking and Finance* 1:249–76.

Meyer, P., and H. Pifer. 1970. Prediction of bank failures. *Journal of Finance* 25:853–68.

Myers, J., and E. Forgy. 1963. The development of numerical credit evaluation systems. *Journal of the American Statistical Association* September:799–806.

O'Connor, M. 1973. On the usefulness of financial ratios to investors in common stocks. *Accounting Review* April:339–52.

Ohlson, J. 1980. Financial ratios and the probabilistic prediction of bankruptcy. *Journal of Accounting Research* 18:109–31.

Orgler, Y. 1970. A credit scoring model for consumer loans. *Journal of Money Credit and Banking* November:435–525.

Perry, L., and T. Cronan. 1986. A note on rank transformation discriminant analysis. *Journal of Banking and Finance* 10:605–10.

Perry, L., T. Cronan, and G. Henderson. 1985. Industry classification, ordinal data and bond rating decision models. *Decision Science* Winter:14–24.

Pinches, G., and J. Trieschman. 1977. Discriminant analysis, classification results and financially distressed property–liability insurers. *Journal of Risk and Insurance* 44:289–98.

Santomero, A., and J. Vinso. 1977. Estimating the probability of failure for commercial banks and the banking system. *Journal of Banking and Finance* September:185–205.

SAS. 1995. *User's Guide: The LOGISTIC Procedure*, Version 6, Volume 2, pp. 1077–121. Cary, NC: SAS.

Scott, J. 1981. The probability of bankruptcy: a comparison of empirical predictions and theoretical models. *Journal of Banking and Finance* 5:317–44.

Sinkey, J. 1975. A multivariate statistical analysis of the characteristics of problem banks. *Journal of Finance* 29:21–35.

So, J. 1987. Some empirical evidence on the outliers and the non-normal distribution of financial ratios. *Journal of Business Finance and Accounting* 14:483–96.

Whittington, G. 1980. Some basic properties of accounting ratios. *Journal of Business Finance and Accounting* Summer:219–32.

Wilcox, J. 1971. A simple theory of financial ratios as predictors of failure. *Journal of Accounting Research* Autumn:389–95.

Zavgren, C. 1983. The prediction of corporate failure: the state of the art. *Journal of Accounting Literature* Spring:1–38.

Zavgren, C. 1985. Assessing the vulnerability to failure of american industrial firms: a logistic analysis. *Journal of Business Finance and Accounting* 12:19–45.

Zavgren, C., M. Dugan, and J. Reeve. 1988. The association between probabilities of bankruptcy and market responses. A test of market anticipation. *Journal of Business Finance and Accounting* 15:27–95.

Zmijewski, M. 1984. Methodological issues related to the estimation of financial distress prediction models. *Journal of Accounting Research* 22(Supplement):58–86.

4

Score Performance

A high-quality score is expected to perform well in distinguishing between "bad" and "good" risk individuals. From a statistical point of view, it is unlikely that indications of a score are correct in 100% of cases. There exist methods that assess and enhance the power of a score in order to keep the error margin to a minimum. The power of a score can deteriorate or improve in time, or vary across different populations. In order to avoid flaws in individual risk prediction, scores need to be monitored and adjusted, if necessary. The main diagnostic tool used by the professionals for score monitoring is the so-called performance curve, which is conceptually close to the determination coefficient R^2 in a linear regression model. In general, financial institutions are reluctant to disclose to the public information about their own diagnostic tools. Therefore, it is hard to learn about the monitoring techniques from the theoretical or applied literature.

Formally, the score monitoring consists in applying various goodness-of-fit measures to the risk-prediction model for the endogenous dichotomous risk variable Y_i. In this chapter, the prediction of individual risk is denoted by $\hat{Y}_i$ and is defined below as an indicator whose value depends on the score value S_i:

$$\hat{Y}_i = \begin{cases} 1 & \text{if } S_i \geqslant s, \\ 0 & \text{if } S_i < s. \end{cases}$$

The prediction is "good risk" ($\hat{Y}_i = 1$) or "bad risk" ($\hat{Y}_i = 0$) depending on whether the value of score S_i for individual i is greater than or less than some threshold s. Score S_i and threshold s determine the scoring procedure. The performance and selection curves are functional measures of goodness-of-fit, based on the conditional distribution of risk given covariates. By the duality of the approach to risk prediction (see Chapter 2), an equivalent functional measure—called the discriminant curve and based on the conditional distribution of covariates given risk—is also available for score monitoring. Empirical illustrations are given in the last part of the chapter.

4.1 Performance and Selection Curves

4.1.1 Definitions

The performance and selection curves provide a graphical display of score performance. Formally, these two types of curve are functional goodness-of-fit measures, defined in parametric and implicit forms. The parametric forms naturally depend on threshold s, and contain terms which need to be clarified before the definitions are given. For ease of exposition, let us drop the individual index i, and assume again that the individual under study is a credit applicant. Recall that, for a given s, an individual is believed to be "good risk" and is approved for a loan if $S \geqslant s$.

(1) For a given s, $P[S \geqslant s]$ is the probability of "good risk." Its empirical equivalent is the rate of accepted credit applications, called the *market share*.

(2) $P[Y = 0 \mid S \geqslant s]/P[Y = 0]$ is the conditional probability that the applicant is "bad risk" despite the fact that she scored high enough to qualify for credit, divided by the marginal probability that a credit applicant is "bad risk." Its empirical equivalent is the rate of bad risk individuals in the population of customers who qualify for credit, in the sense that their score value S exceeds threshold s, divided by the rate of bad risk individuals in the whole population of credit applicants.

(3) $P[S \geqslant s \mid Y = 0]$ is the conditional probability that a score high enough to qualify for credit is obtained by a "bad risk" applicant. Its empirical equivalent is the rate of credit applications accepted among bad risk individuals.

The performance and selection curves are traced out in a two-dimensional plane with coordinates x and y. The x-axis and y-axis of the plane are denoted in curve definitions below as $x(s)$ and $y(s)$, and correspond to (1) and (2) for the performance curve, and to (1) and (3) for the selection curve, respectively. The values of expressions (1), (2), and (3) vary between 0 and 1 depending on the selection threshold s.

The notation $x(s)$, $y(s)$ emphasizes the role of threshold s: the point in the plane with coordinates $(x(s_1), y(s_1))$ corresponds to threshold s_1, while the point in the plane with coordinates $(x(s_2), y(s_2))$, corresponds to threshold s_2.

Definition 4.1. The *performance curve* of score S is defined in parametric form as the set of points with coordinates $(x(s), y(s))$:

$$\left. \begin{aligned} x(s) &= P[S \geqslant s], \\ y(s) &= \frac{P[Y = 0 \mid S \geqslant s]}{P[Y = 0]}, \end{aligned} \right\} \quad s \text{ varying.}$$

The implicit form of the performance curve is function $y = \mathcal{P}(x)$. The performance curve tells us how the proportion of bad risks, mistakenly qualified for credit because of score values above the threshold s, will evolve when the rate of acceptance increases. The acceptance rate increases when threshold s is lowered.

Definition 4.2. The *selection curve* of score S is defined in parametric form as the set of points with coordinates $(x(s), y(s))$:

$$\left. \begin{aligned} x(s) &= P[S \geqslant s], \\ y(s) &= P[S \geqslant s \mid Y = 0], \end{aligned} \right\} \quad s \text{ varying.}$$

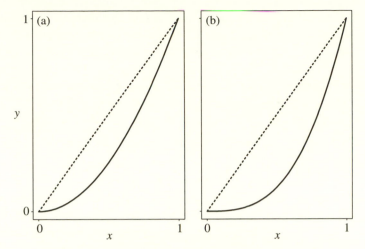

Figure 4.1. Patterns of performance and selection curves:
(a) performance curve; (b) selection curve.

The implicit form of the selection curve is the function $y = \mathscr{S}(x)$.

Since

$$P[S \geqslant s \mid Y = 0] = \frac{P[Y = 0 \mid S \geqslant s]}{P[Y = 0]} P[S \geqslant s],$$

the selection curve tells us how the proportion of high scores among the "bad risk" applicants evolves when the rate of acceptance increases. The acceptance rate increases when threshold s gets lower.

The two curves are related as follows:

$$\mathscr{S}(x) = x \mathscr{P}(x). \tag{4.1}$$

When the scoring function S is well-specified, the quality of selection is expected to increase when the selection rules get tougher. Therefore, both the performance and selection curves are expected to be increasing functions of s.

Let us now illustrate graphically the shapes of selection and performance curves. First, we focus on the performance curve. For a very small threshold s close to zero, all applications are accepted. Therefore the x-coordinate is $P[S \geqslant s] = 1$ and the y-coordinate is $P[Y = 0 \mid S \geqslant s]/P[Y = 0] = P[Y = 0]/P[Y = 0] = 1$. Thus, for threshold s close to 0, the coordinates of the corresponding point on the performance curve are $(1, 1)$. Similarly, for a large threshold s close to 1, the coordinates of the corresponding point on the performance curve are $(0, 0)$. Therefore, the performance curve passes through the points $(0, 0)$ and $(1, 1)$.

Similar reasoning leads us to the conclusion that any selection curve passes through the points $(0, 0)$ and $(1, 1)$. Some typical patterns of the performance and selection curves are shown in Figure 4.1.

The performance and selection curves are used for monitoring the customer-selection procedure. For example, the curves can detect deterioration in the quality of customers resulting from an increase of the market share, obtained by lowering threshold s.

Note also that the performance and selection curves remain invariant when score S is replaced by score S^* which preserves the same risk ordering. Indeed, if $S^* = h(S)$, where h is an increasing function (such as log or exponential), we get

$$x^*(s) = P[S^* > s] = P[S > h^{-1}(s)] = x[h^{-1}(s)],$$
$$y^*(s) = y[h^{-1}(s)].$$

The performance curves based on scores S and S^* are identical, that is, two different parametrizations in terms of s and $h^{-1}(s)$, respectively, yield the same performance curve.

4.1.2 Desirable Properties of a Score

In order to get correct risk classification of individuals, the dependence between score S and risk variable Y has to be positive. This means that the score value should be high when $Y = 1$ ("good risk") and low when $Y = 0$ ("bad risk"), and that the performance and selection curves should be increasing functions of Y, or equivalently of function $g(Y)$, where g itself is increasing. Proposition 4.3 below determines under what conditions the performance and selection curves satisfy this requirement. Technically, the conditions of positive dependence concern the covariances and conditional expectation of Y and S. Therefore, Proposition 4.3 consists of three statements which define positive dependence of performance and selection curves in terms of marginal and conditional covariance and expectation. The proofs of all results are provided in Appendix 4.5.

Proposition 4.3.

(i) *The performance curve (respectively, the selection curve) lies below the line $y = 1$ (respectively, the 45° line) if and only if $\text{Cov}[g(Y), h(S)] \geqslant 0$ for any increasing functions g, h.*

(ii) *The performance curve is increasing if and only if $\text{Cov}[g(Y), h(S) \mid S \geqslant s] \geqslant 0$ for any increasing functions g, h and any threshold s.*

(iii) *The selection curve is increasing and convex if and only if the prediction $E[g(Y) \mid S = s]$ is an increasing function of s for any increasing function g.*

Among the conditions of positive dependence between Y and S, condition (i) is the least restrictive, while condition (iii) is the most stringent. A score which satisfies the more restrictive condition of positive dependence is preferred to other scores.

Let us investigate which property of positive dependence is satisfied by the canonical score $S = P[Y = 1 \mid X]$.

Proposition 4.4. *Let X be a set of individual covariates and let $S = P[Y = 1 \mid X]$ be the associated canonical score. Then the selection curve of the canonical score is increasing and convex.*

Proof. We obtain

$$E[g(Y) \mid S] = g(0) + [g(1) - g(0)]P[Y = 1 \mid S].$$

Moreover,

$$P[Y = 1 \mid S] = E[P[Y = 1 \mid S, X] \mid S]$$
$$= E[P[Y = 1 \mid X] \mid S]$$
$$= S.$$

Therefore, $E[g(Y) \mid S] = g(0) + [g(1) - g(0)]S$ is an increasing function of S, when g is increasing. The canonical score satisfies the most restrictive condition of positive dependence: (iii) in Proposition 4.3. $\square$

We can conclude that the canonical score is preferred to other scores and yields an increasing and convex selection curve. In practice, the canonical score is used as a benchmark for comparison of selection curves obtained from other scores. In particular, the convexity of those selection curves can be assessed by comparing them with the selection curve of the canonical score. Nonconvexity of a selection curve implies that the underlying score is less performant than a canonical score, and needs to be improved (the technique of score improvement is discussed in the next section).

4.1.3 *Comparison of Scores*

The main use of performance and selection curves, other than for the analysis of performance of a single score, is the comparison of performance of different scores. However, the selection curves depend, not only on the underlying score, but also on the population under study. For this reason we need to establish an adequate preference ordering.

Definition 4.5. In population Pop$_1$ score S_1 is more discriminatory than score S_2 in population Pop$_2$ if and only if the selection curve (respectively, performance curve) computed from (S_1, Pop_1) lies below the selection curve (respectively, performance curve) computed from (S_2, Pop_2).

In practice, preference ordering serves the following purposes.

(i) The comparison of performance of two different scores S_1 and S_2 in the same population: for instance, such as comparing a new score to an old one.

(ii) The comparison of performance of the same score in two different subpopulations. These subpopulations may be simultaneously controlled in order to distinguish the categories of customers for whom a given selection procedure works in the most efficient manner.

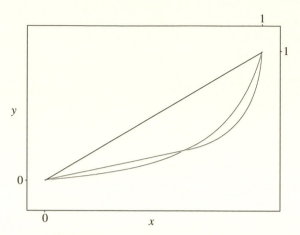

Figure 4.2. Comparison of scores.

(iii) Also, the same population of individuals may be examined at different times. In such a case, the evolution of the performance of a given score in time is examined to determine whether the score needs to be updated.

The preference ordering based on comparison of the performance and selection curves forms a partial ordering. Two scores applied to the same population can be incomparable: for instance, when the first one performs better in the subpopulation of bad risks and the second one performs better in the subpopulation of good risks.

The preference ordering is automatically satisfied by two canonical scores, one of which is based on an information set larger than the other one (see Gourieroux (1992) for a proof). This result is described in the following proposition.

Proposition 4.6. *Let us consider two canonical scores* S_1, S_2 *computed from the same population* Pop. *Let us assume that the first score is based on a set of covariates* X_1, *which is larger than the set of covariates* X_2 *of the second score. Then canonical score* S_1, *based on the larger information set, performs better than score* S_2.

Proposition 4.6 allows us to determine the bounds of selection curves (respectively, performance curves). This is done by considering the following two extreme situations: (1) lack of information about the individual (individual covariates are unobserved or missing), and (2) complete information (no risk) about the individual.

The canonical scores are, respectively,

(1) no information, $S_2 = P[Y = 1]$,

i.e., the score is equal to the marginal probability that the individual will be "good risk"; and

(2) complete information, $S_1 = P[Y = 1 \mid Y] = Y$.

We observe the risk associated with the individual and we know she is "good."

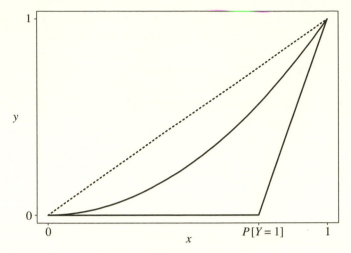

Figure 4.3. Bounds for selection curves.

The bounds of selection curves are established as follows. The upper bound is determined by the 45° line corresponding to the lack of information. Thus, any selection curve has to lie below the 45° line. The lower bound is established by the equation

$$
y = \begin{cases} 0 & \text{if } x \leqslant P[Y = 1], \\ 1 + \dfrac{x - 1}{P[Y = 0]} & \text{otherwise,} \end{cases} \tag{4.2}
$$

and corresponds to complete information.

When score S is defective, in that the associated selection curve is not increasing and convex, it can be improved by a well-chosen transformation to a canonical score (Gourieroux 1992).

Proposition 4.7. *For any score $\tilde{S}$, the score $S = P[Y = 1 \mid \tilde{S}]$ is a canonical score which performs better than $\tilde{S}$.*

The more powerful score is obtained by calculating the conditional probability that an individual will be good risk given the value of the defective score for that individual.

Strict improvement is achieved when $\tilde{S}$ and S are not one-to-one increasing functions of one another. In practice, it is useful to draw the selection curves of the initial score $\tilde{S}$ and of the improved score $P[Y = 1 \mid \tilde{S}]$ to see for which categories of individuals the most significant improvement was obtained.

4.2   Discriminant Curves

The preference ordering introduced in Section 4.1 was based on the conditional distribution of risk given covariates. Let us now consider the dual approach based on the conditional distribution of covariates given risk, and introduce an alternative score performance measure called the discriminant curve.

Suppose that score S is based on a set of covariates and is continuously valued. The density and survivor functions of the score, conditional on $Y = 0$ (respectively, $Y = 1$), are denoted by f_0, G_0 (respectively, f_1, G_1). Let us recall that the conditional survivor function is the following conditional probability:

$$G_j(s) = P[S \geqslant s \mid Y = j], \quad j = 0, 1.$$

The inverse of survivor function $G_0(s)$ is the value of threshold s at which the survivor function is evaluated. Let us denote that value by x:

$$x = G_0^{-1}(s) \longleftrightarrow P[S \geqslant x \mid Y = 0] = G_0.$$

The inverse of $G_1(s)$ can be found in an analogous way.

The discriminant curve is an alternative graphical goodness-of-fit representation for score performance.

4.2.1 Definitions

Definition 4.8. The *discriminant curve* of the score S is $D(x) = G_1 \circ G_0^{-1}(x)$.

One can think of the discriminant curve as the probability that score S is higher than threshold x for a good risk credit applicant, where x is the inverse of the survivor function for a bad risk applicant.

The discriminant curve is increasing in x, which takes values between 0 and 1 like the score itself. Therefore the x-axis of the two-dimensional plane in which the discriminant curve is traced covers the interval $[0, 1]$. The discriminant curve takes the value 0 at 0 and the value 1 at 1, and is invariant with respect to any increasing transformation of the score. The shape of the discriminant curve reflects positive dependence between the score value and risk Y. In particular, its concavity follows from Proposition 4.9 below.

Proposition 4.9. *The discriminant curve is concave if and only if* $E[g(Y) \mid S = s]$ *is an increasing function of s for any increasing function g.*

Proof. Indeed, we obtain

$$\frac{d\mathcal{D}(x)}{dx} = \frac{f_1[G_0^{-1}(x)]}{f_0[G_0^{-1}(x)]}.$$

The function $\mathcal{D}$ is concave if and only if the discriminant ratio $f_1(s)/f_0(s)$ is an increasing function of s. This ratio,

$$f_1(s)/f_0(s) = \frac{p_0}{p_1} \frac{P[Y = 1 \mid S = s]}{1 - P[Y = 1 \mid S = s]},$$

increases with s if and only if $P[Y = 1 \mid S = s]$ increases with s, which is the condition of Proposition 4.3 (iii) (see also the proof of Proposition 4.4). $\square$

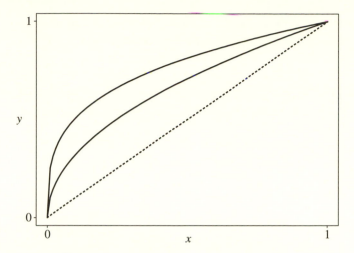

Figure 4.4. Comparison of discriminant curves.

To explain the role of the discriminant curve in evaluating the performance of a score, let us consider two extreme situations. When a score is completely useless for distinguishing between good and bad risks $G_1 = G_0$, and the discriminant curve coincides with the 45° line.

Suppose that distributions G_0 and G_1 are concentrated at two distinct values a_0 and a_1 with $a_1 > a_0$. Then, for any threshold value x different from 0 and 1, $G_0^{-1}(x) = a_0$ and $\mathcal{D}(x) = G_1 \circ G_0^{-1}(x) = G_1(a_0) = 1$. The discriminant curve takes the value 0 at 0, $D(x) = 0$ if $x = 0$, and is a flat line with ordinate 1, $D(x) = 1$, for all $x > 0$.

Since the discriminant curve of the most powerful score is a horizontal line at 1, one can argue that the closer a discriminant curve lies to 1, the better the score that curve is designed for. This remark leads us to the next topic: *discriminant ordering*.

Definition 4.10. Score S_1 applied to supbopulation Pop_1 is more discriminatory than score S_2 applied to subpopulation Pop_2 if and only if the discriminant curve associated with (S_1, Pop_1) lies above the discriminant curve associated with (S_2, Pop_2).

A relationship exists between the selection and discriminant curves and between the orderings based on each type of curve. This result follows from the equivalence of the dual approaches to risk prediction. The relationship between the selection and discriminant curves can be formally expressed as follows.

Proposition 4.11.

(i) *If function $\mathcal{S}$ is invertible, we have*

$$\mathcal{S}(x) = (p_1 \mathcal{D} + p_0 \, \text{Id})^{-1}(x).$$

(ii) (S_1, Pop_1) *performs better than* (S_2, Pop_2) *if and only if the discriminant curve associated with* (S_1, Pop_1) *lies above the discriminant curve associated with* (S_2, Pop_2).

Proof. (i) The selection curve admits the parametric specification, which can be rewritten by explicitly introducing the survivor functions G_1 and G_0:

$$x(s) = P[S \geqslant s] = p_1 G_1(s) + p_0 G_0(s),$$
$$y(s) = P[S \geqslant s \mid Y = 0] = G_0(s).$$

By considering the new parametrization with $u = G_0(s)$, we get the new parametric form,

$$x(u) = (p_1 \mathcal{D} + p_0 \, \mathrm{Id})(u),$$
$$y(u) = u,$$

and the implicit form,

$$\mathcal{S}(x) = [p_1 \mathcal{D} + p_0 \, \mathrm{Id}]^{-1}(x).$$

(ii) This property follows directly from the relationship between $\mathcal{S}$ and $\mathcal{D}$. □

4.2.2 Linear Discriminant Analysis

In the linear discriminant model, the score arises as a linear combination of basic covariates, which are conditionally normally distributed. Therefore, the score is also conditionally normal with distribution $N[m_0, \sigma^2]$ in subpopulation $Y = 0$, and $N(m_1, \sigma^2)$ in subpopulation $Y = 1$. Therefore,

$$G_1(s) = P[S \geqslant s \mid Y = 1] = \Phi\left(\frac{s - m_1}{\sigma}\right), \qquad G_0(s) = \Phi\left(\frac{s - m_0}{\sigma}\right),$$

where Φ is the c.d.f. of the standard normal. The discriminant curve is given by

$$y = \mathcal{D}(x) = G_1 \circ G_0^{-1}(x) = \Phi\left(\frac{m_1 - m_0}{\sigma} + \Phi^{-1}(x)\right).$$

Under normality, the discriminant curves belong to a parametric family, parametrized by $\mu = (m_1 - m_0)/\sigma$. The larger this parameter is, the more powerful the score.

4.3 Demand Monitoring, Credit Granting, and Scores

The following example illustrates the use of diagnostic tools, including performance curves, for the assessment of consumer credit scoring.

4.3.1 Time-Varying Quality of Credit Applicants

In Chapter 3 we saw that a credit score has to be estimated from the sample of customers who have established credit histories and for whom a value $Y_i = 0$ or $Y_i = 1$ of the risk variable has been observed and recorded. Once the estimates become available, the score can be used to assess the individual risk associated with new credit applicants. This procedure is based on an implicit assumption that the new credit applicants belong to the same population as the past ones, and that no structural change, relevant to the scoring system, has occurred. For example, if single and unemployed persons in the population of past applicants were considered "bad risk," a dramatic change would occur if among the new applicants all single unemployed persons were shown to repay their debt in a timely and consistent manner. It is important that a score has the ability of detecting and tracing out any structural changes in the population of applicants. Structural changes may be due to a variety of factors, such as competition among credit institutions who specialize in financial products that attract individuals with some specific characteristics, or an increase in the market share of one these institutions.

The following procedure can be used to detect the occurrence of structural changes in time. First, among the customers of a bank we distinguish a representative group of "past" and "new" loan holders. The score values for each person in each group are available from the records. We divide the score values into K categories k, $k = 1, \ldots, K$. Next, we take the sample of "past" customers and divide it into subsamples in the following way: the first subsample contains all customers with score values in category $k = 1$, the second subsample contains all those with score level $k = 2$, and so on. Each subsample has its own probability function of risk, provided by the fraction of customers with default in debt payment, $Y_i = 0$, and without default, $Y_i = 1$. The probability functions of risk for all score categories of past applicants are denoted $p_{0,k}, k = 1, \ldots, K$.

All steps of the procedure are then repeated for the group of "new" customers. The probability functions of risk for all score categories of new customers are denoted $p_{c,k}, k = 1, \ldots, K$

Finally, we compare the K probability functions of risk $p_{0,k}, k = 1, \ldots, K$, in the "past" applicants group with $p_{c,k}, k = 1, \ldots, K$, for the "new" group (see Table 4.1). A measure of change in risk distribution is a scalar *stability index*, defined by

$$\text{stab} = \sum_{k=1}^{K} (p_{c,k} - p_{0,k}) \log\left(\frac{p_{c,k}}{p_{0,k}}\right). \tag{4.3}$$

By definition, the stability index is nonnegative. When its value is less than 0.1, we conclude that the structure of demand has not been significantly modified.

Table 4.1 illustrates structural change in the population of customers of Bank UOMe Inc. Their credit score can take any positive value, and is divided into four categories given in column 1. Four groups of customers are distinguished. The "past"

Table 4.1. Population change in time with respect to risk.

Score	Benchmark	April–June	July–Sep	Oct–Dec
< 100	22.5	21.0	20.5	19.0
$100 \leqslant \cdots < 200$	20.0	20.5	19.0	18.0
$200 \leqslant \cdots < 250$	30.0	30.5	31.0	32.0
$\geqslant 250$	27.5	28.0	29.5	31.0
Stability index	0.000	0.001	0.004	0.135

Table 4.2. Population change in time with respect to income.

Covariate: monthly income (hundreds of euros)	Benchmark	Oct–Dec
< 5	12.5	16.0
$5 \leqslant \cdots < 10$	25.0	29.0
$10 \leqslant \cdots < 20$	30.0	27.0
$20 \leqslant \cdots < 30$	25.0	24.0
$\geqslant 30$	7.5	4.0

applicants group is referenced as "Benchmark" (column 2). The new customers are divided into three cohorts depending on which month of the current year their credit application was approved (columns 3–5). The entries in the table provide the default rate in each score category for each cohort of customers. For example, by looking at the first row, we conclude that the probability of no default for individuals with score values from the lowest category has diminished across cohorts. By looking at the last row, we find an opposite effect concerning individuals with the highest score values; their probability of no default has increased. The inference is not fully rigorous in the sense that no tests have been conducted to see whether the differences in default probabilities are statistically significant. From that point of view, the values of the stability index are more reliable. They are given in the last row of Table 4.1. The results indicate that no structural change has occurred.

If there is evidence in favor of structural change, then it is insightful to determine what type of change it is. This can be done by tracing the evolution of risk structure, with respect to main explanatory variables in the score (see Table 4.2). For example, we observe that changes often concern the income of applicants, and are often driven by the effects of extreme (low or high) incomes.

Table 4.2 presents the data for five categories of monthly income levels, measured in hundreds of euros (column 1). The subsamples of customers with incomes belonging to each category were selected from the "Benchmark" sample and from the "October–December" sample. The second (respectively, third) column provides the repartition of income in the "Benchmark" (respectively, October–December)

Table 4.3. Credit-granting decision.

Score	Total	Accepted	Rejected
< 100	2 860	277	2 583
$100 \leqslant \cdots < 200$	4 040	3 845	195
$200 \leqslant \cdots < 300$	3 933	3 903	30
$300 \leqslant \cdots$	2 429	2 428	1
Total	13 262	10 453	2 809
Exceptions from rule	503	277	226

sample. We observe that the new customers have smaller incomes than the "Benchmark" sample.

4.3.2 Analysis of Credit-Granting Decision

In practice, indications provided by the computed score values, on which applications should be accepted or denied, are not necessarily followed by credit officers in their final decision making. Therefore, differences arise between the outcomes of decisions based rigorously on the score, and those based on the subjective evaluation by credit officers. The reasons are as follows: (1) access to relevant information not accounted for by the score, but available to credit officers, (2) score distortion, and (3) fraud. Below, we illustrate the practice of decision making by Bank UOMe Inc. in 2003, which has an official rule of accepting credit applications with score values higher than $s = 100$. Table 4.3 shows data on the exceptions to the rule. The score values of credit applicants under study were divided into four categories: from less than 100, as the lowest category, to greater than 300, as the highest. Column 2 shows the total number of credit applicants with the score value from each of the four categories. Columns 3 and 4 show how many among the applications in each score category were accepted (column 3) and rejected (column 4). The outcomes of wrong (or ambiguous) decisions are underlined. For example, if the rule of threshold $s = 100$ were strictly implemented, all applicants with scores below that threshold should be denied credit. From the first row of Table 4.3 we see that out of 2869 applications with an insufficient score value, 277 applications were accepted. Rows 2–4 pertain to applicants whose score values satisfy the threshold requirement. In spite of that, some applications were denied: 195 in row 2, 30 in row 3, and 1 in row 4, which is very surprising, given that the score value of that individual was among the highest possible.

The second last row of Table 4.3 shows the total number of all applications (column 2), the total number of those accepted (column 3), and the total number of those denied (column 4). The last row gives the number of exceptions to the rule: there are 277 such decisions among the acceptances, and 226 among the rejections, giving a total of 503.

Table 4.4. Credit officer auditing.

Credit officer	Default predicted by the score	Observed default
A	7.8%	7.7%
B	7.5%	9.2%
C	8.2%	8.4%
⋮	⋮	⋮
Total	7.9%	8.0%

It is unknown whether the exceptions to the rule were due to human error or were the outcomes of deliberate decisions of credit officers, aware of important factors other than those accounted for in the score. As mentioned earlier, credit officers have some degree of discretion in their decision making, and are allowed to make exceptions for appropriate reasons.

The credit officers may decide to grant credit to high-risk customers. *Ex post*, some of these decisions can be proven correct, while others are proven to be mistaken. To monitor the rate of erroneous decisions, banks maintain a database for auditing their employees. Table 4.4 shows the data concerning three credit officers from Bank UOMe Inc, with personal identifiers A, B, C.

The data on past performance in Table 4.4 allow us to assess the efficiency of decisions made by A, B, and C. Column 2 shows the predicted rate of defaults on credits formerly approved by the score, for each credit officer. Column 3 gives the *ex post* observed rate of default among the costumers of each credit officer. When the observed default rate is lower than the expected one, the credit officer applies rules that are tougher than the score. This is the case for officer A, although the rate of default among loans approved by him is only marginally lower than the expected one. When the observed default rate is much greater than the expected rate, the credit officer is too liberal. This applies to officer B, whose default rate is much greater then 7.5. One possible rationale for granting credit to risky individuals often involves a strategic objective of the bank, such as an overall increase in market share. Otherwise, the credit officers may subjectively consider some particular covariate irrelevant. Finally, there is a chance the officers commit fraud by granting credit to applicants who are very risky.

One has to keep in mind that even for contracts with the same initial characteristics (credit amount, interest rate, maturity, and so on), the risk measured in terms of number of default occurrences can be different from risk measured in terms of severities, that is the dollar amounts of financial losses (see Table 4.5).

Table 4.5 provides the data on loans granted by Bank UOMe Inc. Column 1 distinguishes the five score value categories. Column 2 shows the predicted risk. For example, the probability of default is 18% for applicants with score values

Table 4.5. Risk dynamics: occurrence and severity.

Score	Predicted risk	Observed risk January		Observed risk February	
		Number	1000$	Number	1000$
< 100	18%	45	324	27	234
100 ⩽ ··· < 200	12%	90	864	59	708
200 ⩽ ··· < 250	8%	160	1680	119	1560
250 ⩽ ··· < 300	4%	60	792	73	1012
⩾ 300	3%	15	306	30	390
Total		370	3970	308	3904

Table 4.6. Evolution of risk by generations.

Generation	Sept 1990	Dec 1990	March 1991	June 1991	Sept 1991	Dec 1991	March 1992
Oct–Dec 1989	1.7	3.0	2.9	3.5	1.7	2.2	2.5
Jan–March 1990	1.1	1.7	1.5	2.9	1.7	1.9	2.1
April–June 1990	0.9	1.8	2.4	2.6	1.4	1.9	2.5
July–Sept 1990	0.0	1.5	1.9	2.4	2.5	1.9	2.4
Oct–Dec 1990	—	0.1	1.4	2.5	1.6	1.5	1.4
Jan–March 1991	—	—	0.3	1.9	1.8	2.2	2.8
April–June 1991	—	—	—	0.4	1.5	2.0	2.3
July–Sept 1991	—	—	—	—	0.5	1.7	2.3
Oct–Dec 1991	—	—	—	—	—	0.3	1.1
Jan–March 1991	—	—	—	—	—	—	0.1
Total	1.0	1.9	1.9	2.4	1.7	1.7	1.9

less than 100. The predicted default rates for the four remaining score categories are 12%, 8%, 4%, and 3%, respectively. Columns 3 and 4 contain the data on occurrence and severity of losses incurred in January. These can be compared with entries in columns 5 and 6 which present the same records one month later. It seems that the average risk of default occurrence has diminished in time for individuals with poor score values.

To make a final comment on the statistical results concerning the change in average occurrence and severity of default in time, one has to be aware that defaults recorded in different months may be associated with different generations of borrowers. The correction for the *generation effect* (or *cohort effect*) requires performing a dynamic analysis of risk (Table 4.6).

The columns of Table 4.6 show the consecutive months at which default rates were recorded for each generation. The last row of Table 4.6 provides aggregate results concerning a mixture of different generations, which are often difficult to

Table 4.7. Construction of performance curve.

Score	Fraction of total applicants	Acceptance rate	Default rate level 1	Default rate level 2	Default rate level 3
$0 \leqslant \cdots < 50$	11.3%	8.2%	17.2%	9.4%	2.8%
$50 \leqslant \cdots < 100$	11.2%	12.4%	15.4%	7.1%	2.0%
$100 \leqslant \cdots < 150$	9.8%	73.6%	9.8%	4.8%	1.4%
$150 \leqslant \cdots < 200$	10.2%	87.2%	5.6%	3.1%	0.8%
$200 \leqslant \cdots < 250$	30.0%	94.3%	4.1%	2.3%	0.3%
$\geqslant 250$	27.5%	99.1%	2.3%	1.5%	0.1%

interpret. By looking at the rows, generation by generation, we observe that default rates increase during the first three to four months of the loan, after which they have a tendency to drop.

4.3.3 Performance Curves

Performance curves can be used to monitor potential distortions in a score. If the indications of a score were strictly implemented (given an imposed threshold s_0), we could only observe the portion of the performance curve for $S \geqslant s_0$. On the other hand, if the score was completely disregarded, then loan applications that do not meet the minimum score requirement would be approved. The less consideration is given to the score, the more often such decisions can be made. Table 4.7 shows the data on acceptance rates and defaults associated with varying score levels. Three types of default are distinguished and ranked with respect to increasing severity in columns 4–6.

For borrowers in all score categories, the highest default rates are associated with the class of low severity (column 4). In the classes of moderate severity (column 5), default rates are slightly lower, and they drop again when we move to the class of highest severity (column 6).

Finally, we show in Figure 4.5 two performance curves for the same score evaluated at two different dates. Recall that the lower the curve is, the better the score performance.

4.4 Concluding Remarks

The main diagnostic tools for qualitative risk analysis are the performance and discriminant curves. Of these, the performance curve is more suitable for the analysis of risk based on qualitative models. It visualizes the relative probability of default in a selected population as a function of the market share. The curves provide a graphical display that features positive dependence between the score and the dichotomous risk variable. The curves also allow for comparison of score performances across different samples of individuals and at different points in time. In practice, performance

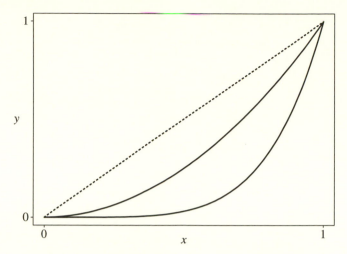

Figure 4.5.   Performance curves at two different dates.

and selection curves are among many components in a battery of diagnostic tools designed for score monitoring. Other summary statistics considered may include data on the evolution of the number of credit applicants in time and the outcomes of auditing among the credit officers.

Further readings on positive dependence are available in Lehmann (1966), Kimeldorf and Sampson (1987), Schriever (1987), and Suppes (1970). In marketing, the performance curve is called the "richness curve" (see Novak et al. 1992).

4.5   Appendix: Positive Dependence

Proof of the First Part of Proposition 4.3

(i) Since Y is a dichotomous qualitative variable, any function $g(Y)$ admits a linear form $g(Y) = g(1)Y + g(0)(1 - Y)$, and the condition $\mathrm{Cov}(g(Y), h(S)) \leqslant 0$, for any increasing functions g, h, is equivalent to $\mathrm{Cov}(Y, h(S)) \leqslant 0$, for any increasing function h.

(ii) Since any increasing function h can be written as an increasing limit of positive linear combinations of indicator functions $\mathbf{1}_{S \geqslant s_0}$, s_0 varying, the latter condition becomes

$$\mathrm{Cov}[Y, \mathbf{1}_{S \geqslant s_0}] \geqslant 0, \quad \forall s_0.$$

(iii) By expanding this condition, we obtain

$$\mathrm{Cov}[Y, \mathbf{1}_{S \geqslant s_0}] = \mathrm{Cov}[E(Y \mid S), \mathbf{1}_{S \geqslant s_0}]$$
$$= \mathrm{Cov}[P(Y = 1 \mid S), \mathbf{1}_{S \geqslant s_0}] \geqslant 0, \quad \forall s_0.$$

Equivalently, we obtain

$$\mathrm{Cov}[P(Y = 0 \mid S), \mathbf{1}_{S \geqslant s_0}] = P[Y = 0, \ S \geqslant s_0] - P[Y = 0]P[S \geqslant s_0] \leqslant 0, \quad \forall s_0,$$

or

$$y(s_0) = \frac{P[Y = 0 \mid S \geqslant s_0]}{P[Y = 0]} \leqslant 1.$$

Proof of the Second Part of Proposition 4.3

By applying the same arguments to the joint distribution of Y, S, conditional on $S \geqslant s_1$, where $s_1 < s_0$, we obtain

$$\frac{P[Y = 0 \mid S \geqslant s_0, \ S \geqslant s_1]}{P[Y = 0 \mid S \geqslant s_1]} \leqslant 1, \quad \forall s_1 < s_0,$$

$$\iff \frac{y(s_0)}{y(s_1)} = \frac{P[Y = 0 \mid S \geqslant s_0]}{P[Y = 0 \mid S \geqslant s_1]} \leqslant 1, \quad \forall s_1 < s_0,$$

which is the condition for a decreasing $y(\cdot)$ function. The result is derived by observing that $x(\cdot)$ is also decreasing.

Proof of the Third Part of Proposition 4.3

For convenience, let us assume a continuous score, with p.d.f. f and survivor function G. The selection curve is defined by

$$x(s) = G(s), \qquad y(s) = \int_s^{\bar{s}} P[Y = 0 \mid S = u] f(u) \, du / P[Y = 0],$$

where $\bar{s}$ is the maximum admissible value of the score.

Therefore the implicit equation of the selection curve is

$$\delta(x) = \frac{1}{P[Y = 0]} \int_{G^{-1}(x)}^{\bar{s}} P[Y = 0 \mid S = u] f(u) \, du.$$

Its first-order derivative,

$$\frac{d\delta(x)}{dx} = \frac{P[Y = 0 \mid S = G^{-1}(x)]}{P[Y = 0]},$$

is always positive.

The selection curve is convex if and only if $x \longrightarrow (d\delta(x)/dx)$ is increasing, or if and only if $s \longrightarrow P[Y = 0 \mid S = s]$ is decreasing, which provides the result.

References

Gouriéroux, C. 1992. Courbes de performances et de discrimination. *Annales d'Economie et de Statistique* 28:107–23.

Lehmann, E. 1966. Some concepts of dependence. *Annals of Mathematical Statistics* 37:1137–53.

Kimeldorf, G., and A. Sampson. 1987. Positive dependence orderings. *Annals of the Institute of Statistics and Mathematics* 39:113–28.

Novak, T., de Leeuw, J., and B. McEroy. 1992. Richness curves for evaluating market segmentation. *Journal of Marketing Research* 29:254–67.

Schriever, B. 1987. An ordering for positive dependence. *Annals of Statistics* 15:1208–14.

Suppes, P. 1970. *A Probabilistic Theory of Causality*. Amsterdam: North-Holland.

5

Count Data Models

The risk models discussed so far are based on the dichotomous risk variable, which indicates whether or not a loss event occurs. In this chapter, we will investigate how many loss events occur per unit of time or, equivalently, how frequent the loss events are. In technical terms, counting the number of losses per unit of time means shifting our attention to risk viewed as a count variable. In the insurance system, for example, important count variables include the number of claims on one policy in one year, the number of payments on one policy in one year, and the number of losses to the insurer or the insured in one year. These count variables of claims or losses represent individual risks, and need to be predicted, for example, when the pure premium is computed for new policyholders, or when future premiums are updated, based on past experience. In general, problems regarding risk in the insurance system will provide a framework for the discussion of various models and examples. Accordingly, we will borrow from insurance terminology and refer to the count variable of risk as the "number of claims" or "claim count" interchangeably in the text.

In the first approach, the number of claims can be modeled and predicted by the Poisson regression model. This basic specification for count variables will allow us to establish a relationship between the count variable risk models and the models based on the dichotomous qualitative variable of risk covered in Chapters 3 and 4. In practice, there exists some idiosyncratic risk related to individual insurance contracts which also has to be insured. For this reason, the underlying assumption of the basic Poisson regression model seems quite unrealistic. When this assumption is relaxed, we get various extensions to the Poisson regression model. These variations consist of treating the residual heterogeneity of insureds as a distinct unobserved random variable. Two cases are distinguished; when the heterogeneity distribution is left unspecified, the model becomes semi-parametric. Under the assumption of a gamma heterogeneity distribution, the model becomes a negative binomial model, with observable covariates. In automobile insurance, the negative-binomial model is used to derive closed-form updating formulas for the policy premium (bonus-malus scheme). An application that illustrates how automobile insurance premiums are determined is given at the end of the chapter.

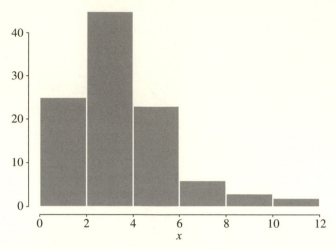

Figure 5.1.   Histogram of a Poisson distribution.

5.1   Poisson Regression

The Poisson regression is the basic count variable model for individual risks. It is easy to estimate and interpret, but relies on some strong simplifying assumptions. Before introducing the Poisson regression, we provide some insights on the Poisson distribution of a single count variable and its moments.

5.1.1   The Model

A count variable Y is often assumed to be Poisson distributed $\mathcal{P}(\lambda)$. The probability function (referred to as the density in the remainder of this chapter) of the Poisson variable is

$$P[Y = y] = \exp(-\lambda)\frac{\lambda^y}{y!}, \quad y = 0, 1, 2, \ldots, \qquad (5.1)$$

where λ is the intensity parameter. The Poisson distribution is generally unimodal and skewed, with the first- and second-order moments given by

$$EY = \lambda, \qquad VY = \lambda. \qquad (5.2)$$

Its particular feature is that the mean and variance are equal.

The *Poisson regression model* arises as an extension of (5.1). In particular, in the Poisson regression model, the intensity λ depends on the values of observable covariates for each individual (or contract) i. Since λ varies across individuals, its notation changes to λ_i. The standard specification of individual intensity is

$$\lambda_i = \exp(z_i'\theta), \qquad (5.3)$$

where θ is a vector of unknown parameters and z_i is a vector whose components are various transformations of individual characteristics x_i. The exponential function in (5.3) ensures that individual intensity parameters are positive.

In the Poisson regression model, the risk count variables $Y_1, \ldots, Y_n$ are independent, conditional on the covariates, and the conditional distribution of Y_i is $\mathcal{P}[\exp z_i'\theta]$. In particular,

$$E[Y_i \mid x_i] = V[Y_i \mid x_i] = \exp(z_i'\theta). \tag{5.4}$$

The Poisson regression model is intrinsically heteroskedastic, meaning that the variance of each count is different.

The Poisson regression model suggests the use of a specific score for rating individuals in the sample with respect to risk. This score is $S_i = z_i'\theta$. The higher the score is, the higher the expected number of claims and the higher its variation. Thus, contrary to the approach adopted in previous chapters, a high value of this score indicates bad risk.

5.1.2 Maximum Likelihood Estimator

The Poisson regression is a parametric model with the following log-likelihood function:

$$L(\theta) = \log\left\{ \prod_{i=1}^{n} \left[\exp(-\exp z_i'\theta) \frac{\exp(y_i z_i'\theta)}{y_i!} \right] \right\}$$

$$= \sum_{i=1}^{n} \{y_i z_i'\theta - \exp(z_i'\theta) - \log(y_i!)\}.$$

The log-likelihood function is concave with respect to θ. The maximum likelihood estimator is derived from the first-order conditions

$$\frac{\partial L(\hat{\theta}_n)}{\partial \theta} = 0 \iff \sum_{i=1}^{n} [y_i - \exp(z_i'\hat{\theta}_n)]z_i = 0. \tag{5.5}$$

$\hat{u}_i = y_i - \exp(z_i'\hat{\theta}_n)$ is the residual associated with individual i, that is, the difference between the observed and fitted count variable. Thus, the first-order conditions in (5.5) are equivalent to the orthogonality conditions for residuals and explanatory variables (as in standard linear or logit models). In particular, the residuals sum up to zero, provided that the covariates include a constant term.

The second-order derivative of the log-likelihood function is

$$\frac{\partial^2 L}{\partial \theta \partial \theta'}(\theta) = -\sum_{i=1}^{n} z_i z_i' \exp(z_i'\hat{\theta}_n).$$

According to the theory of maximum likelihood, the estimator $\hat{\theta}_n$ is consistent and asymptotically normal. The estimated variance matrix of $\hat{\theta}_n$ is

$$\hat{V}(\hat{\theta}_n) = \left[-\frac{\partial^2 L(\hat{\theta}_n)}{\partial \theta \partial \theta'} \right]^{-1} = \left[\sum_{i=1}^{n} z_i z_i' \exp(z_i'\hat{\theta}_n) \right]^{-1}. \tag{5.6}$$

5.1.3   Relationship with the Dichotomous Qualitative Model

A dichotomous qualitative variable can be easily associated with any count variable of risk in the following manner. Let us assume that Y is the number of claims. We define

$$Y^* = \begin{cases} 1 & \text{if } Y > 0, \\ 0 & \text{otherwise.} \end{cases}$$

The variable Y^* indicates the occurrence of at least one claim. Therefore, $Y^* = 1$ for bad risk individuals. The conditional distribution of Y_i^* given covariates is

$$P[Y_i^* = 1 \mid x_i] = 1 - P[Y_i = 0 \mid x_i]$$
$$= 1 - \exp(-\exp z_i'\theta), \tag{5.7}$$

which is the so-called *Gompit regression model* for dichotomous variables.

The unknown parameter θ can be estimated by the maximum likelihood method from a sample of indicator values $Y_i^*, i = 1, \ldots, n$. Since the qualitative information is incomplete, this estimator is less accurate than the estimator based on count data discussed earlier in the text. It arises as the solution of the following optimization:

$$\max_{\theta} \sum_{i=1}^{n} \{y_i^* \log[1 - \exp(-\exp z_i'\theta)] - (1 - y_i^*) \exp z_i'\theta\}.$$

The estimator value is found by numerical maximization.

5.2   The Negative-Binomial Regression

One drawback of the Poisson regression model is that it involves a constraint of equality on the conditional mean and conditional variance of the count variable. In empirical research, the data seem to reject the mean-variance equality, and the fit of the model is often poor. As a remedy, an additional degree of freedom can be gained by introducing an unobservable *heterogeneity factor*. It accounts for the effects of all characteristics of sampled individuals that, although potentially relevant, are not included among the explanatory variables. Technically, the heterogeneity factor is a random variable, which is supposed to follow a gamma distribution. A Poisson regression with gamma distributed heterogeneity yields the *negative-binomial regression model*. The negative-binomial regression model is used in the automobile insurance system for updating insurance premiums, that is, for determining *the bonus-malus scheme*.

5.2.1   Model with Gamma Heterogeneity

Individual intensity λ_i was specified in Section 5.1 as a deterministic function of observable covariates. Let us now assume that all individuals comply with that scheme, yet some explanatory variables have been omitted because they are unobserved, or are considered irrelevant. More specifically, the variable μ_i will account for all characteristics of individual i that distinguish his/her behavior from the average computed, given the set of observable characteristics included in the model. Under the new approach, individual intensity can be written as

$$\lambda_i = \exp(z_i'\theta + \varepsilon_i) = \mu_i \exp(z_i'\theta), \tag{5.8}$$

where μ_i (or ε_i) is the latent (unobserved) variable, called the *heterogeneity factor* or the *omitted heterogeneity*.

The negative-binomial regression model is defined in two steps. First, we assume that the conditional distribution of Y_i, given both x_i and μ_i, is Poisson distributed $\mathcal{P}[\mu_i \exp z_i'\theta]$; second, we specify the conditional distribution of μ_i given covariates as a gamma distribution $\gamma(A, A)$ with density

$$f(\mu) = A^A \mu^{A-1} \frac{\exp(-A\mu)}{\Gamma(A)}, \tag{5.9}$$

where the $\Gamma(\cdot)$ function is defined by $\Gamma(A) = \int_0^\infty \exp{-\mu\mu^{A-1}} \, d\mu, \ A > 0$. There is an additional equality constraint on the two parameters of the gamma distribution that yields $E\mu = 1$. This constraint on the expected heterogeneity factor is not too restrictive, provided that a constant term is included among the observable covariates.

Since the variance of the heterogeneity factor is equal to $V\mu = 1/A$, we obtain the first- and second-order conditional moments of risk given the observable covariates:

$$\begin{aligned}
E(Y_i \mid x_i) &= E[E(Y_i \mid x_i, \mu_i) \mid x_i] \\
&= E[\mu_i \exp z_i'\theta \mid x_i] \\
&= \exp(z_i'\theta); \\
V(Y_i \mid x_i) &= E(V(Y_i \mid x_i, \mu_i) \mid x_i) + V(E(Y_i \mid x_i, \mu_i) \mid x_i) \\
&= E[\mu_i \exp z_i'\theta \mid x_i] + V[\mu_i \exp z_i'\theta \mid x_i] \\
&= \exp(z_i'\theta) + (1/A) \exp(2z_i'\theta).
\end{aligned}$$

The presence of unobservable heterogeneity removes the equality restriction concerning the two first conditional moments, which was binding in the Poisson regression model. As a consequence, the conditional variance can be larger than, or equal to, the conditional mean. When A decreases there is more heterogeneity among the individuals, and the overdispersion ratio $V(Y_i \mid x_i)/E(Y_i \mid x_i)$ increases. In the limiting case $A \to +\infty$, the gamma distribution degenerates to a point mass at $\mu = 1$, so that we end up with the Poisson regression model where $V(Y_i \mid x_i) = E(Y_i \mid x_i)$.

The negative-binomial regression model depends on the two following types of parameter: vector θ contains the sensitivity coefficients of the observable explanatory variables, and scalar A measures the amount of heterogeneity. All the parameters can be estimated by the maximum likelihood method, based on the conditional density of the count variable, given the observable covariates. The conditional density is derived by integrating out the unobservable heterogeneity factor, as follows:

$$
\begin{aligned}
f(y_i \mid x_i) &= \int_0^\infty \exp[-\mu \exp(-z_i'\theta)]\mu^{y_i} \frac{\exp(y_i z_i'\theta)}{y_i!} A^A \mu^{A-1} \frac{\exp(-A\mu)}{\Gamma(A)} \, d\mu \\
&= \frac{A^A \exp(y_i z_i'\theta)}{y_i! \Gamma(A)} \int_0^\infty \exp -\mu[A + \exp(-z_i'\theta)]\mu^{y_i+A-1} \, d\mu \\
&= \frac{\Gamma(y_i + A)}{\Gamma(y_i + 1)\Gamma(A)} \frac{[(1/A) \exp z_i'\theta]^{y_i}}{[1 + (1/A) \exp z_i'\theta]^{y_i+A}}.
\end{aligned}
\tag{5.10}
$$

This expression is the density of a negative-binomial count variable. The likelihood function of the negative-binomial regression is equal to the logarithm of the product of expression (5.10) evaluated for each individual i across the sample. It can be maximized numerically with respect to A and θ. This procedure directly yields maximum likelihood estimates.

5.2.2   The Bonus-Malus Scheme

The negative-binomial model provides a simple framework for updating the policy premiums in automobile insurance; it is also known as the bonus-malus scheme. Let us consider policyholder i, who has been insured in years $t = 1, \ldots, T$. We denote the observed number of accidents in which she was involved in any year by $Y_{i,t}, t = 1, \ldots, T$, and her potential number of accidents in the next year by $Y_{i,T+1}$. We assume that the risk variables represented by accident counts in each year are independent, conditional on the observable covariates $x_{i,t}, t = 1, \ldots, T, T+1$, and unobservable individual factors μ_i. The annual accident counts have the following distributions:

$$
Y_{i,t} \sim \mathcal{P}[\mu_i \exp(z_{i,t}'\theta)], \quad t = 1, \ldots, T+1,
$$

where the $z_{i,t}$ are some known transformations of basic covariates $x_{i,t}$.

The heterogeneity factor has marginal distribution $\gamma(A, A)$, called the *prior*, which represents the *a priori* knowledge about the heterogeneity factor, unrelated to any past experience of the policyholder. This knowledge needs to be updated, based on new driving records collected each year.

The updated knowledge about the heterogeneity factor will, in turn, allow for updating the premium paid by the policyholder for automobile insurance. If the experience of our policyholder is consistently better than the average computed in a given rating class of individuals with similar characteristics, then she deserves a reduction in her policy premium. In fact, some policyholders are better risks than expected in a given rating class of individuals due to their intrinsic characteristics, reflected by the heterogeneity factor. Therefore, the insurer needs to establish how much of the difference in the experience of a given policyholder is due to random variation in her driving experience and how much is due to the fact that the policyholder really is a better or worse risk than the average for the given rating class.

Obviously, the more past information the insurer has on a given policyholder, the more credible the policyholder's own experience.[1]

To perform the premium updating, we first compute the conditional distribution of factor μ_i given past information $Y_{i,1}, \ldots, Y_{i,T}$, called the *posterior distribution*. This is done in Section 5.2.2.1 below. The updating of the insurance premium is explained in Section 5.2.2.2.

5.2.2.1 *The Posterior Distribution of the Heterogeneity Factor*

The joint distribution of $(Y_{i,1}, \ldots, Y_{i,T}, \mu_i)$, conditional on the observable covariates, is

$$l(y_{i,1}, \ldots, y_{i,T}, \mu_i \mid x)$$

$$= \prod_{t=1}^{T} \left\{ \exp[-\mu_i \exp z'_{i,t} \theta] \frac{\mu_i^{y_{i,t}} \exp(y_{i,t} z'_{i,t} \theta)}{y_{i,t}!} \right\} \frac{1}{\Gamma(A)} A^A \mu_i^{A-1} \exp(-A\mu_i)$$

$$= \exp\left[-\mu_i \sum_{t=1}^{T} \exp(z'_{it}\theta) \right] \frac{\mu_i^{\sum_{t=1}^{T} y_{i,t}} \exp[\sum_{t=1}^{T} y_{i,t} z'_{i,t} \theta]}{\prod_{t=1}^{T}(y_{i,t})!}$$

$$\times \frac{1}{\Gamma(A)} A^A \mu_i^{A-1} \exp(-A\mu_i).$$

The posterior distribution of heterogeneity is derived using the Bayes formula:

$$l(\mu_i \mid y_{i,1}, \ldots, y_{i,T}, x)$$

$$= \exp\left(-\mu_i \left[A + \sum_{t=1}^{T} \exp z'_{i,t} \theta \right] \right) \mu_i^{A + \sum_{t=1}^{T} y_{i,t} - 1}$$

$$\times \left(A + \sum_{t=1}^{T} \exp z'_{i,t} \theta \right)^{(A + \sum_{t=1}^{T} y_{i,t})} \frac{1}{\Gamma(A + \sum_{t=1}^{T} y_{i,t})}. \qquad (5.11)$$

This expression defines a gamma distribution, with degrees of freedom parameter $A + \sum_{t=1}^{T} y_{i,t}$ and scale parameter $A + \sum_{t=1}^{T} \exp(z'_{i,t}\theta)$. More concisely, it can be written as

$$l(\mu_i \mid y_{i,1}, \ldots, y_{i,T}, x) = \gamma\left[A + \sum_{t=1}^{T} y_{i,t}, A + \sum_{t=1}^{T} \exp(z'_{i,t}\theta) \right]. \qquad (5.12)$$

The prior and posterior distributions belong to the same gamma family. Therefore, only the two parameters of the gamma distribution need to be updated in order to update the whole posterior distribution when new records are added to individual experience. More specifically, the parameters of the posterior distribution depend on the sequence of past accidents (or claims[2]) through term $\sum_{t=1}^{T} y_{i,t}$, which is a sufficient summary statistic of individual risk experience.

---

[1] For more on credibility theory see Klugman et al. (2004).

[2] The number of accidents may be different from the number of claims. A policyholder may not file a claim when an accident entails losses of an amount lower than the deductible. Similarly, the anticipation

5.2.2.2   *The Pure Premium*

Let us assume that the dollar amount lost due to an accident is independent of the total number of accidents, and that the expected dollar amount paid per accident is C_{T+1} in year $T + 1$.[3] The pure premium at date T is defined as the total expected amount to be payed in year $T + 1$ and is given by

$$P_{i,T} = C_{T+1}E(Y_{i,T+1} \mid x_{i,t},\ t = 1, \ldots, T + 1,\ y_{i,t},\ t = 1, \ldots, T)$$
$$= C_{T+1}\exp(z'_{i,t+1}\theta)E[\mu_i \mid x_{i,t},\ t = 1, \ldots, T + 1,\ y_{i,t},\ t = 1, \ldots, T].$$

Since the posterior expectation of heterogeneity is the mean of gamma distribution (5.12), we can substitute it for expectation in the last formula to arrive at the following:

$$P_{i,T} = C_{T+1}\exp(z'_{i,T+1}\theta)\frac{A + \sum_{t=1}^{T} y_{i,t}}{A + \sum_{t=1}^{T} \exp(z'_{i,t}\theta)}. \tag{5.13}$$

5.2.2.3   *The Bonus-Malus Scheme*

The pure premium formula (5.13) allows us to distinguish three essential premium updating components: (1) the inflation factor, (2) the change of risk priors, and (3) the effect of learning about the heterogeneity factor from past experience. These components are obtained by computing the relative increment of the premium $P_{i,T+1}/P_{i,T}$:

$$\frac{P_{i,T+1}}{P_{i,T}} = \frac{C_{T+2}}{C_{T+1}}\frac{\exp(z'_{i,T+2}\theta)}{\exp(z'_{i,T+1}\theta)}\frac{\hat{\mu}_{i,T+1}}{\hat{\mu}_{i,T}}, \tag{5.14}$$

where $\hat{\mu}_{i,T}$ denotes the expected heterogeneity factor computed at the end of period T. The ratio of expected heterogeneity factors in the two consecutive years is a necessary input for a model with unobservable heterogeneity. The inflation term is the increment of cost C_t from year $T + 1$ to $T + 2$. The change in risk priors is reflected by the ratio of terms $\exp(z'_{i,t}\theta)$ evaluated in years $T + 1$ and $T + 2$, consecutively.

Formula (5.14) for insurance policy premium updating can be interpreted as follows: if the observed number of accidents $y_{i,T+1}$ is greater than the expected number of accidents $\exp(z'_{i,T+1}\theta)$, then $\hat{\mu}_{i,T+1}/\hat{\mu}_{i,T}$ is larger than one. This is the case of malus, and the premium has to increase, ceteris paribus. Thus, our statistical evidence reveals that our policyholder is higher risk than the average policyholder in his/her score rating category.

5.2.2.4   *Time-Invariant Observable Covariates*

The premium updating in the case of time-invariant explanatory variables $z_{i,t} = z_i$, $\forall t$, is of particular interest, as it allows us to see the long-term effect of learning

---

of an increase in future premiums (through malus) motivates a car owner not to report a minor accident even when the damage exceeds the deductible by a little.

[3] The cost of claim and the cost of settlement may be different from the amount paid by the insurer, due to the effect of the deductible, for example.

from past experience. When the explanatory variables are fixed in time, the expected heterogeneity factor is

$$\hat{\mu}_{i,T} = \frac{A + \sum_{t=1}^{T} y_{i,t}}{A + T \exp(z_i'\theta)}$$
$$= \frac{A/T + \bar{y}_{i,T}}{A/T + \exp z_i'\theta},$$

where $\bar{y}_{i,T}$ is the average number of accidents per year computed over the first T years. Accordingly, the pure premium is

$$P_{i,T} = C_{T+1} \exp z_i'\theta \frac{A/T + \bar{y}_{i,T}}{A/T + \exp z_i'\theta}. \tag{5.15}$$

When no records on past individual experience are available (limiting case: $T = 0$), the pure premium is $P_{i,0} = C_1 \exp z_i'\theta$. It depends only on the prior individual characteristics. In the insurance literature, the pure premium is often referred to as the manual rate. When the observed individual history spans a very long period of time (i.e., consists of a very large number of observations; that is, in the limiting case $T \to \infty$), we get

$$\lim_{T\to\infty} \bar{y}_{i,T} = \mu_i \exp z_i'\theta, \qquad \lim_{T\to\infty} \hat{\mu}_{i,T} = \mu_i, \qquad \lim_{T\to\infty} (P_{i,T} - C_{T+1}\mu_i) = 0.$$

The unobservable heterogeneity factor becomes known and the premium no longer depends on the prior risk covariates x_i. In other words, when the set of observations of individual experience increases, the insurer learns more and more about the policyholders. This learning process allows the insurer to adjust the compensation scheme. At the beginning of the first contract with an unknown policyholder, the insurer only has information about individual covariates x_i, but no information on past driving records. Therefore, the policy premium paid by a new policyholder depends on x_i only. In some sense, within the class of new policyholders with similar score ratings, the good risks finance indemnities paid to the bad risks. The insurance contracts imply coverage across the insureds in a rating class. As time goes on, the insurer acquires more and more knowledge about policyholders whose experience keeps growing and becomes more credible. To these policyholders a different type of coverage is available. Each policyholder compensates his own losses from his own past policy premiums which keep accumulating. These insurance contracts imply coverage over time, where premiums collected from a given policyholder form a "savings account" that covers indemnities paid in bad periods.

5.3 Semi-Parametric Analysis

As mentioned before, two types of extensions to the basic Poisson regression exist. The first type is based on a parametric approach to modeling the heterogeneity factor as a gamma variable. This approach leads to the negative-binomial model. The second type is nonparametric, in that no particular distributional form of heterogeneity factor is imposed.

The assumption that the heterogeneity factor is gamma distributed can be seen as a drawback of the negative-binomial model. When this assumption is wrong, the model is misspecified. Misspecification, in turn, can entail bad evaluation of the pure premium and inadequate premium updating.

In this section, we consider a less restrictive semi-parametric specification. It bridges the gap between the fully parametric and fully nonparametric approaches. In the semi-parametric setup, the heterogeneity factor is allowed to follow an unspecified density, but its generic parameters, which are the mean and variance, are constrained to be finite.

The set of assumptions on the semi-parametric model is as follows.

(a) The risk (count) variables $Y_{i,t}$, $i = 1, \ldots, n$, $t = 1, \ldots, T$, are independent, conditional on the observable covariates and the heterogeneity factor, and have the following conditional Poisson distributions:

$$Y_{i,t} \sim \mathcal{P}[\mu_i \exp(z'_{i,t}\theta)], \quad i = 1, \ldots, n, \ t = 1, \ldots, T.$$

(b) The heterogeneity factors μ_i, $i = 1, \ldots, n$, are independent, with identical p.d.f. g, with mean 1 and variance η^2.

5.3.1   *Mean and Variance Estimators*

The semi-parametric model includes parametric specifications of the first- and second-order moments of the count variables of risk given the observable covariates:

$$
\begin{aligned}
E(Y_{i,t} \mid x_{i,t}) &= E[E(Y_{i,t} \mid x_{i,t}, \mu_i) \mid x_{i,t}] \\
&= E[\mu_i \exp z'_{i,t}\theta] \\
&= \exp(z'_{i,t}\theta), \qquad\qquad\qquad\qquad\qquad (5.16)
\end{aligned}
$$

$$
\begin{aligned}
V[Y_{i,t} \mid x_{i,t}] &= V[E(Y_{i,t} \mid x_{i,t}, \mu_i) \mid x_{i,t}] + E[V(Y_{i,t} \mid x_{i,t}, \mu_i) \mid x_{i,t}] \\
&= V[\mu_i \exp(z'_{i,t}\theta)] + E[\mu_i \exp(z'_{i,t}\theta)] \\
&= \eta^2 \exp(2z'_{i,t}\theta) + \exp(z'_{i,t}\theta). \qquad\qquad (5.17)
\end{aligned}
$$

These conditional moment restrictions suggest that consistent estimators of θ and η^2 can be found by minimizing the distance between the observed claim counts and their conditional expectations. Let us first consider estimation of parameter θ. We introduce the nonlinear least squares (NLS) estimator, defined by

$$\tilde{\theta} = \arg\min_{\theta} \sum_i \sum_t [y_{i,t} - \exp z'_{it}\theta]^2.$$

NLS estimation is known to be consistent when the number of observations tends to infinity. However, $\tilde{\theta}$ is not fully efficient since the endogenous variables $Y_{i,t}$ are not Gaussian. To solve this difficulty, Gourieroux et al. (1984) propose using the maximum likelihood estimator of θ from the Poisson regression model, that is, to set the heterogeneity factor equal to zero. Such a model is obviously misspecified as it disregards an important feature of the data. However, it turns out that the resulting estimator has good asymptotic properties. This so-called *pseudo-* (or quasi-) *maximum likelihood estimator* is defined as

$$\hat{\theta} = \arg\min_{\theta} \sum_i \sum_t [y_{i,t} z'_{i,t}\theta - \exp(z'_{i,t}\theta) - \log(y_{it}!)]. \tag{5.18}$$

It has been proven that the pseudo-maximum likelihood estimator is consistent despite the misspecification due to omitted heterogeneity. Nonetheless, it is not fully efficient, but in practice it is shown to be more efficient than the NLS estimator.

Once a consistent estimator of parameter θ is computed, a consistent estimator of the variance of the heterogeneity factor η^2 can also be derived. The expression of the conditional variance of count $Y_{i,t}$ is

$$V(Y_{i,t} \mid x_{i,t}) = E((Y_{i,t} - \exp z'_{i,t}\theta)^2 \mid x_{i,t})$$
$$= \eta^2 \exp(2z'_{i,t}\theta) + \exp(z'_{i,t}\theta).$$

Let us define the residuals as the differences between the observed and conditionally expected counts:

$$\hat{u}_{i,t} = y_{i,t} - \exp(z'_{i,t}\hat{\theta}_T).$$

A consistent estimator of η^2 is obtained by regressing

$$\hat{u}_{i,t}^2 - \exp z'_{i,t}\hat{\theta}_T \quad \text{on} \quad \exp(2z'_{i,t}\hat{\theta}_T).$$

5.3.2 *Estimation of the Heterogeneity Distribution*

Knowledge of the conditional first- and second-order moments is generally insufficient for computing the pure premium and for its updating, since these require knowledge of the whole heterogeneity distribution, rather than knowledge of parameter η^2 only. Therefore, the heterogeneity distribution needs to be estimated. Two different procedures are available and are described below.

(i) The first approach assumes that the heterogeneity distribution belongs to a large parametric family, $g_\alpha(\mu)$, α varying, say. For instance, this distribution can be a mixture of gamma distributions $\sum_{j=1}^{J} \pi_j \gamma(A_j, A_j)$, where the parameter set includes weights π_j, degrees of freedom A_j, and the number of terms J tends to infinity with the number of observations. Then parameter α is estimated by maximizing the log-likelihood function:

$$\hat{\alpha} = \arg\max_{\alpha} \sum_i \sum_t \log \left[\int \exp(-\mu \exp z'_{it}\hat{\theta}) \frac{(\mu \exp z'_{it}\hat{\theta})^{y_{it}}}{y_{it}!} g_\alpha(\mu) \, d\mu \right].$$

Restricting the heterogeneity distribution to be a gamma mixture enables us to find closed-form expressions of integrals which appear in the likelihood function.

(ii) The second approach relies on the moment conditions, which serve to identify the Laplace transform (or moment-generating function) of the heterogeneity
distribution. We have

$$E[\exp\{Y_{i,t}\log(1 - v\exp(-z'_{it}\theta))\} \mid z_{it}]$$
$$= E[E[\exp\{Y_{i,t}\log[1 - v\exp(-z'_{it}\theta)]\} \mid z_{it}, \mu_i] \mid z_{it}]$$
$$= E[\exp\{-\mu_i\exp z'_{it}\theta[1 - [1 - v\exp(-z'_{it}\theta)]]\} \mid z_{it}]$$
$$= E(\exp{-v\mu_i}) = \psi(v), \quad \text{say.}$$

A consistent estimator of the Laplace transform is

$$\hat{\psi}(v) = \frac{1}{N}\sum_i\sum_t(1 - v\exp{-z'_{it}\hat{\theta}})^{y_{it}},$$

where N denotes the total number of observations. The moment-generating function
along with the density and cumulative distribution functions are three alternative and
equivalent representations of the probabilistic properties of a random variable. Once
the heterogeneity distribution has been estimated nonparametrically, it is possible
to compare it with a gamma distribution, in order to test the goodness-of-fit of the
binomial regression model.

5.3.3   *Determination of the Premium*

The determination and updating of insurance premiums are based on some predictive
distributions, which are the distributions of future claim counts $Y_{i,T+1}$ (say), given
the past counts of claims $Y_{i,1}, \ldots, Y_{i,T}$. For instance, let us consider driver i who
held an automobile insurance policy in the past two years ($T = 2$) and filed two
claims $Y_{i,1} = y_{i,1}$, $Y_{i,2} = y_{i,2}$ in that period. We need to find the conditional
distribution of $Y_{i,3}$ given $Y_{i,1} = y_{i,1}$, $Y_{i,2} = y_{i,2}$.

To accomplish this we have to choose between the semi-parametric model
discussed above and the fully parametric negative-binomial model. The semi-
parametric model relies on weaker assumptions and from that point of view is
preferable to the parametric one. However, under the semi-parametric approach, the
computation of predictive distributions is technically more difficult. In contrast, the
parametric negative-binomial model provides simple premium updating formulas
in a straightforward way. Loosely speaking, once the structural parameter θ and the
heterogeneity distribution of μ are estimated, it is possible to simulate and draw
$Y^s_{i,1}, Y^s_{i,2}, Y^s_{i,3}, s = 1, \ldots, S$, in the joint distribution of $Y_{i,1}, Y_{i,2}, Y_{i,3}$ after replacing
the parameters by their estimates, and next to find the conditional distribution of $Y_{i,3}$
given $Y_{i,1} = y_{i,1}$, $Y_{i,2} = y_{i,2}$ by considering the ratio of approximate frequencies
$\hat{P}(Y_{i,3} = y_{i,3}, Y_{i,2} = y_{i,2}, Y_{i,1} = y_{i,1})/(\hat{P}(Y_{i,2} = y_{i,2}, Y_{i,1} = y_{i,1}))$. Clearly this
method is less accurate when the number of conditioning variables is high, that is,
when the policyholder under study has established a long history of past experience.
On the other hand, one can expect that only a limited number of such conditional

probabilities would have to be computed since, in practice, the conditioning variables admit very few values. The number of claims filed by one policyholder in one year is in most cases 0, 1, or 2.

5.4 Applications

5.4.1 Car Insurance

As mentioned earlier, the Poisson and negative-binomial models are commonly used in automobile insurance (see the list of references). The endogenous variable is the annual number of claims of a given type (bodily injury or property damage) for a given category of insurance contracts. The models provide the score values for rating the individuals, given their personal characteristics. Despite the fact that the estimated scores depend significantly on the population of interest and type of contract, some explanatory variables are common to most of them.

5.4.1.1 Risk Factors

Below is an incomplete list of explanatory variables that appear in the expressions of scores for rating individual risks.

(a) Use of the car. So far we have considered the counts of claims per year, because conventionally one year is the standard length of an insurance contract. In general, risk, defined as the number of claims expected to be filed during a time period, depends on the length of that time period, and also on the use of the car. The intensity of car use varies among individuals and changes in time. In order to account for these two effects, some proxy variables are included among the explanatory ones. These represent, for example,

   (i) the expected annual mileage in categories, such as up to 10 000 km per year, 10–20 000, etc. (in some countries, such as Sweden, it is routinely verified *ex post* after a claim incidence),

  (ii) the type of use (personal or professional use, agricultural or nonagricultural use), type of engine (gasoline or diesel), and so on.

(b) Car's characteristics. Some variables determine if the car is more or less easy to drive:

   (i) engine power,

  (ii) features such as turbo versus nonturbo engine, color (black, red, or other), car model,

 (iii) weight of car,

 (iv) age of car,

  (v) maintenance.

(c) Driver's experience. Some variables representing driver's experience are *ex ante* measures of risk, and are known before the first claim is filed; other variables are *ex post* measures based on the driving records; these contain more information about the risk associated with a given driver.

Among the *ex ante* measures, we distinguish the following:

  (i) number of years licensed;

 (ii) type of driving school attended;

(iii) driver's age;

(iv) some characteristics of the driving licence, such as being authorized to drive an ambulance, a bus, to carry explosives or radioactive materials, to drive government automobiles, or a car with manual transmission (United States).

The *ex post* variables summarize the driving history. These include the following:

  (i) number of claims and amount paid to cover them in the last two or three years;

 (ii) bonus-malus coefficient;

(iii) number of demerit points;

(iv) fines for traffic law violations such as speeding, impaired driving, and so on.

(d) Safe driving. Some exogenous variables are correlated with driving habits. The "good risk" individuals drive responsibly and safely. They can sometimes be distinguished from other individuals in the sample because of personal characteristics, such as marital status or professional and financial standing. More insights on individual risks can come from information on the following:

   (i) gender (women are more cautious than men);

  (ii) professional status (employed, unemployed, retired);

 (iii) age,

 (iv) marital status (married, not married, divorced (high risk)), with or without children;

  (v) the indicators of specific professions, such as government employee (low risk), university professor (low risk), blue collar worker (low risk), taxi driver (high risk), student (high risk);

 (vi) the number of years in the current job, or the number of years at the same address;

(vii) credit history (good or bad; some credit scores may appear among the explanatory variables);

(viii) the deductible chosen by the policyholder, which may reflect the driver's expectation of his own risk (this is an adverse selection argument).

(e) The average speed. Proxies are used to assess the average speed of the vehicle. Of particular importance are the following geographical characteristics:

(i) the territory;

(ii) the type of agglomeration.

In a large town, the number of accidents tends to be high, although most incidents are small collisions rather than big accidents. Moreover, depending on the territory, different rules may apply, especially those that determine the speed and alcohol-consumption limits.

(f) Other factors. These include the requirement to wear glasses while driving or to undergo a routine medical check-up.

(g) Cross-effects. By examining the types of automobile insurance policies issued by different insurance companies, one can collect a set of covariates x, which are common knowledge. A given insurer can gain a competitive edge by improving the accuracy of risk assessment by adequately accounting for the cross-effects between the covariates. This task is much more difficult, as it is hard to identify the relevant cross-effects. The following cross-effects may be insightful:

(i) {use of car for business operation} × {profession} (a proxy for the mileage and the speed),

(ii) {gender} × {age of the driver},

(iii) {age of the car} × {mileage declared} (the correlation between these variables is generally negative, except for some individuals),

(iv) {family situation} × {age} (a young father is often a responsible and safe driver).

5.4.1.2 *Count of Claims and Total Amount Paid*

Differentiating the automobile insurance premiums with respect to individual characteristics is usually based on the statistical analysis of the number of claims, rather than on the costs of claims. This approach is only valid under certain specific assumptions regarding the average dollar amount paid per claim. For ease of exposition, we will refer to the amount paid on a claim as the cost of that claim (this is the cost for the insurance company). Let us denote the number of claims by Y and the cost of claim j by C_j. The total cost of all claims filed in a given period is equal to

$$C = \sum_{j=1}^{Y} C_j,$$

where by convention we set $\sum_{j=1}^{0} C_j = 0$.

The expected total cost is

$$E[C \mid X] = E\left[\sum_{j=1}^{Y} C_j \,\middle|\, X\right].$$

This expression involves two sources of randomness, since both Y and C_j, j varying, are random. In the special case, when the number of claims and the costs are independent variables, and the costs are identically distributed (conditional on the exogenous variables), we obtain

$$E[C \mid X] = E\left[E\left(\sum_{j=1}^{Y} C_j \mid X, Y\right) \,\middle|\, X\right]$$

$$= E\left(\left[\sum_{j=1}^{Y} E(C_j \mid X, Y)\right] \,\middle|\, X\right)$$

$$= E\left(\sum_{j=1}^{Y} E(C_j \mid X) \,\middle|\, X\right)$$

$$= E[Y E(C_1 \mid X) \mid X]$$

$$= E(Y \mid X) E(C_1 \mid X).$$

This result tells us that the analysis of the total expected cost of all claims of a given individual can be performed by separately predicting the number of claims and the cost per claim. The rating of insurance contracts, with respect to the total expected cost, then becomes a mixture of the rating with respect to the number of claims and of the rating with respect to the expected cost per claim. This second rating will, in particular, depend on some price effects, such as the present value estimate of the car.

It is important to note that the assumption of independence between the number of claims and the cost per claim is not satisfied in the whole population of policyholders in a given country, for example. This is due to the large number of low-cost collisions in big cities, and the low number of high-cost accidents in the rural areas. These less frequent accidents in rural areas have a higher probability of entailing bodily injuries or deaths. To illustrate, we provide the data on occurrence, average cost per claim, and expected cost (pure premium) for France in 1987.

In order to see the dependence between the claim counts and costs, we compute the correlation between the samples of size 4, formed by the entries in columns 2 and 3 in the middle part of Table 5.1 concerning the male drivers. The correlation coefficient is 0.96. We conclude that there is evidence of a very strong correlation between the claim counts and costs.

However, despite the fact that claim counts and costs are dependent in the whole population of policyholders, they can become conditionally independent when the set of exogenous variables and the cross-effects are appropriately chosen to this end.

Table 5.1. The pure premium decomposition
(benchmark: 100 for the representative driver).

Category	Claim occurrence	Average cost per claim	Pure premium
Male	99	102	101
Female	104	94	97
Male < 21 years	225	191	430
Male $21 \leqslant \cdots < 25$	173	131	226
Male $25 \leqslant \cdots < 30$	125	117	145
Male $\geqslant 30$	89	92	82
Licensed to drive in current year	275	169	470

Table 5.2. Effect of profession (France, 1985).

Profession	Kilometers per year
Farmer	10 500
Trader	15 600
Artisan	14 700
Executive	18 400
Employee	12 200
Worker	12 600

5.4.2 Presentation of Results

The estimation of a count data model by a statistical software package such as SAS produces the estimated coefficients, standard errors, and test statistics. However, for practitioners these outputs may be hard to interpret. In practice, any change in insurance premiums can be implemented only once it is approved by the insurer, as well as tested on some typical risks.

5.4.2.1 Relations between Variables

Prior to estimation, it is necessary to collect information on the relationships between the variables of interest. This concerns the effect of candidate exogenous variables on risk, as well as correlations between the (sets of) exogenous variables. The last issue concerns detection of (quasi-) collinearity. The existence of collinearity can be examined by computing empirical correlations, or by using graphical methods of display (scatterplot).

It is also important to justify the use of proxies, by examining relations between the observed exogenous variables and unobserved factors. Insight into such relationships

Table 5.3. Effect of gender (France, 1985).

Gender	Kilometers per year
Male	13 100
Female	11 200

Table 5.4. Effect of the age of the driver.

Age of the driver	Kilometers per year
< 25	13 200
$25 \leqslant \cdots < 30$	14 000
$30 \leqslant \cdots < 50$	13 500
$50 \leqslant \cdots < 60$	11 800
$60 \leqslant \cdots < 65$	11 000
$\geqslant 65$	8 200

Table 5.5. Effect of the year (France).

Year	Kilometers per year
1975	13 100
1980	11 700
1985	12 600

can be gained from additional surveys. Tables 5.2–5.4 show various proxies that indicate the number of kilometers driven per year.

Interestingly, we observe a nonlinear relationship between the age of the driver and the number of kilometers driven per year. The mileage increases in the first two rows when age increases from "less than 25" to "between 25 and 30," and decreases steadily for higher age categories displayed in the subsequent rows. This empirical finding points to the importance of dividing the age variable into various classes, in order to evaluate its nonlinear effect on risk.

Tables 5.5 and 5.6 show that the effect of individual characteristics such as age, gender, and profession may vary in time, due to changing economic conditions (such as gasoline price). This is an argument in favor of introducing into the scores some time-varying explanatory variables or trends (Besson and Partrat 1992).

Table 5.6 shows the evolution of nominal gas prices and total gas consumption in France. In the period 1977–85, the price of gas has increased in both real and nominal terms. It seems preferable to use nominal instead of real (inflation discounted) gas prices due to the fact that drivers adjust their individual gas consumption with respect

Table 5.6. Effect of the gasoline price on consumption.

Year	Price (French francs)	Consumption (m^3)
1977	2.31	18 534 200
1978	2.42	19 469 200
1979	2.75	19 651 700
1980	3.27	19 780 700
1981	3.72	20 409 200
1982	4.32	20 519 500
1983	4.65	20 919 000
1984	5.04	21 153 900
1985	5.74	21 047 500

to changes in nominal prices that they perceive directly at a gas station. An increase in total gas consumption can follow either from an overall increase in the number of cars in the country, a general increase in mileage per car, or an increase in the engine power of cars. All these changes can increase the number and severity of claims due to car accidents. Tables 5.5 and 5.6 suggest that time and gas price are related to risk and can be used as explanatory variables in risk models.

5.4.2.2 Estimation Results

As mentioned earlier, the outputs of standard statistical software for estimation of Poisson and negative-binomial regression models are difficult to interpret for people unfamiliar with basic econometrics. The main difficulty in interpreting the output is due to the transformation of exogenous quantitative variables into qualitative variables, by partitioning their sets of admissible values into distinct categories (alternatives). For identification purposes, one (arbitrary) category has to always be deleted when the regression is estimated. Next, the estimated coefficients on the indicator variables (dummies) of the remaining categories need to be interpreted as differences between the effect of each category included, and the one deleted.

Moreover, in a Poisson model, the expected number of claims is $\exp z'\theta$. If z is a vector of indicators associated with a segmentation of the population into subpopulations ($z_k = 1$ if individual belongs to subpopulation k), the expected number of claims in subpopulation k is $\exp \hat{\theta}_k$. Consequently, it may be more insightful to estimate and report the expected number of claims $\exp \hat{\theta}_k$, rather than $\hat{\theta}_k$ alone.

The interpretation changes when the indicator functions are not associated with any segmentation. Let us consider two basic exogenous covariates x_1, x_2 and indicator functions $z_{1,l}, l = 1, \ldots, L$ (respectively, $z_{2,k}, k = 1, \ldots, K$), that represent a partition of the set of values of x_1 (respectively, x_2). If $\hat{\theta}_{1,l}$ and $\hat{\theta}_{2,k}$ denote the estimated coefficients on $z_{1,l}$ and $z_{2,k}$, the expected number of claims for a contract

Table 5.7. Estimated multiplicative factors for variable "professions."

Alternative	Civic liability	Total claims	Rank for civic liability	Rank for total claims
Public sector	0.763	0.757	2	2
Police officer	0.693	0.692	1	1
Private sector	0.835	0.815	4	5
Retired	0.783	0.777	3	3
Student	0.985	0.795	6	4
Artisan	0.983	0.961	5	6

with $z_{1,l} = z_{2,k} = 1$ is equal to

$$\exp(\hat{\theta}_{1,l} + \hat{\theta}_{2,k}) = \exp\hat{\theta}_{1,l} \exp\hat{\theta}_{2,k}.$$

We get a multiplicative formula, where $\exp\hat{\theta}_{1,l}$ is a multiplicative factor to be considered for category l of covariate x_1.

As an illustration, a Poisson model is estimated from a population of French automobile insurance policyholders in the year 1988. The following five explanatory variables are considered: age of car, premium on policy (bonus-malus), professional occupation, territory of residence, and vehicle rating group. They all are transformed into qualitative variables with distinct alternatives. Table 5.7 contains the marginal multiplicative factor $\exp\hat{\theta}_{1,l}$ of variable "professions" for two types of coverage: civic liability and comprehensive coverage. The alternatives are ranked in ascending order in the two last columns.

In order to estimate a regression model which provides a good fit to the data, we need to find the optimal set of regressors, as well as an optimal segmentation scheme of regressors into various categories. To accomplish this, we may need to experiment with different sets of explanatory variables, as well as various segmentation schemes. Some statistical software is equipped with macro commands that help select a set of relevant explanatory variables and their categories (see, for example, SAS, model selection procedure). It is insightful to take a look at the first stages of segmentation in order to see the relevant characteristics considered. Table 5.8 shows the first steps of an automatic multi-step segmentation procedure.

The procedure consists of several steps. In step 1, the covariate "bonus-malus" is used for segmentation of the whole sample. Two groups (segments) of individuals are distinguished: the covariate "bonus-malus" is equal to 0.5 for individuals in segment 1, and is not equal to 0.5 for individuals in segment 2. Next, in step 2, the covariate "bonus-malus" is used again to divide segment 2 into two categories of individuals. Individuals with "bonus-malus" covariate values less than or equal to 0.64 and not equal to 0.5 belong to the first category, while individuals with "bonus-malus" covariate values greater than 0.64 belong to the second category. In step 3, the covariate "age of car" is considered, and is used for further segmentation of

Table 5.8. Steps in segmentation (for civic liability).

Index of the segmented class	Number of classes	Segmenting variables
1	2	Bonus-malus $= 0.5$
2	3	Bonus-malus $\leqslant 0.64$
1	4	Age of car $\leqslant 8$
2	5	Car group rate $\leqslant 7$
3	6	Car group rate $\leqslant 9$
1	7	Car group rate $\leqslant 10$
4	8	Car group rate $\leqslant 8$
2	9	Car group rate $\leqslant 11$
9	10	Car group rate $\leqslant 9$
3	11	Territory $\geqslant 3$
1	12	Artisan $\times$ professional use

segment 1. The next steps in the segmentation procedure are based on other variables, such as "car group" and "territory." The automated segmentation procedure ends when the most significant cross-effects in the sample of individuals are revealed.

It is interesting to compare the estimation results produced by the Poisson regression and the negative-binomial models, in order to check for any evidence of the effects of unobserved heterogeneity.

Below, we provide empirical results on the heterogeneity among drivers in the province of Quebec, Canada (Dionne and Vanasse 1989). Table 5.9 compares the estimates produced by the Poisson and negative-binomial models. It shows the estimated coefficients on selected alternatives of relevant covariates, including the additional heterogeneity estimate (which was set equal to zero in the Poisson regression). In this example, the heterogeneity coefficient is found to be significant and the Poisson model is rejected. However, the scores estimated from the Poisson regression and negative-binomial models are very close. In particular, both specifications provide the same ranking of individuals. The main difference concerns the level of the pure premium. The negative-binomial model suggests a higher premium than the Poisson regression, in order to compensate for nondiversifiable risk associated with unobserved heterogeneity.

5.4.2.3 Additional Output

There are additional practical outcomes of model estimation. For example, for some particular individuals pure premiums are computed. Next, these premiums are compared with the premiums prevailing in the industry, and the evolution of these premiums with respect to past claim experience is examined. In Table 5.10 we describe the evolution of premiums based on the negative-binomial model (Dionne and Vanasse 1989) computed for a female of age 30 who lives in Montreal and is authorized to

Table 5.9. Comparison of the Poisson and negative-binomial models.

Variable	Poisson		Negative binomial	
	Coefficient	$|t|$-ratio	Coefficient	$|t|$-ratio
Required to wear glasses	−0.35	1.86	−0.07	1.66
Licensed to drive a car with automatic transmission	1.41	1.99	1.42	1.46
Region: Trois-Rivieres	0.14	1.26	−0.14	1.22
Female, age 25–35 years	−0.35	1.37	−0.35	1.30
Heterogeneity	—	—	0.68	3.9

Table 5.10. Pure premium.

Year	Number of claims				
	0	1	2	3	4
0	85.8	—	—	—	—
1	82.4	138.6	194.8	251.0	307.2
2	79.3	133.4	187.5	241.5	295.6
3	76.4	128.5	180.6	232.7	284.8

drive vehicles of weight less than 10 tonnes, except for public transportation vehicles. The premium is a function of the time t that has elapsed since the first insurance contract and of the past numbers of accidents per year.

In year 0, the person pays the premium based on an average driving record in her rating category (the homogeneity assumption). In year 1, she pays a different premium depending on the number of claims filed. If she had no accidents, her premium drops to 82.4, compared with the initial rate of 85.8. In contrast, if she was involved in four accidents, her premium increases to 307.2. If she maintains a clear driving record, with no accidents for two (respectively, three) consecutive years, her premium keeps decreasing to 79.3 (respectively, 76.4) after two (respectively, three) years of experience. Four accidents along with three years experience entail a premium lower than four accidents along with one year of experience (284.8 compared with 307.2), since the frequency of claims is lower.

5.5 Concluding Remarks

Individual risk can be partly assessed by considering the number of claims filed on an insurance policy in a given period. This approach consists of examining a count variable of risk. The variation of claim counts can be successfully explained by an appropriately chosen set of individual covariates. The basic count data model is the Poisson regression model, which can be extended to the negative-binomial regression model to account for unobserved individual heterogeneity. In practice, the negative-binomial regression is used for the updating of premiums in automobile insurance.

Good references for further reading on automobile insurance are Lemaire (1985) and Gourieroux (1999a,b). Other applications of count data models concern, for example, worker absenteeism, annual number of days on strike (Delgado and Kniesner 1997), health insurance (Cameron et al. 1988), bank failures (Davutyan 1989), and research and development (Hausman et al. 1984). The estimation and testing procedures for Poisson and negative-binomial regression models are available in the *SAS/STAT User's Guide*[4].

References

Barnett, A., M. Abraham, and V. Schimmel. 1979. Airline safety: some empirical findings. *Management Science* 25:1045–56.

Besson, J., and C. Partrat. 1992. Trend et systèmes de bonus-malus. *ASTIN Bulletin* 22:11–31.

Brannas, K., and P. Johansen. 1996. Panel data regression for counts. *Statistical Papers* 37:191–213.

Cameron, A., and P. Trivedi. 1998. *Regression Analysis of Count Data*. Cambridge University Press.

Cameron, A., and P. Trivedi. 1999. Essentials of count data regression. In *Companion in Econometric Theory* (ed. B. Baltagi). Oxford: Blackwell.

Cameron, A., P. Trivedi, F. Milne, and J. Pigott. 1988. A microeconometric model of the demand for health care and health insurance in Australia. *Review of Economic Studies* 55:85–106.

Campbell, J. 1934. The Poisson correlation function. *Proceedings of the Edinburgh Mathematical Society* 2:18–26.

Chalk, A. 1986. Market forces and airline safety: the case of DC-10. *Economic Inquiry* 24:43–60.

Cummins, J., and A. Powell. 1980. The performance of alternative models for forecasting automobile insurance paid claim costs. *ASTIN Bulletin* 11:91–106.

Davutyan, N. 1989. Bank failures as Poisson variates. *Economic Letters* 29:333–38.

Delgado, M., and T. Kniesner. 1997. Count data models with variance of unknown form: an application to a hedonic model of worker absenteeism. *Review of Economics and Statistics* 79:41–49.

Dionne, G., and C. Vanasse. 1989. A generalization of automobile insurance rating models: the negative binomial distribution with a regression component. *ASTIN Bulletin* 19:199–221.

Edwards, C., and J. Gurland. 1961. A class of distributions applicable to accider is. *Journal of the American Statistical Association* 56:503–17.

Ganio, L., and D. Schafer. 1992. Diagnostics for overdispersion. *Journal of the American Statistical Association* 87:795–804.

Golbe, D. 1986. Safety and profits in the airline industry. *Journal of Industrial Economics* 34:305–18.

---

[4] Available at http://www.id.unizh.ch/software/unix/statmath/sas/sasdoc/stat.

Gourieroux, C. 1989. *Econométrie des Variables Qualitatives*, 2nd edn, Chapter X. Paris: Economica.

Gourieroux, C. 1999a. *Statistique de l'Assurance*. Paris: Economica.

Gourieroux, C. 1999b. Econometrics of risk classification in insurance. *Geneva Papers for Risk and Insurance* 24:119–37.

Gourieroux, C., and J. Jasiak. 2000. Nonlinear panel data models with dynamics heterogeneity. In *Panel Data Econometrics: Future Directions* (ed. J. Krishnakumar and E. Ronchetti), pp. 127–47. Elsevier.

Gourieroux, C., A. Monfort, and A. Trognon. 1984. Pseudo maximum likelihood methods: application to Poisson models. *Econometrica* 52:701–20.

Graham, D., and M. Bowes. 1979. Do finances influence airline safety, maintenance and services? Report to the Civil Aeronautics Board, Contract 78-C-60. Public Research Institutes, Center for Naval Analysis.

Gurmu, S. 1991. Tests for detecting overdispersion in the positive Poisson regression model. *Journal of Business and Economics Statistics* 9:215–22.

Hamdan, M., and H. Al-Bayyati. 1971. Canonical expansion of the compound correlated bivariate Poisson distribution. *Journal of the American Statistical Association* 66:390–93.

Hausman, J., B. Hall, and Z. Griliches. 1984. Econometric models for count data with an application to the patents–R&D relationship. *Econometrica* 52:909–38.

Jung, J. 1968. On automobile insurance rate making. *ASTIN Bulletin* 5:41–48.

Kanafani, A., and T. Keeler. 1989. New entrants and safety: some statistical evidence on the effects of airline deregulation. In *Safety Performance under Deregulation* (ed. L. Moses and I. Savage). Oxford University Press.

Klugman, S. A., H. H. Panjer, and G. E. Willmot. 2004. *Loss Models; from Data to Decisions*, 2nd edn. Wiley.

Lawless, J. 1987. Negative binomial and mixed Poisson regression. *The Canadian Journal of Statistics* 15:209–25.

Lemaire, J. 1985. *Automobile Insurance: Actuarial Models*. Dordrecht: Kluwer-Nijhoff.

Lee, L. 1986. Specification test for Poisson regression models. *International Economic Review* 27:687–706.

Mullahy, J. 1986. Specification and testing in some modified count data models. *Journal of Econometrics* 33:341–65.

Ramaswamy, V., E. Anderson, and W. De Sarbo. 1993. A disaggregate negative binomial regression procedure for count data analysis. *Management Science* 40:405–17.

Rose, N. 1989. Financial influence on airline safety. In *Safety Performance Under Deregulation* (ed. L. Moses and I. Savage). Oxford University Press.

Rose, N. 1990. Profitability and product quality: economic determinants of airline safety performance. *Journal of Political Economy* 98:944–64.

Van Eeghen, J., E. Greup, and J. Nijssen. 1984. *Rate making*. Surveys of Actuarial Studies, Volume 2. Rotterdam: Nationale-Nederlanden, N.V.

Wang, P., M. Puterman, I. Cockburn, and N. Le. 1996. Mixed Poisson regression models with covariate dependent rates. *Biometrics* 52:381–400.

Wedel, M., W. De Sarbo, J. Bult, and V. Ramaswany. 1993. A latent class Poisson regression model for heterogenous count data. *Journal of Applied Econometrics* 8:397–411.

Winkelmann, R. 1995. Duration dependence and dispersion in count data models. *Journal of Business and Economic Statistics* 13:467–74.

Winkelmann, R. 1997. *Count Data Models: Econometric Theory and Application to Labor Mobility* Springer.

6

Durations

The last type of risk variable discussed in this book is the duration variable, or, equivalently, the time-to-loss. This approach to risk assessment emphasizes the timing of a loss event. The following durations are commonly encountered in insurance and finance: the time-to-death from the date insurance was purchased for a life insurance policy; the time from occurrence of a disabling event to recovery or death for a health insurance policy; the time-to-default on a loan; and the time-to-prepayment on a loan or a mortgage that terminates early.

Like any random variable, a duration variable can be defined by its density and moment-generating functions. What makes the duration analysis more complex is that the distributional properties of a duration variable are better depicted by survivor, hazard and expected residual lifetime functions. The first part of this chapter presents the probabilistic framework and provides examples of commonly encountered families of duration distributions. An important property of durations is the so-called positive and negative duration dependence. It concerns the relationship between the probability of an instantaneous occurrence of a loss event and the time elapsed prior to that event.

The models for individual risk assessment are discussed in the second part of the chapter. The duration-based risk models share some common features with the count data models covered in Chapter 5, regarding the structure and main assumptions. The basic parametric model is the so-called exponential regression. Just as with the Poisson regression model, it can be extended by incorporating an additional variable that represents unobserved individual heterogeneity. This approach leads to the Pareto regression. Two types of semi-parametric models are also available. These are the accelerated and proportional hazard models, distinguished by the effects of explanatory variables on the hazard function. Compared with the fully parametric models, they offer alternative, less restrictive specifications, but may require more advanced estimation techniques. The applications concerning the calculation of pension premiums, corporate bond pricing and prepayment analysis appear at the end of the chapter.

6.1   Duration Distributions

6.1.1   Characterizations of a Duration Distribution

The distribution of a random duration Y can be defined by its density function f, or its cumulative distribution function F. However, the specificity of duration analysis requires the introduction of additional concepts such as the survivor function, the hazard function and the expected residual lifetime.

6.1.1.1   The Survivor Function

The term "survivor function" originates from the analysis of the residual lifetime of individuals or various objects that depreciate in time. The survivor function S is given by

$$S(y) = P[Y \geqslant y] = 1 - F(y). \tag{6.1}$$

The survivor function evaluated at point y is the probability that a person (object) will live for at least y years. It takes values between 0 and 1 and is decreasing in y. At $y = 0$ the survivor function is equal to 1. For growing values of y the survivor function decreases, and for large values of y it approaches zero asymptotically.

The first derivative of the survivor function at any point is equal to the negative density of the random variable Y evaluated at that point.

6.1.1.2   The Hazard Function (Hazard Rate)

The hazard function (rate) is also known by many other names, depending on the area of study. For example, in demographic studies the term *instantaneous mortality rate* at age y is used. The notion is quite intuitive. The instantaneous mortality rate at age y is the probability that the person will die very shortly after reaching age y, provided that she reaches age y. The instantaneous mortality rate is the following function of age y:

$$\lambda(y) = \lim_{dy \to 0} \frac{1}{dy} P[y \leqslant Y < y + dy \mid Y \geqslant y]. \tag{6.2}$$

The term $y + dy$ in the last expression represents age "y" plus a short instant. In general, hazard functions (rates) are formally defined in exactly the same way as the instantaneous mortality rate, but concern duration variables other than human lifetime.

Definition 6.1. The hazard function is defined by

$$\lambda(y) = \lim_{dy \to 0} \frac{1}{dy} P[y \leqslant Y < y + dy \mid Y \geqslant y], \quad \forall y \in \mathbb{R}^+.$$

The hazard function evaluated at y is the probability that a duration will terminate shortly after y, given that the object or person is alive for y units of time.

By writing the probabilities in terms of survivor functions, the relationship between the hazard function and the survivor function can be established:

$$\lambda(y) = \lim_{dy \to 0} \frac{1}{dy} \frac{P[y \leqslant Y < y + dy]}{P[Y \geqslant y]}$$

$$= \lim_{dy \to 0} \frac{1}{dy} \frac{S(y) - S(y + dy)}{S(y)}$$

$$= -\frac{1}{S(y)} \frac{dS(y)}{dy},$$

$$\lambda(y) = \frac{f(y)}{S(y)}. \tag{6.3}$$

A hazard function fully characterizes the duration distribution since the survivor function (and hence the distribution function) of any duration variable can be derived from a given hazard function.

Proposition 6.2. $S(y) = \exp[-\int_0^y \lambda(u) \, du], \forall y \in \mathbb{R}^+$.

Proof. From expression (6.3) of the hazard function, we get

$$\lambda(y) = -\frac{1}{S(y)} \frac{dS(y)}{dy} = -\frac{d \log S(y)}{dy}.$$

Then, we solve this equation for $S(y)$ by integrating:

$$S(y) = K \exp \left[-\int_0^y \lambda(u) \, du \right],$$

where the constant $K = 1$, since $S(0) = 1$. $\qquad \square$

As mentioned before, the hazard function is known by several different names and always defines the instantaneous chance of quitting a state. When the duration variable represents time spent in a given state of a Markov chain, the term (instantaneous) exit rate is used. "Mortality rate" is employed in demographic studies of residual lifetime. The *"prepayment rate"* concerns the loans repaid by borrowers prior to the termination dates of their credit agreements (see Section 6.4.3). In other applications, we find terms such as *purchasing rate, failure rate, bankruptcy rate, intensity*, and so on.

6.1.1.3 The Expected Residual Lifetime

The expected residual lifetime at y is the expected remaining life conditioned on staying alive up to time y. Formally it is defined as follows.

Definition 6.3. The *expected residual lifetime* is

$$r(y) = E[Y - y \mid Y \geqslant y], \quad \forall y \in \mathbb{R}^+.$$

It is easy to show that the expected residual lifetime (also called the *mean excess function*) fully characterizes a duration variable. In this respect is it similar to the hazard function (and obviously to the survivor, density and cumulative distribution functions). This property follows from a one-to-one relationship between the expected residual lifetime and the survivor function given below (see Appendix 6.6):

$$r(y) = \frac{1}{S(y)} \int_y^\infty S(u)\,du, \qquad \forall y \in \mathbb{R}^+, \tag{6.4}$$

$$S(y) = \frac{r(0)}{r(y)} \exp\left[-\int_0^y \frac{du}{r(u)} \right], \quad \forall y \in \mathbb{R}^+. \tag{6.5}$$

In particular, for $y = 0$, we get

$$r(0) = E(Y) = \int_0^\infty S(u)\,du. \tag{6.6}$$

We illustrate the relationship between expected residual lifetime and survivor function as follows: we assume that the expected residual lifetime is an affine function of time and we determine the associated duration distribution.

Example 6.4. Let us assume an affine form of the expected residual lifetime:

$$r(u) = \alpha + \beta u,$$

with $\beta > 0$. We first find the survivor function:

$$
\begin{aligned}
S(y) &= \frac{\alpha}{\alpha + \beta y} \exp - \int_0^y \frac{du}{\alpha + \beta u} \\
&= \frac{\alpha}{\alpha + \beta y} \exp - \frac{1}{\beta} \log\left(\frac{\alpha + \beta y}{\alpha} \right) \\
&= \left(\frac{\alpha + \beta y}{\alpha} \right)^{-1/\beta + 1}.
\end{aligned}
$$

This survivor function is associated with a Pareto distribution (see Section 6.2.2). Hence, the duration variable with affine expected residual lifetime is Pareto distributed.

6.1.2 Duration Dependence

The duration dependence describes the relationship between the exit rate and the time spent in a given state (such as the state of driving without accidents) by an individual. Technically, it is determined by the form of the hazard function, which can be decreasing, increasing, or constant. One can think of the negative (positive) duration dependence in a sequence of loss events occurring randomly in time. If the duration dependence is negative (respectively, positive), then the more time has elapsed since the last loss event, the smaller (respectively, greater) the probability of an *instantaneous* occurrence of another loss.

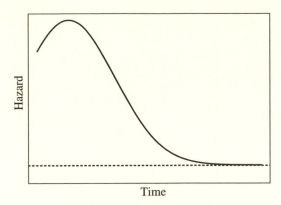

Figure 6.1. Bankruptcy rate.

(a) Negative duration dependence. Negative duration dependence is associated with decreasing hazard functions. Examples of negative duration dependence can be found in automobile insurance. The longer the time a policyholder has driven the car without getting involved in a road accident, the better the revealed driving ability and the lower the probability of being involved in an accident in the near future.

(b) Positive duration dependence. Positive duration dependence characterizes durations with increasing hazard functions. Due to depreciation, we typically observe that the longer an instrument has been in operation, the higher its failure rate, that is, the probability that it fails instantaneously.

(c) Absence of duration dependence. There is no relationship between the exit rate and the duration. The hazard function is constant. This means that the probability of quitting the state of driving without accidents does not depend on the duration in that state. The assumption of no duration dependence is often imposed as a simplifying assumption, especially when some individual explanatory variables are included in the model.

In empirical research, the forms of hazard functions have to be examined one by one. They may display quite complicated patterns, and be nonmonotone. For example, Figure 6.1 illustrates a typical hazard function representing the rate of bankruptcy.

A newly created firm has a low probability of failure. However, between six months and two years later the bankruptcy rate increases sharply. Later, it shows a tendency to diminish for companies that remained in business for a fairly long time, acquired more experience, and became better known to their customers and suppliers.

6.1.3 *Basic Duration Distributions*

Let us discuss some commonly encountered parametric distributions of a single duration variable.

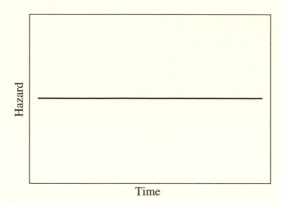

Figure 6.2.   The hazard function of an exponential distribution.

6.1.3.1   Exponential Distribution

The exponentially distributed durations feature no duration dependence. Therefore they have a constant (flat) hazard function:

$$\lambda(y) = \lambda, \quad y \in \mathbb{R}^+, \tag{6.7}$$

where λ is a positive real number. The exponential survivor function and density function are

$$S(y) = \exp(-\lambda y), \qquad f(y) = \lambda \exp(-\lambda y). \tag{6.8}$$

The mean and standard deviation of an exponential distribution are equal:

$$EY = \frac{1}{\lambda}, \qquad VY = \frac{1}{\lambda^2}. \tag{6.9}$$

The expected residual lifetime is constant, equal to $1/\lambda$.

6.1.3.2   The Gamma Distribution

The family of gamma distributions depends on two positive parameters a and v. The p.d.f. is given by

$$f(y) = \frac{a^v y^{v-1} \exp(-ay)}{\Gamma(v)}, \tag{6.10}$$

where $\Gamma(v) = \int_0^\infty \exp(-y) y^{v-1} \, dy$.

When $v = n$ is integer valued, $\Gamma(n) = (n-1)!$ and the gamma distribution can be obtained by summing up n independent exponentially distributed durations with intensity parameter $\lambda = a$.

The hazard function has a complicated integral form,

$$\lambda(y) = \left[\int_0^\infty \left(\frac{u}{y} + 1 \right)^{v-1} \exp(-au) \, du \right]^{-1},$$

and its pattern depends on parameter v as follows.

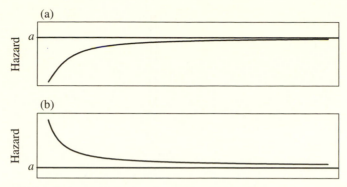

Figure 6.3. The hazard function of a gamma distribution: (a) $\nu > 1$; (b) $\nu < 1$.

(i) If $\nu > 1$, the hazard function increases from 0 to a.

(ii) If $\nu = 1$, the distribution simplifies to an exponential distribution.

(iii) If $\nu < 1$, the hazard function is decreasing from $+\infty$ and approaches an asymptote at a.

Thus, the gamma distributed durations can display various types of duration dependence, as indicated by different forms of hazard functions.

The mean and variance of the gamma duration variable are

$$EY = \frac{\nu}{a}, \qquad VY = \frac{\nu}{a^2}. \tag{6.11}$$

6.1.3.3 The Weibull Distribution

The Weibull duration variable is obtained from a power transform Y^b, $b > 0$, of an exponentially distributed duration variable with parameter a (instead of λ).

The Weibull survivor function is $S(y) = \exp(-ay^b)$, $\forall y \in \mathbb{R}^+$. The density and hazard functions are

$$f(y) = aby^{b-1}\exp(-ay^b), \quad \forall y \in \mathbb{R}^+, \tag{6.12}$$

$$\lambda(y) = aby^{b-1}, \qquad\qquad \forall y \in \mathbb{R}^+. \tag{6.13}$$

The hazard function is increasing for $b > 1$, and decreasing for $b < 1$.

Note that the increasing Weibull hazard function does not approach an asymptote.

6.1.3.4 Log-Normal Distributions

The density and hazard functions can be derived as follows. If the log-duration variable follows a normal distribution,

$$\log Y \sim N[m, \sigma^2],$$

then its density is

$$f(y) = \frac{1}{\sigma y}\varphi\left(\frac{\log y - m}{\sigma}\right), \tag{6.14}$$

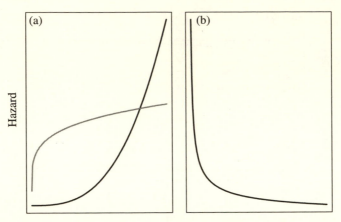

Figure 6.4.   The hazard function of a Weibull distribution: (a) $b > 1$; (b) $b < 1$.

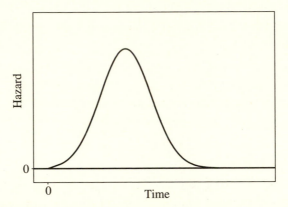

Figure 6.5.   The hazard function of the log-normal distribution.

and its hazard function is

$$\lambda(y) = \frac{1}{y} \frac{(1/\sigma)\varphi((\log y - m)/\sigma)}{1 - \Phi((\log y - m)/\sigma)}, \qquad (6.15)$$

where φ and Φ denote the p.d.f. and the c.d.f. of the standard normal.

The log-normally distributed durations have nonmonotone hazard functions. The nonmonotonicity of the hazard function is illustrated in Figure 6.5. For small values of y, the hazard function is increasing. Next, for larger values of the argument it becomes a decreasing function.

6.2   Duration Models

We now turn our attention to modeling individual risks, using the durations as endogenous risk variables. Like any of the previously discussed risk models, the duration model needs to accommodate the effects of observable and unobservable individual characteristics. Let us denote the observable covariates by x_i. First, a simple parametric model is presented which disregards unobservable heterogeneity. It is called the exponential regression. Next, we assume that unobserved heterogeneity is represented by a gamma distributed random variable. By incorporating this additional variable, the simple model is extended to a Pareto regression. Among semi-parametric models, the proportional and accelerated hazard models are discussed below.

6.2.1 The Exponential Regression Model

The model is based on the exponential distribution of durations. Accordingly, it assumes that the hazard rate is constant in time, but allows for variation of hazard rate across individuals. This is accomplished by specifying the hazard rate as an exponential function of a set of explanatory variables:

$$\lambda_i = \exp(z_i'\theta), \tag{6.16}$$

where θ is a vector of unknown parameters and the z_i are the transformations of initial covariates x_i. Since the individual hazard function λ_i does not depend on the duration y_i, the exponential regression features no duration dependence.

The conditional p.d.f. of the duration variable given the covariates is

$$
\begin{aligned}
f(y_i \mid x_i; \theta) &= \lambda_i \exp(-\lambda_i y_i) \\
&= \exp(z_i'\theta) \exp(-y_i \exp(z_i'\theta)).
\end{aligned} \tag{6.17}
$$

The parameter θ can be estimated by using the maximum likelihood method from the sample of n independent vectors of individual observations on the covariates and risk durations (x_i, y_i), $i = 1, \ldots, n$. The conditional log-likelihood function is

$$
\begin{aligned}
\log l(y \mid x; \theta) &= \sum_{i=1}^{n} \log f[y_i \mid x_i; \theta] \\
&= \sum_{i=1}^{n} (z_i'\theta - y_i \exp(z_i'\theta)).
\end{aligned}
$$

The first-order conditions are

$$\frac{\partial \log l(y \mid x; \hat{\theta})}{\partial \theta} = 0$$

$$\Longleftrightarrow \quad \sum_{i=1}^{n} z_i (1 - y_i \exp(z_i'\hat{\theta})) = 0$$

$$\Longleftrightarrow \quad \sum_{i=1}^{n} z_i \exp(z_i'\hat{\theta})[y_i - \exp(-z_i'\hat{\theta})] = 0. \tag{6.18}$$

Since the conditional expectation of the duration variable is $E[Y_i \mid x_i] = \exp(-z_i'\theta)$, the first-order conditions are equivalent to the orthogonality conditions for explanatory variables and residuals: $\hat{u}_i = y_i - \exp(-z_i'\hat{\theta})$, multiplied by "weights" $z_i \exp(z_i'\hat{\theta})$. Similar results were established earlier in the text for the Poisson and logit models.

Since the variance differs across individuals in the sample, the exponential model is heteroskedastic.

6.2.2 The Exponential Model with Gamma Heterogeneity

Recall that omitted individual heterogeneity, introduced in the previous chapter, is a random variable that captures the effects of individual covariates that are not included among the explanatory variables. The omitted individual heterogeneity reflects the idiosyncratic risk of individuals. It is denoted by μ_i and introduced into the individual hazard rate of the exponential regression model yielding

$$\lambda_i = \mu_i \exp(z_i'\theta). \tag{6.19}$$

To carry out analytical computations, we assume that the omitted heterogeneity is gamma $\gamma[A, A]$ distributed, where the equality of the two parameters is imposed so that $E\mu_i = 1$.

In order to build the log-likelihood function, we need to find the expression for the conditional distribution of durations given the observable covariates only. It is derived from $f(y_i \mid x_i, \mu_i)$ by integrating out omitted heterogeneity μ with density $\Pi(\mu; A)$ as follows:

$$
\begin{aligned}
f(y_i \mid x_i; \theta, A) &= \int_0^\infty f(y_i \mid x_i, \mu; \theta)\Pi(\mu; A)\, d\mu \\
&= \int_0^\infty \mu \exp(z_i'\theta) \exp[-y_i \mu \exp(z_i'\theta)] \frac{A^A \mu^{A-1} \exp(-A\mu)}{\Gamma(A)}\, d\mu \\
&= \frac{A^A \exp(z_i'\theta)}{\Gamma(A)} \int_0^\infty \exp\{-\mu[A + y_i \exp(z_i'\theta)]\}\mu^A\, d\mu \\
&= \frac{A^A \exp(z_i'\theta)}{[A + y_i \exp(z_i'\theta)]^{A+1}} \frac{\Gamma(A+1)}{\Gamma(A)},
\end{aligned}
$$

$$f(y_i \mid x_i; \theta, A) = \frac{A^{A+1} \exp(z_i'\theta)}{[A + y_i \exp(z_i'\theta)]^{A+1}}. \tag{6.20}$$

The conditional distribution of durations given the observable covariates is a Pareto distribution. The associated conditional survivor function is

$$
\begin{aligned}
S(y_i \mid x_i; \theta, A) &= \int_{y_i}^\infty \frac{A^{A+1} \exp(z_i'\theta)}{[A + u \exp(z_i'\theta)]^{A+1}}\, du \\
&= \frac{A^A}{[A + y_i \exp z_i'\theta]^A},
\end{aligned}
$$

and the conditional hazard function is

$$\lambda(y_i \mid x_i; \theta, A) = \frac{A \exp(z_i'\theta)}{A + y_i \exp(z_i'\theta)}. \tag{6.21}$$

The conditional hazard of the Pareto regression is a decreasing function of duration. Hence, the Pareto regression model features negative duration dependence. The heterogeneity parameter A provides a natural measure of this dependence. The smaller the heterogeneity parameter is, the stronger the negative duration effect. In the limiting case $A = \infty$, we get $\mu_i = 1$, $\lambda(y_i \mid x_i; \theta, A) = \exp(z_i'\theta)$; there is no duration dependence and the Pareto regression model simplifies to an exponential regression model.

The log-likelihood function of the Pareto regression model is

$$\log l(y \mid x; \theta, A) = \sum_{i=1}^{n} \log f(y_i \mid x_i; \theta, A)$$

$$= \sum_{i=1}^{n}\{(A+1)\log A + z_i'\theta - (A+1)\log[A + y_i \exp(z_i'\theta)]\}.$$

The first-order conditions with respect to θ and A are

$$\frac{\partial \log l(y \mid x; \theta, A)}{\partial \theta} = \sum_{i=1}^{n} z_i \left\{ 1 - \frac{(A+1)y_i \exp z_i'\theta}{A + y_i \exp z_i'\theta} \right\}$$

$$= A \sum_{i=1}^{n} \frac{z_i[1 - y_i \exp z_i'\theta]}{A + y_i \exp z_i'\theta} = 0,$$

$$\frac{\partial \log l(y \mid x; \theta, A)}{\partial A} = n \log A + n\frac{A+1}{A} - \sum_{i=1}^{n} \log(A + y_i \exp z_i'\theta)$$

$$- \sum_{i=1}^{n} \frac{A+1}{A + y_i \exp z_i'\theta} = 0.$$

The ML estimators of θ and A are obtained by numerical maximization of the log-likelihood function.

6.2.3 *Heterogeneity and Negative Duration Dependence*

A comparison of the exponential and Pareto regression models allows us to comment on the effect of omitted heterogeneity, and its impact on duration dependence. The analysis is performed in a simplified framework that allows us to focus on this objective. The simplification consists of disregarding all the observable individual characteristics. Then, the conditional distribution of durations given the omitted heterogeneity factor μ_i is exponential with parameter $\lambda_i = \mu_i$. The conditional and marginal survivor functions are, respectively,

$$S(y_i \mid \mu_i) = \exp(-\mu_i y_i),$$

$$S(y_i) = \int_0^\infty \exp(-\mu y_i)\Pi(\mu)\,d\mu.$$

The conditional and marginal hazard functions are, respectively,

$$\lambda(y_i \mid \mu_i) = \mu_i,$$

$$\lambda(y_i) = -\frac{d \log S(y_i)}{dy}$$

$$= -\frac{1}{S(y_i)} \frac{dS(y_i)}{dy}$$

$$= \frac{\int_0^\infty \exp(-\mu y_i)\mu \Pi(\mu)\,d\mu}{\int_0^\infty \exp(-\mu y_i)\Pi(\mu)\,d\mu}. \tag{6.22}$$

The marginal hazard rate is an expectation of the individual hazard rate μ_i taken with respect to a modified probability distribution with p.d.f.

$$\Pi_{y_i}(\mu) = \exp(-\mu y_i)\Pi(\mu)/\int_0^\infty \exp(-\mu y_i)\Pi(\mu)\,d\mu. \tag{6.23}$$

Using the subscript Π_{y_i} for the expectation taken with respect to the modified probability, we get

$$\lambda(y_i) = E_{\Pi_{y_i}}[\lambda(y_i \mid \mu_i)] = E_{\Pi_{y_i}}(\mu_i). \tag{6.24}$$

We find that, contrary to the exponential model, the individual hazard function depends on duration y_i. Thus, adding omitted heterogeneity transforms a model without duration dependence into a model which features duration dependence. The question is, what type of duration dependence can be created in this way? The answer is found by taking the first-order derivative of the hazard function with respect to y.

Proposition 6.5. *The marginal hazard function features negative duration dependence.*

Proof. Let us consider the first-order derivative of the marginal hazard function. We get

$$\frac{d\lambda(y_i)}{dy} = \frac{-\int_0^\infty \mu^2 \exp(-\mu y_i)\Pi(\mu)\,d\mu}{\int_0^\infty \exp(-\mu y_i)\Pi(\mu)\,d\mu} + \frac{[\int_0^\infty \exp(-\mu y_i)\mu \Pi(\mu)\,d\mu]^2}{[\int_0^\infty \exp(-\mu y_i)\Pi(\mu)\,d\mu]^2}$$

$$= -E_{\Pi_{y_i}}\mu_i^2 + [E_{\Pi_{y_i}}(\mu_i)]^2$$

$$= -V_{\Pi_{y_i}}\mu_i \leqslant 0.$$

$\square$

We conclude that the duration-dependence is negative and is related to the variance of heterogeneity (computed with respect to modified probability Π_{y_i}).

The previous results are easy to interpret by considering the example of two categories of individuals with respective (hazard) exit rates $\mu_1 > \mu_2$. The first category has a higher exit rate than the second one. For this reason individuals in the first category are called the *movers*. Individuals in the second subcategory are

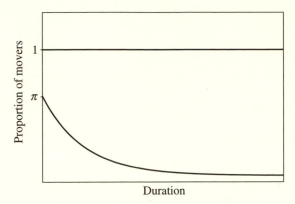

Figure 6.6. Evolution of population structure.

called the *stayers*. The structure of the whole population at date 0 is given by the proportion of movers, $\Pi_1 = \Pi$, and stayers, $\Pi_2 = 1 - \Pi$. The exit rate defined in condition (6.22) becomes

$$\lambda(y) = \frac{\Pi_1 S_1(y)\mu_1 + \Pi_2 S_2(y)\mu_2}{\Pi_1 S_1(y) + \Pi_2 S_2(y)}. \tag{6.25}$$

It can be interpreted as follows: between dates 0 and y, some individuals quit the population. Among them are some movers, and some stayers. The survivor functions (the probabilities of staying) in the two categories of individuals are different: $S_1(y) = \exp(-\mu_1 y) < S_2(y) = \exp(-\mu_2 y)$. The outflow of individuals results in a change of the structure of population remaining at date y. The new structure is given by the new proportions of movers and stayers which are, respectively,

$$\Pi_1(y) = \Pi_1 S_1(y)/[\Pi_1 S_1(y) + \Pi_2 S_2(y)], \qquad \Pi_2(y) = 1 - \Pi_1(y). \tag{6.26}$$

Since $S_1(y) < S_2(y)$, the proportion of movers at date y is less than that at date 0, which implies $\lambda(y) < \lambda(0) = \Pi_1\mu_1 + \Pi_2\mu_2$. As time goes on, for large y, $\Pi_2(y)$ tends to one. All movers tend to quit, so that the remaining population consists of stayers only and becomes homogeneous.

The mover–stayer phenomenon illustrates the negative duration dependence, which arises as a consequence of omitted individual heterogeneity. In the example discussed above, individual heterogeneity was implicitly assumed to be time invariant. It is possible to impose time-dependent individual heterogeneity that, for example, increases as time progresses, or, equivalently, as the individual grows older. Age-dependent individual heterogeneity also exists under moral hazard and can be illustrated by the following example: a driver makes unobservable efforts e_{iy}, say, to avoid accidents, that is, to "stay" in the state of no demerit points or zero claims in the insurance history. This effort depends on age y and impacts the exit rate $\lambda(y \mid e_{iy})$. The higher the individual effort is, the more chances to maintain clean accident-free records. Likely, the effort depends on the expected malus if an accident occurs, which itself is time varying, due to regular premium updating.

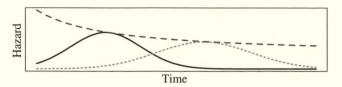

Figure 6.7. Individual hazard functions for the accelerated hazard model.

6.3 Semi-Parametric Models

The semi-parametric duration models consist of a parametric scoring function and an unconstrained *baseline distribution*. We describe below the accelerated and proportional hazard models and the associated estimation methods.

6.3.1 Accelerated Hazard Model

Individual durations are assumed to be identically distributed up to an individual time change (*time deformation*). More precisely, we have

$$Y_i \exp(z_i'\theta) \sim f_0, \tag{6.27}$$

where f_0 is the unconstrained baseline distribution and $\exp(z_i'\theta)$ defines the unit of deformed time. The conditional hazard function given the observable covariates is

$$\lambda(y_i \mid x_i; \theta, f_0) = \lambda_0[y_i \exp(z_i'\theta)] \exp(z_i'\theta), \tag{6.28}$$

where the baseline hazard λ_0 corresponds to the f_0 distribution. The forms of score-dependent hazard functions of the accelerated hazard model are displayed in Figure 6.7.

The model involves two types of unknown parameter: the vector θ of constant parameters, and the functional parameter f_0. A consistent two-step estimation method for the two types of parameter is as follows: taking logarithms on both sides of (6.27) yields the following linear regression:

$$\log Y_i = -z_i'\theta + u_i, \tag{6.29}$$

where the variables $\exp u_i$ are i.i.d. with unknown distribution f_0. By introducing a constant term among the regressors, it is always possible to constrain distribution f_0 so that $Eu_i = 0$. Parameter θ can be consistently estimated by ordinary least squares (OLS) from the regression of log-durations $\log y_i$ on explanatory variables z_i. Let us denote the OLS estimator by $\hat{\theta}$.

The baseline distribution is estimated in the second step. This is done by computing the residuals $\hat{u}_i = \log y_i + z_i'\hat{\theta}$ from the linear regression above and approximating the baseline density by the sample density of exponential residuals: $\exp \hat{u}_i = y_i \exp z_i'\hat{\theta}, i = 1, \ldots, n$. Among simple, consistent density estimators are the histogram and kernel-smoothed density estimators, available in any statistical software.

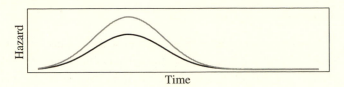

Figure 6.8. Individual hazard functions for the proportional hazard model.

6.3.2 *Proportional Hazard Model*

This model is based on homothetic conditional hazard functions. The individual hazard is proportional to the baseline hazard, with a parametric score as the proportionality coefficient:

$$\lambda(y_i \mid x_i; \theta, f_0) = \exp(z_i'\theta)\lambda_0(y_i), \qquad (6.30)$$

where λ_0 is an unconstrained baseline hazard function. The admissible forms of hazard functions in the proportional hazard model are displayed in Figure 6.8.

The parameter θ can be consistently estimated by the *partial maximum likelihood* method introduced by Cox (1975). The approach is as follows. First, we rank the duration data in ascending order, $y_{(1)} < y_{(2)} < \cdots < y_{(n)}$, under an implicit assumption that the observed duration values are distinct. Then we consider the subsample at risk (or *Population-at-Risk* (PaR)), made up of individuals with durations greater than that of the ith individual:

$$\mathcal{R}_{(i)} = \{j : y_{(j)} \geqslant y_{(i)}\}.$$

The probability that the first individual to quit subsample $\mathcal{R}_{(i)}$ will be individual (i) is given by

$$
\begin{aligned}
p_{(i)}(\theta, \lambda_0) &= \frac{\lambda[y_{(i)} \mid x_{(i)}; \theta, \lambda_0]}{\sum_{j \in \mathcal{R}_{(i)}} \lambda[y_{(j)} \mid x_{(j)}; \theta, \lambda_0]} \\
&= \frac{\exp(z_{(i)}'\theta)}{\sum_{j \in \mathcal{R}_{(i)}} \exp(z_{(j)}'\theta)}.
\end{aligned}
$$

This probability no longer depends on the baseline distribution. The partial maximum likelihood estimator of θ is defined by

$$
\begin{aligned}
\hat{\theta} &= \arg\max_{\theta} \sum_{i=1}^{n} \log p_{(i)}(\theta, \lambda_0) \\
&= \arg\max_{\theta} \sum_{i=1}^{n} \log \left\{ \frac{\exp(z_{(i)}'\theta)}{\sum_{j \in \mathcal{R}_{(i)}} \exp(z_{(j)}'\theta)} \right\}. \qquad (6.31)
\end{aligned}
$$

The expression of the partial log-likelihood is similar to the log-likelihood for a logit model. Therefore, it can be maximized by using standard statistical software.

6.4 Applications

In actuarial calculus, a common problem concerns the evaluation of the current value of a sequence of future random payoffs, defined as the sum of their discounted expectations. Solving this type of problem requires the use of duration models. Below, we provide some examples of actuarial calculus in application to pension funds, corporate bonds, and consumer loans.

6.4.1 Pension Fund

Let us consider an individual contract for a retirement pension. To simplify the computations, the premium and the pension annuities are defined in continuous time. The contract comes into effect when the individual reaches age y. The individual pays a premium rate $m(y, A)$ until either the contractual retirement age A or death, whichever happens first. During the retirement period, the retiree receives a pension at rate pe. The premium rate and the annuity rate are supposedly time-independent. The computations are performed under the assumption of a zero risk-free interest rate.

A risk-neutral insurance company determines the pure premium at the beginning of the contract by equating the expected negative and positive payoffs. If Y denotes the lifetime of an individual, the payoffs are balanced when

$$m(y, A)E[\min(Y, A - y) \mid Y \geqslant y] = pe \, E[\max(Y - A, 0) \mid Y \geqslant y].$$

The premium paid by the individual over the time remaining to retirement $A - y$, or time-to-death, has to be equal to pension annuities received in the period between retirement and death. By replacing the expectations by integrals, we can solve this equation for $m(y, A)$.

Proposition 6.6. *The pure premium for the pension contract is*

$$m(y, A) = pe \, \frac{\int_A^\infty S(u) \, du}{\int_y^A S(u) \, du}.$$

Proof. See Appendix 6.6.2.   □

The pure premium is proportional to the annuity rate with the coefficient of proportionality depending on both y and A. The premium increases with age y, at which time the contract becomes effective. It tends to infinity in the limiting case $y = A$, that is, when the contract is signed at the same time as the person retires from work.

A more detailed computation can be done for a specific survivor function.

Example 6.7. For an exponential distribution, the pension premium is

$$m(y, A) = pe \, \frac{-\exp -\lambda u|_A^\infty}{-\exp -\lambda u|_y^A} = pe \, \frac{1}{\exp \lambda(A - y) - 1}.$$

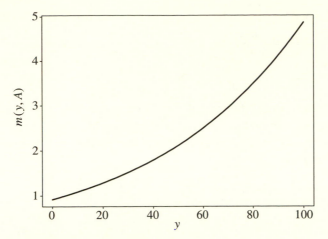

Figure 6.9. Premium rate.

The premium depends only on time-to-retirement $A - y$. This result illustrates the "lack of memory" of an exponential distribution. The premium as a function of the age at which an individual signs the contract is plotted in Figure 6.9.

6.4.2 Interest Rate Spreads

Let us consider a loan with initial balance B_0 and constant monthly payment m in H units of time. If the default probability of the borrower is zero, and the risk-free interest rate is r, the bank will determine the amount of the (actuarial) pure monthly payment from the following equation:

$$
\begin{aligned}
B_0 &= \frac{m}{1+r} + \frac{m}{(1+r)^2} + \cdots + \frac{m}{(1+r)^H} \\
&= m \frac{1}{1+r} \frac{1 - (1/(1+r)^H)}{1 - (1/(1+r))} \\
&= \frac{m}{r} \frac{(1+r)^H - 1}{(1+r)^H}.
\end{aligned}
$$

The (pure) monthly payment is the amount m that solves the equality between the initial debt (principal) and the sum of future discounted payoffs over H months. The pure monthly payment is

$$
m = B_0 \frac{r(1+r)^H}{(1+r)^H - 1}. \tag{6.32}
$$

If the probability of default is not equal to zero, the last formula needs to be modified. Let us denote the time-to-default (with the time origin set at the date when credit was granted) by Y and assume that after Y the borrower will not repay even a fraction of the remaining balance. For a loan with the same initial balance and maturity as before, the monthly payment is computed from the following equality (Fons 1994):

$$B_0 = \frac{m}{1+r} P[Y \geqslant 1] + \cdots + \frac{m}{(1+r)^H} P[Y \geqslant H]$$

$$= m \left\{ \frac{S(1)}{1+r} + \cdots + \frac{S(H)}{(1+r)^H} \right\}. \tag{6.33}$$

In this expression, each future installment is not only discounted with respect to the interest rate, but also with respect to the probability of default in the future, prior to the contractual term. The actuarial interest rate (yield) γ is determined from the following equality:

$$\frac{1}{1+\gamma} + \cdots + \frac{1}{(1+\gamma)^H} = \frac{(1+\gamma)^H - 1}{\gamma(1+\gamma)^H}$$

$$= \frac{S(1)}{1+r} + \cdots + \frac{S(H)}{(1+r)^H}. \tag{6.34}$$

It comes as no surprise that rate γ is larger than the risk-free interest rate. The positive spread $s = \gamma - r > 0$ compensates the bank for risk of default. Let us illustrate the computation of the yield for an exponentially distributed duration.

Example 6.8. For an exponential duration with default rate λ, we get

$$\frac{S(1)}{1+r} + \cdots + \frac{S(H)}{(1+r)^H} = \frac{\exp -\lambda}{1+r} + \cdots + \frac{\exp(-\lambda H)}{(1+r)^H}$$

$$= \frac{\exp -\lambda}{1+r} \frac{1 - (\exp -\lambda/(1+r))^H}{1 - (\exp -\lambda/(1+r))}.$$

The yield is the solution of the above equation,

$$\gamma = \exp \lambda (1+r) - 1,$$

and the spread of interest rate is given by

$$s = \gamma - r = (1+r)[\exp \lambda - 1]. \tag{6.35}$$

It increases with λ. The higher the default rate is, the higher the discount factor. Therefore, a risky borrower has to pay higher installments than the nonrisky borrower examined earlier.

The above computation establishes a link between the interest rate on a personal loan and the risk of default. By analogy one can find an equivalent relationship between corporate default risk and the interest rate on a corporate bond. Let us assume that market prices of corporate bonds reflect the underlying fundamental risk of corporate default. Let us denote by $\gamma_{j,H,t}$ the yield at t on the corporate bond of firm j with residual maturity H, and by $r_{H,t}$ the yield of the Treasury bond with the same maturity. Solving for λ the spread formula in (6.35) yields the following approximation of the probability of default of firm j between times t and $t + H$:

$$\hat{\lambda}_{j,H,t} = \log \left[1 + \frac{\gamma_{j,H,t} - r_{H,t}}{1 + r_{H,t}} \right]. \tag{6.36}$$

The instantaneous probability of default (default rate) varies across firms, maturities, and dates. When it is constant in time, the approximations $\hat{\lambda}_{j,H,t}$ are almost independent of H, t. Otherwise, a term structure of default arises that can be analyzed in detail using relation (6.34). More precisely, if bonds at different maturities $h = 1, \ldots, H$ are traded on the market, from (6.34) it follows that

$$\frac{[1 + \gamma_{j,h,t}]^h - 1}{\gamma_{j,h,t}[1 + \gamma_{j,h,t}]^h} = \frac{\hat{S}_{j,t}(1)}{1 + r_{h,t}} + \cdots + \frac{\hat{S}_{j,t}(h)}{(1 + r_{h,t})^h}, \quad h = 1, \ldots, H. \quad (6.37)$$

where $\hat{S}_{j,t}(h)$ is the approximated survivor probability at time t for maturity h. The sequence of (market) values of survivor function, $\hat{S}_{j,t}(1), \ldots, \hat{S}_{j,t}(H)$, can be computed by solving the recursive system (6.37). The fact that approximated survivor functions depend on time is due to changes in the amount of information available.

Determining survivor function from market prices requires perfect competition on financial markets. Among the conditions that need to be satisfied are the following: (1) all agents on the market are equally informed; (2) the corporate bonds are liquid at all maturities (except when default occurs). In practice, these conditions are never satisfied. Despite that, the computation method discussed above can serve the following purposes.

(i) Comparison of the approximation of duration distributions based on market prices with the probabilities of default evaluated from the balance sheet of a firm, or inferred from the standard credit rating of firm, provided by Standard & Poor's or Moody's or Fitch.

(ii) Introduction of appropriately transformed interest rate spreads as additional explanatory variables into the standard score formula (see (6.36)), and the testing of their significance. In the same spirit, the one-year term-deposit rate announced by a bank can also be included in the score, since it reveals the cost of refinancing.

6.4.3 Prepayment Analysis

A prepayment on a loan, such as a mortgage, that terminates early may entail financial losses to a credit institution. In particular, losses may be incurred when the loan is refinanced without the possibility of prepayment.

Securitization is an important tool of refinancing used by credit institutions. The idea is to transform a pool of credits into financial assets tradable on a secondary financial market. To simplify the description of this transformation, we consider a pool of homogeneous consumer credits granted on the same date, with identical maturity and fixed interest rates. The pool is split into 10 000 shares, say, which are sold on the market. These provide to each buyer 1/10 000 of the payoff generated by the pool, including the payments of the principal and interest. Under the condition of no default or prepayment, these assets become fixed-income securities and resemble risk-free bonds. However, their future payoffs become uncertain, due to the risk of default or prepayment. While in practice the risk of default is insured, the risk of prepayment is not. The lack of coverage has an impact on the price of these contingent assets. Most analytical studies of prepayment concern the *mortgage-backed securities*, which are the major assets of this type in the United States. The empirical results are usually based on aggregate data, even when a heterogenous pool of credits is examined (see, for example, Bartholomew et al. 1988; Richard and Roll 1989; Hayre et al. 1989; Frachot and Gourieroux 1995). We report below some empirical results concerning car loans for new-car purchases,[1] which are based on individual data. The database is generated from records on French securitization (see De Toldi et al. 1995). Since this is a short-term loan of a rather small amount, prepayments made in order to benefit from a change in interest rates are rare, and the main reason for prepayment is essentially the purchase of another car.

6.4.3.1   *Estimation of Prepayment Rates*

Seasonality is an important feature in the dynamics of car purchases. Typically, in certain months of the year, more cars are sold. These monthly seasonal effects concern first-car purchases, as well as replacements of old cars by more recent models.

The model below explains the dynamics of car loan durations. At some point in time τ_i, an individual signs a car loan agreement. At a later point in time $\tau_i + h$, the same person terminates the loan by prepaying the debt. The dates τ_i and $\tau_i + h$ are related to the seasonal patterns in car purchases. Technically, our model is a semi-parametric proportional hazard model with seasonal effects. It is designed for individual data sampled at the frequency of one month:

$$\lambda_{i,\tau_i}(h) = \lambda_0(h) \exp\left[z_i'b + \sum_{s=1}^{12} C_{1,s}\xi_s(\tau_i) + \sum_{s=1}^{12} C_{2,s}\xi_s(\tau_i + h) \right], \qquad (6.38)$$

where λ_0 is a baseline hazard function, $\xi_s(\tau_i)$ and $\xi_s(\tau_i + h)$ are the indicators of the month in which the car loan is granted and of the month at which the loan is terminated, respectively. $C_{1,s}$ and $C_{2,s}$ are the associated seasonal coefficients, called the seasonal entry and exit coefficients, respectively. No individual covariates are included.

Model (6.38) was estimated on data for four-year-term car loans. (There also exist two-year-term car loans, but these cannot be securitized.) The estimated seasonal coefficients are given in Table 6.1, and the pattern of baseline hazard is plotted in Figure 6.10. Due to lack of space, the estimated variance–covariance matrix of seasonal coefficients with $24 \times 25/2 = 300$ elements is not reported.

Table 6.1 reports the values of seasonal entry and exit coefficients for each month of the year. The absolute values of the seasonal exit coefficients are, on average,

---

[1] These car loans have to be distinguished from new lease contracts.

Table 6.1. Seasonal coefficients.

	January	February	March	April	May	June
Seasonal entry coefficient	0.059	0.024	0.006	0.033	−0.052	−0.037
Seasonal exit coefficient	−0.131	−0.197	0.054	0.203	0.029	0.104

	July	August	September	October	November	December
Seasonal entry coefficient	−0.092	0.001	0.037	0.030	0.006	−0.015
Seasonal exit coefficient	0.100	−0.284	−0.177	0.012	0.085	0.201

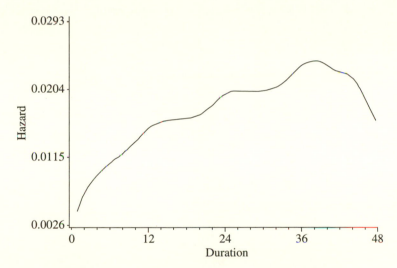

Figure 6.10. Baseline hazard function (after smoothing).

larger than the absolute values of the seasonal entry coefficients. The seasonal effects revealed by the model are as follows: there is a spike in the rate of prepayment in April (row 3 for exit, column 5 for April). This is the time of year when car dealers receive new vehicle models, which are displayed at the National French automobile fair in November. Another seasonal increase in prepayments is observed in December. This effect is related to some specific tax rules for car owners. During the summer holidays, we observe negative values of seasonal entry coefficients. This finding suggests that in the summer, the car market is very slow.

Figure 6.10 displays the baseline hazard (exit) rate as a function of car loan duration (from 0 to 48 months). The exit rates associated with the baseline hazard function vary between 1.5% and 2.5% per month. They increase with the age of the car, except for credit agreements close to the termination date (a decrease of prepayment rate is observed after 36 months). The rates of prepayment are quite high: 12% for the first year, 16% for the second and third years, 12% for the last year. Only 44% of car loan agreements terminate at the expiry date. There are local maxima in months 12, 24, and 36. Their presence may be due to the effects of marketing. Indeed, advertisements encouraging consumers to replace their old cars are mailed at each anniversary of the car purchase by the car dealer (or at each anniversary of the credit agreement by the credit institution, respectively).

6.4.3.2 *Payoff Patterns*

Using the results of the prepayment duration model, one can identify the patterns of future payoffs generated by a pool of car loans. Let us consider credit contracts that begin on the same date 0, terminate in H units of time, and have identical monthly interest rates equal to γ. The original balances $B_{0,i}$ are allowed to be different. The loans are to be repaid in equal monthly payments. The monthly payment on loan i is

$$m_i = B_{0,i} \frac{\gamma(1+\gamma)^H}{(1+\gamma)^H - 1},$$

and the balance remaining unpaid after h months is

$$B_{h,i} = B_{0,i} \frac{(1+\gamma)^H - (1+\gamma)^h}{(1+\gamma)^H - 1}.$$

The monthly payment is divided into two parts. One part covers repayment of the principal,

$$P_{h,i} = B_{0,i} \frac{\gamma(1+\gamma)^{h-1}}{(1+\gamma)^H - 1},$$

and the second one covers the interest,

$$I_{h,i} = B_{0,i}\gamma \frac{(1+\gamma)^H - (1+\gamma)^{h-1}}{(1+\gamma)^H - 1}.$$

In the absence of a prepayment penalty, the payoff generated by individual car loan i in month h is a random variable, which takes one of the following three possible values:

$$Z_{h,i} = \begin{cases} 0 & \text{with probability } 1 - S_i(h), \\ B_{h,i} + m_i & \text{with probability } p_i(h), \\ m_i & \text{with probability } S_i(h+1) = S_i(h) - p_i(h). \end{cases}$$

The expected payoff generated in month h by the entire pool of credits $i = 1, \ldots, n$ is the sum of individual payoffs:

$$E\left(\sum_{i=1}^n Z_{h,i}\right) = \sum_{i=1}^n [(B_{h,i} + m_i)p_i(h) + m_i S_i(h+1)]$$

$$= \sum_{i=1}^n [B_{h,i} p_i(h) + m_i S_i(h)].$$

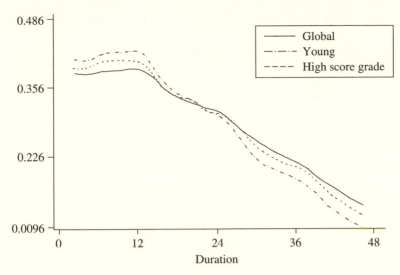

Figure 6.11. Expected payoff.

Figure 6.11 shows the total expected payoffs generated by the April entry cohort (solid line) as a function of the month. The cohort is divided up according to age and score value. The expected payoffs generated by the categories "young" and "high score" are depicted by the dashed lines. For all categories the payoffs increase or are steady in the first year, and decrease steadily to zero in years 2, 3, and 4.

In securitized credits, it is common to separate the payoffs into repayments of the principal and of the interest. There exist tradable financial assets associated with each of them, called the IO (*interest only*) and PO (*principal only*) strips, which belong to the category of credit derivatives. The financial properties of these stripped securities are different. Figures 6.12 and 6.13 compare the monthly expected payoffs, the monthly standard errors on payoffs, and the Sharpe performances (measured as the ratio of expected payoff and standard error) for IO and PO strips as functions of the month. The payoff generated by the IO strip is a linearly decreasing function. Its performance drops quickly in the first five months, and then decreases slowly to zero. The payoff generated by the PO strip fluctuates heavily. It increases sharply in the first five months and decreases steadily, while displaying strong seasonal effects, to zero. The performance of the PO strip is very different from that of the IO strip because at maturity the principal is repaid. Therefore, the PO strip performance displays an upward trend and ends up at 1 instead of 0. Apart from the tendency to increase, there is also some variation related to seasonal effects.

6.5 Concluding Remarks

The duration approach to risk assessment shares common features with the count data analysis. Depending on the presence or absence of omitted individual hetero-geneity, we distinguish a family of simple parametric models, such as the exponential

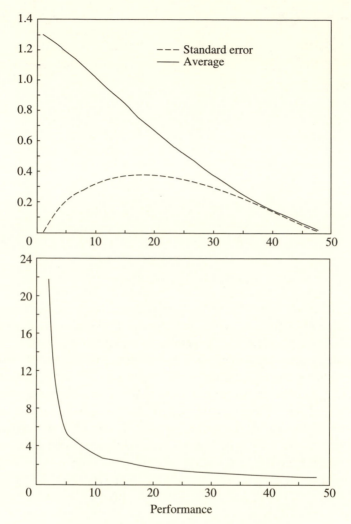

Figure 6.12.   Characteristics of interest payments.

regression model, and a family of more advanced specifications based on the Pareto distribution. What sets apart the duration based approach is the information conveyed in complex descriptive statistics such as survivor functions and hazard rates. The behavior of a hazard function is determined by the type of duration dependence featured by a given duration variable. In the semi-parametric framework it is possible to leave the pattern of the hazard function unconstrained, and to distinguish the proportional or accelerated effects of explanatory variables.

There exists a large body of literature on duration models including surveys and books such as Cox (1962), Kalbfleich and Prentice (1980), Cox and Oakes (1984), Heckman and Singer (1984), Gourieroux and Jasiak (1990), Lancaster (1990), Lee

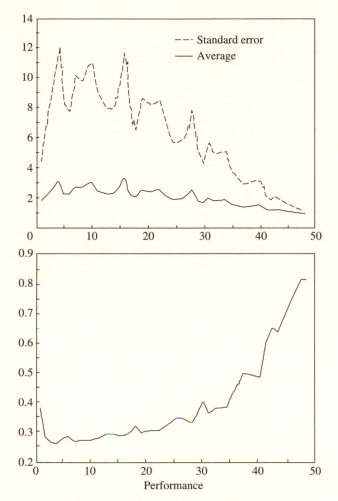

Figure 6.13. Characteristics of principal payments.

(1992), and Van den Berg (2001). The main economic application of duration models concerns unemployment analysis and is not referenced in this chapter, except for unemployment insurance (Meyer 1990). Other well-known domains of application are automobile insurance, life insurance, health economics (Hartman and Watts 1978), credit risk, mailing, and purchase intensities (see, for example, Gupta 1991).

6.6 Appendix

6.6.1 *Expected Residual Lifetime*

$$r(y) = E[Y - y \mid Y \geqslant y]$$
$$= \int_y^\infty (u - y) \frac{f(u)}{S(y)} \, \mathrm{d}u = -\frac{1}{S(y)} \int_y^\infty (u - y) \, \mathrm{d}S(u).$$

Therefore, by integrating by parts, we get

$$r(y) = -\frac{S(u)}{S(y)}(u-y)\Big|_y^\infty + \frac{1}{S(y)}\int_y^\infty S(u)\,du$$

$$= \frac{1}{S(y)}\int_y^\infty S(u)\,du. \tag{6.39}$$

This relationship can be easily inverted. Indeed we get

$$-\frac{1}{r(y)} = \frac{-S(y)}{\int_y^\infty S(u)\,du} = \frac{d}{dy}\log\left[\int_y^\infty S(u)\,du\right].$$

We deduce

$$-\int_0^y \frac{du}{r(u)} = \log\left[\int_y^\infty S(u)\,du\right] - \log\left[\int_0^\infty S(u)\,du\right], \tag{6.40}$$

$$\exp-\int_0^y \frac{du}{r(u)} = \frac{1}{r(0)}\int_y^\infty S(u)\,du. \tag{6.41}$$

Finally, by substitution into Equation (6.39) we obtain

$$S(y) = \frac{r(0)}{r(y)}\exp-\int_0^y \frac{du}{r(u)}.$$

6.6.2 Computation of the Premium Rate for the Pension Contract

We get

$$E[\min(Y, A) - y \mid Y \geqslant y]$$

$$= \frac{1}{S(y)}\int_y^\infty \min(u-y, A-y)f(u)\,du$$

$$= \frac{1}{S(y)}\int_y^A (u-y)f(u)\,du + \frac{A-y}{S(y)}\int_A^\infty f(u)\,du$$

$$= -\frac{S(u)}{S(y)}(u-y)\Big|_y^A + \frac{1}{S(y)}\int_y^A S(u)\,du + (A-y)\frac{S(A)}{S(y)}$$

$$= \frac{1}{S(y)}\int_y^A S(u)\,du.$$

Similarly, we have

$$E[\max(Y-A, 0) \mid Y \geqslant y] = \int_A^\infty (u-A)\frac{f(u)}{S(y)}\,du$$

$$= \frac{\int_A^\infty S(u)\,du}{S(y)}.$$

The formula of Proposition 6.6 follows directly.

References

Bartholomew, L., J. Berk, and R. Roll. 1988. Adjustable rate mortgages prepayment behaviour. *Housing Finance Review* 7:31–46.

Cox, D. R. 1962. *Renewal Theory*. London: Methuen.

Cox, D. R. 1972. Regression models and life tables. *Journal of the Royal Statistical Society* B 34:187–220.

Cox, D. R. 1975. Partial likelihood. *Biometrika* 62:269–76.

Cox, D. R., and D. Oakes. 1984. *Analysis of Survival Data*. London: Chapman & Hall.

De Toldi, M., C. Gourieroux, and A. Monfort. 1995. Prepayment analysis for securitization. *Journal of Empirical Finance* 2:45–70.

Fons, J. 1994. Using default rates to model the term structure of credit risk. *Financial Analyst Journal* September:25–31.

Frachot, A., and C. Gourieroux. 1995. *Titrisation et Remboursements Anticipés*. Paris: Economica.

Gourieroux, C., and J. Jasiak. 1999. Durations. In *Companion in Econometric Theory* (ed. B. Baltagi). Oxford: Blackwell.

Gupta, S. 1991. Stochastic Models of interpurchase time with time dependent covariates. *Journal of Marketing Research* 28:1–15.

Hartman, R., and C. Wattes. 1987. The determination of average hospital length of stay: an economic approach. *Quarterly Review of Economics and Business* 18:83–96.

Hayre, L., K. Lauterbach, and C. Mohebbi. 1989. Prepayment models and methodologies. In *Advances and Innovations in the Bond and Mortgage Markets* (ed. F. J. Fabozzi), pp. 259–304. Chicago, IL: Probus Publishing

Heckman, J. 1981. Heterogeneity and state dependence. In *Studies in Labor Markets* (ed. S. Rosen). University of Chicago Press.

Heckman, J., and B. Singer. 1974. Econometric duration analysis. *Journal of Econometrics* 24:63–132.

Heckman, J., and B. Singer. 1984. The identifiability of the proportional hazard model. *Review of Economic Studies* 52:231–41.

Jarrow, R., and S. Turnbull. 1992. Drawing the analogy. *Risk Magazine* 5:63–71.

Kalbfleisch, J., and R. Prentice. 1980. *The Statistical Analysis of Failure Time Data*. Wiley.

Kennan, J. 1985. The duration of contract strikes in U.S. manufacturing. *Journal of Econometrics* 28:5–28.

Lee, E. 1992. *Statistical Methods for Survival Data Analysis*. Wiley.

Meyer, B. 1990. Unemployment insurance and unemployment spells. *Econometrica* 58:757–82.

Kiefer, N. 1984. A simple test for heterogeneity in exponential models of duration. *Journal of Labor Economics* 2:539–49.

Kim, I., K. Ramaswamy, and S. Sundaresan. 1993. Does default risk affect the valuation of corporate bonds? A contingent claims model. *Financial Management* Autumn:117–31.

Lancaster, T. 1985. Generalized residuals and heterogenous duration models, with application to the Weibull model. *Journal of Econometrics* 28:155–69.

Lancaster, T. 1990. *The Econometric Analysis of Transition Data*. Cambridge University Press.

Lee, L. 1984. Maximum likelihood estimation and a specification test for normal distributional assumption for accelerated failure time models. *Journal of Econometrics* 24:159–79.

Merton, R. 1974. On the pricing of corporate debt: the risk structure of interest rates. *Journal of Finance* 29:449–70.

Richard, S., and R. Roll. 1989. Prepayments on fixed rate mortgage backed securities. *Journal of Portfolio Management* 15:73–82.

Van den Berg, G. 1997. Association measures for durations in bivariate hazard rate models. *Journal of Econometrics* 79:221–45.

Van den Berg, G. 2001. Duration models: specification, identification and multiple durations. In *Handbook of Econometrics* (ed. J. Heckman and E. Leamer), Volume 5, pp. 3381–480. Amsterdam: North-Holland.

7

Endogenous Selection and Partial Observability

The statistical methods introduced in previous chapters concerned samples of individuals drawn randomly from the same population. Under this assumption, all individual observations in a sample are i.i.d., that is, independently and identically distributed. In addition, the endogenous risk variables were assumed to be completely observed. These two assumptions are not always satisfied, for various reasons. In this chapter, we discuss statistical methods applicable to nonhomogeneous samples and partially observed variables. The first part covers estimation of individual risk from stratified samples, under exogenous and endogenous stratification schemes. The model relies on the dichotomous qualitative variable risk representation. We will show that endogenous stratification yields inconsistent risk estimators and results in so-called selectivity bias. The second part of the chapter concerns individual risk modeled by duration variables. In this context, the truncation and censoring in duration data are examined. The bias-correction methods are introduced at the end of the chapter. An example of consumer credit is used to show how the informational content of denied credit applications can be exploited for bias correction. In practice, sample heterogeneity and partial observability are often encountered in longitudinal data. Therefore, these problems will be discussed further in Chapter 10.

7.1 Analysis of Dichotomous Risks from a Stratified Sample

Let us recall the dichotomous quantitative risk variable Y_i, introduced in Chapter 2. Y_i takes the values 0 and 1: $Y_i = 0$ for "bad risk" individuals and $Y_i = 1$ for "good risk" individuals. In Chapter 2, we also discussed the technique of segmentation, which consists of dividing a group of individuals into two categories depending on the predicted value of individual risk: 0 or 1. Below, we show some more advanced techniques for partitioning a group of individuals, and explain the rationale.

7.1.1 Description of the Population and the Sample

For ease of exposition, let the individuals under study be characterized by the following two variables: a qualitative covariate for an individual characteristic X with K alternatives; and the individual risk variable Y that takes the values 0 and 1. As

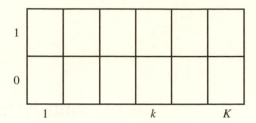

Figure 7.1. Partition of the population.

in all models discussed in the text so far, X is the exogenous variable and Y is the endogenous one.

The population can be partitioned with respect to the value of risk variable Y, and with respect to the value of the covariate X. We end up with the double *stratification* scheme shown in Figure 7.1.

To assess the probability of individual loss, we need to compute the conditional distribution of risk given the covariate. Since the risk takes the values 0 and 1 only, we have to find the following two conditional probabilities:

$$p_1(k) = P[Y = 1 \mid X = k], \qquad\qquad k = 1, \ldots, K, \qquad (7.1)$$
$$p_0(k) = P[Y = 0 \mid X = k] = 1 - p_1(k), \quad k = 1, \ldots, K. \qquad (7.2)$$

The conditional distribution of risk in (7.1), (7.2) involves K unknown parameters $p_1(k), k = 1, \ldots, K$. In order to find the unknown parameters and to evaluate the conditional risk probabilities, we need to consider a sample with the same structure as the population in Figure 7.1.

Let us consider a large sample of size n. Suppose that this sample is partitioned with respect to the same two stratification variables, denoted by Y and X. We denote by $n_{1,k}$ (respectively, $n_{0,k}$) the number of individuals in the sample with $Y_i = 1, X_i = k$ (respectively, $Y_i = 0, X_i = k$). It may seem natural to approximate the unknown conditional probabilities $p_1(k), k = 1, \ldots, K$, by the sample frequencies $\tilde{p}_1(k) = n_{1,k}/(n_{1,k}+n_{0,k}), k = 1, \ldots, K$. This approximation is accurate when the sample is drawn at random from the population, because then the above frequency estimators coincide with the conditional ML estimator shown in Chapter 3. However, for other sampling schemes, the approximations of probabilities by sample frequencies may be inconsistent. To explain this in detail, we consider two stratified sampling schemes below. The first one is stratified with respect to the covariate. The second is stratified with respect to the risk variable.

In practice, the proportion of risky individuals is often quite low. The aim of stratified sampling is to rebalance the risky and nonrisky individuals in the sample by assigning more weight to the risky individuals. A common practice consists of creating a *matched sample*, where one nonrisky individual is assigned to each risky individual.

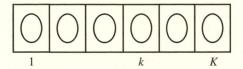

Figure 7.2. Exogenous stratification.

7.1.2 Exogenous Stratification

Exogenous stratification consists of partitioning the population with respect to the exogenous covariate only. In the stratum $(X = k)$, we randomly draw a given number $n_{.k}$ of individuals and record the values of risk variable Y_i for each individual (see the stratification scheme in Figure 7.2).

The log-likelihood function for this exogenously stratified sample is

$$\log L = \sum_{k=1}^{K} [n_{1,k} \log p_1(k) + n_{0,k} \log p_0(k)]$$

$$= \sum_{k=1}^{K} \{n_{1,k} \log p_1(k) + n_{0,k} \log[1 - p_1(k)]\}.$$

Maximizing with respect to $p_1(k)$, $k = 1, \ldots, K$, provides the estimators of unknown parameters $\tilde{p}_1(k) = n_{1,k}/(n_{0,k} + n_{1,k})$, which can be substituted into the conditional probabilities (7.1), (7.2). According to this formula, the ML estimator is equal (and equivalent) to the sample frequency defined as the fraction of "good risk" individuals with $Y_i = 1$ in the group of individuals with characteristic k. Under exogenous stratification, the sample frequency estimator is consistent. This result holds even when the stratified sample is not representative, that is, when the proportion of individuals with a particular covariate value $X = k$ in the sample is not equal to their proportion in the population.

7.1.3 Endogenous Stratification

Endogenous stratification consists of partitioning the population with respect to the endogenous risk variable only (see Figure 7.3 for the stratification scheme). In the stratum $(Y = j)$, $j = 0, 1$, we draw at random a given number $n_{j.}$ of individuals and record the values of observed covariates.

Clearly, endogenous stratification leads to discriminant analysis, so that the log-likelihood function is

$$\log L = \sum_{k=1}^{K} \{n_{1,k} \log p_k(1) + n_{0,k} \log p_k(0)\}, \tag{7.3}$$

where $p_k(j)$ denotes the conditional probability of $X = k$ given $Y = j$. These probabilities are related to the conditional probabilities of interest in (7.1), (7.2) as

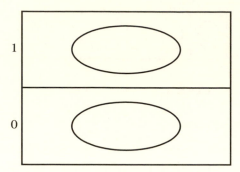

Figure 7.3.   Endogenous stratification.

follows:

$$p_k(1) = \frac{p_1(k)\Pi_k}{\sum_\ell p_1(\ell)\Pi_\ell},\tag{7.4}$$

where $\Pi_k = P[X = k]$ is the marginal probability of the exogenous covariate. Therefore, if all marginal probabilities are known, the ML estimators of the parameters of interest are the solutions of

$$\max_{p_1(k)} \sum_{k=1}^{K} \left\{ n_{1,k} \log\left[\frac{p_1(k)\Pi_k}{\sum_\ell p_1(\ell)\Pi_\ell}\right] + n_{0,k} \log\left[\frac{p_0(k)\Pi_k}{\sum_\ell p_1(\ell)\Pi_\ell}\right] \right\},\tag{7.5}$$

subject to the constraint that the probabilities sum up to one.

The ML estimators can only be computed numerically. They differ from the sample frequency estimators, which have some undesirable properties under endogenous stratification. The sample frequency is the fraction of "good risk" individuals $Y_i = 1$ with covariate value k in the group of all individuals with covariate value k. Indeed, if $n_1.$ and $n_0.$ are large, we obtain

$$\tilde{p}_1(k) = \frac{n_{1,k}}{n_{0,k} + n_{1,k}}$$

$$\sim \frac{n_1. p_k(1)}{n_0. p_k(0) + n_1. p_k(1)}$$

$$\sim \frac{\alpha p_k(1)}{p_k(0) + \alpha p_k(1)},$$

where α is the sampling rate of good risk individuals. This limit is generally different from the parameter of interest $p_1(k)$. Therefore, the sample frequency estimator is not consistent. This effect is called the *selectivity bias*. The proposition below is valid for any logit model, even under additional constraints on the conditional probabilities.

Proposition 7.1. *In an endogenously stratified sample, the sample frequency estimators $\tilde{p}_1(k)$, $k = 1, \ldots, K$, of individual risk probabilities are not consistent, although they provide a correct ranking of individuals.*

Proof. The limiting values of sample frequency estimators are given by

$$\tilde{p}_1(k) \sim \frac{\alpha p_k(1)}{p_k(0) + \alpha p_k(1)}$$
$$= \frac{\alpha p_1(k)(\Pi_k/p_1)}{p_0(k)(\Pi_k/p_0) + \alpha p_1(k)(\Pi_k/p_1)}$$
$$= \frac{(\alpha/\alpha^*)p_1(k)}{p_0(k) + (\alpha/\alpha^*)p_1(k)},$$

where α^* is the proportion of "good risk" individuals in the population. Since $p_0(k) = 1 - p_1(k)$, $\tilde{p}_1(k)$ is an increasing function of $p_1(k)$ in large samples. Therefore $\tilde{p}_1(k)$, k varying, and $p_1(k)$, k varying, provide the same ranking asymptotically. □

7.1.4 The Role of Stratified Samples

The proportion of risky individuals in the population is often very small. Under a random sampling scheme, it is necessary to draw a sample of a very large size in order to observe a sufficient number of risky individuals so that one can discriminate between the two categories of individual. To reduce the sample size, while observing a fair number of risky people, we have to assign more weight to this category. This can be achieved, either by (1) endogenous stratified sampling with, for instance, $n_{1.} = n_{0.}$ and thus α much larger than α^*, or (2) exogenous stratified sampling with more weight assigned to exogenous strata highly correlated with the risk variable.

7.2 Truncation and Censoring in Duration Models

We now turn our attention to durations as risk variables. The data used in duration analysis are often panel data comprising a number of individuals observed over a fixed period of time. A common problem encountered in panel data is the so-called partial observability, either due to censoring or to truncation.

As an illustration, we consider a set of two-year consumer loans granted in January 1999. The associated generation of borrowers is called a *cohort*.

7.2.1 Censoring

Let us assume that a sample is randomly drawn from the cohort and that the individual records are collected from January 1999 until December 1999. In the sample, we distinguish between

(a) individuals with default in 1999;

(b) individuals without default by December 1999.

We are interested in the duration Y_i of time to first default. This duration is completely observed for individuals in subsample (a), whereas we only know that it is larger than one year for individuals in subsample (b). We use the term "right censored" to refer to the duration data in the second subsample (see Figure 7.4).

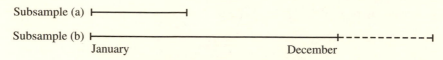

Figure 7.4.   Censoring scheme.

In order to identify the right censored observations, we introduce an indicator variable d_i. The indicator variable takes value 1 if the observed duration is complete, and value 0 if the observation is right censored. The endogenous variables are the indicator variable d_i and the complete duration y_i, when $d_i = 1$. The log-likelihood corresponding to this sampling scheme becomes

$$\log L[d, y \mid x; \theta] = \sum_{i=1}^{n} [d_i \log f(y_i \mid x_i; \theta) + (1 - d_i) \log S(1 \mid x_i; \theta)], \quad (7.6)$$

where the second term pertains to the censored observations.

Example 7.2. The log-likelihood function for the exponential regression model with *right censoring* is

$$\log L(d, y \mid x; \theta) = \sum_{i=1}^{n} d_i z_i' \theta - \sum_{i=1}^{n} (d_i y_i + (1 - d_i)) \exp z_i' \theta$$

$$= \sum_{i=1}^{n} d_i z_i' \theta - \sum_{i=1}^{n} \min(y_i, 1) \exp z_i' \theta.$$

The first-order condition becomes

$$\sum_{i=1}^{n} z_i [d_i - \min(y_i, 1) \exp z_i' \hat{\theta}] = 0,$$

which should be compared with formula (6.18).

7.2.2   Truncation

Let us now assume that in January 2000 we draw a sample of individuals for whom the credit agreement is still in effect, and we keep collecting individual data on this sample until the termination date in December 2000. If the individual credit histories prior to January 2000 are also available, the set of duration data is complete, while the individuals in the sample are endogenously selected. Indeed, we disregard the loan agreements with default prior to December 1999. In such a case, the duration data are said to be *left truncated*. The distribution of duration has to be the conditional distribution given that the credit agreement is still effective after a one-year period.

The log-likelihood function becomes

$$\log L(y \mid x; \theta) = \sum_{i=1}^{n} \log[f(y_i \mid x_i; \theta)/S(1 \mid x_i; \theta)]$$

$$= \sum_{i=1}^{n} \log f(y_i \mid x_i; \theta) - \sum_{i=1}^{n} \log S(1 \mid x_i; \theta). \qquad (7.7)$$

The likelihood function has changed due to replacing the initial p.d.f. of y_i by the conditional p.d.f. given $y_i > 1$.

Example 7.3. The log-likelihood function for the exponential model with *left truncation* is

$$\log L(y \mid x; \theta) = \sum_{i=1}^{n} z_i'\theta - \sum_{i=1}^{n}(y_i - 1) \exp z_i'\theta.$$

The reader should recognize the formula of the exponential regression model (see Section 6.2.1), with the duration y_i from that formula replaced by the residual duration $y_i - 1$. This is a direct consequence of the property of no duration dependence that characterizes the family of exponential distributions.

7.2.3 Competing Risks

In general, the censoring and truncation effects are due to the scope of the available data. However, some selectivity problems may also be generated by individual behaviors. As an illustration, let us consider a life insurance policy backed on a mortgage. When the borrower dies, the insurance company has the responsibility to repay the remaining balance of the mortgage. Therefore, default in mortgage payments is observed only when it occurs prior to the date of death. This is the so-called *competing risks* problem. It can be formalized by introducing the two following latent duration variables:

$$Y_1^* = \text{potential time-to-default,}$$
$$Y_2^* = \text{potential time-to-death.}$$

The observed time-to-default is

$$Y_1 = Y_1^*, \quad \text{when } Y_1^* < \min(Y_2^*, H),$$

where H is the maturity of the mortgage. Otherwise we only know that $Y_1^* > \min(Y_2^*, H)$. This is a censoring effect with a random threshold, which can be assumed to be conditionally independent of default risk, in a first-step approximation.

7.3 Bias Correction Using Rejected Credit Applications

The risk is commonly estimated from observations on customers who were granted a loan or purchased an insurance policy. These individuals have been selected by credit officers or insurance agents, who have the power to reject an application either directly or indirectly by asking a price that a customer cannot afford. The selection procedure reduces the sample of all individuals who applied for credit or insurance to an endogenous subsample of individuals who were successfully selected. If the risk to be estimated is the idiosyncratic risk of any applicant for credit or insurance, the resulting subsample is obviously not representative, as it contains no information on the denied applicants and their individual risks. As a consequence, an individual risk estimator, based on the subsample that contains data on the accepted customers only, is inconsistent and suffers from selectivity bias.

Below, we discuss in detail the selectivity bias, and introduce the bias-detection and bias-correction methods.

7.3.1 Selectivity Bias

Let us introduce a dichotomous default variable that takes the values 0 (no default) or 1 (default), and an exogenous covariate that admits K alternatives. Default will be denoted by $Y_{2,i}$, where the subscript 2 is used to distinguish it from a new dichotomous variable $Y_{1,i}$. $Y_{1,i}$ is an additional dichotomous variable that describes the selection procedure of credit applicants:

$$Y_{1,i} = \begin{cases} 1 & \text{if credit is granted,} \\ 0 & \text{otherwise.} \end{cases}$$

Accordingly, $Y_{1,i}$ is the decision variable.

Let us now consider the conditional probabilities of default given the covariate: $p_1(k) = P[Y_2 = 1 \mid X = k], k = 1, \ldots, K$, and their estimators, which are sample frequencies computed from the set of accepted applications. The estimator $\tilde{p}_1(k)$ will converge to $P[Y_2 = 1 \mid X = k, \ Y_1 = 1]$. It provides a good approximation of the parameter of interest if and only if

$$P[Y_2 = 1 \mid X = k] = P[Y_2 = 1 \mid X = k, \ Y_1 = 1], \tag{7.8}$$

that is, the probability of default given the individual characteristic is equal to the probability that default occurs given the individual characteristic and given that the loan is granted ($Y_1 = 1$). From the Bayes formula, we get

$$P[Y_2 = 1 \mid X = k] = P(Y_1 = 1 \mid X = k)P[Y_2 = 1 \mid X = k, \ Y_1 = 1]$$
$$+ P(Y_1 = 0 \mid X = k)P[Y_2 = 1 \mid X = k, \ Y_1 = 0]. \tag{7.9}$$

Therefore, condition (7.8) is equivalent to

$$P[Y_2 = 1 \mid X = k, \ Y_1 = 1] = P[Y_2 = 1 \mid X = k, \ Y_1 = 0]. \tag{7.10}$$

Condition (7.10) requires that the probabilities of default, given the individual char-acteristic and given the outcome of the selection procedure, are equal regardless of the outcome of the selection procedure, i.e., regardless of whether the loan applica-tion is granted or denied.

This requirement is satisfied for any alternative k of individual characteristic X if, and only if, the dichotomous variables Y_2 and Y_1 are independent, conditional on X.

Proposition 7.4. *The preliminary selection of credit applicants entails no selec-tivity bias if, and only if, the default variable Y_2 and the decision variable Y_1 are independent, conditional on X.*

In practice, when the conditional independence does not hold, it is important to find the rationale behind the decision made by a credit officer or insurance agent. Indeed, they may possess additional information about the applicant that helps elim-inate asymptotic bias and improve the accuracy of predicted risk.

7.3.2 Boundaries for Risk Prediction

When no information about the selection procedure is available, the Bayes for-mula can be used to derive the lower and upper bounds of the risk estimator. More precisely, the bounds concern the conditional probability of "bad risk" given the covariates. Indeed, from (7.9) it follows that

$$P[Y_2 = 1 \mid X = k, \ Y_1 = 1]P[Y_1 = 1 \mid X = k]$$
$$\leqslant P[Y_2 = 1 \mid X = k]$$
$$\leqslant P[Y_2 = 1 \mid X = k, \ Y_1 = 1]P[Y_1 = 1 \mid X = k] + P[Y_1 = 0 \mid X = k].$$
$$(7.11)$$

The bounds can be computed when the selectivity rates in each stratum are known. In practice, the prediction interval can be quite wide, and therefore not sufficiently informative. For instance, if the proportion of accepted applications in a given class $(X = k)$ is equal to 80% and the proportion of good risks in the stratum is 95%, we get

$$76\% \leqslant P[Y_2 = 1 \mid X = k] \leqslant 100\%.$$

In contrast, the bounds produce a reasonably narrow confidence interval when the conditional risk probabilities are *a priori* constrained. In particular, when they are supposed to satisfy a logit model,

$$p_1(k) = [1 + \exp -(\theta_0 + \theta_1 k)]^{-1},$$

we get the following set of boundary conditions:

$$A_k \leqslant \theta_0 + \theta_1 k \leqslant B_k, \quad k = 1, \ldots, K \ (\text{say}).$$

Even when the interval for each k is wide, intervals for θ_0, θ_1 can be narrow, as shown in Figure 7.5, where the bounds on $\theta_0 + \theta_1 k$, k varying, are indicated by straight lines.

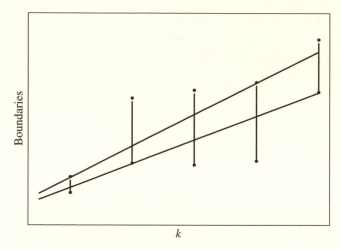

Figure 7.5.   Bounds on the line $\theta_0 + \theta_1 k$.

Table 7.1.   Partial observability.

Risk variable y_2	Decision y_1	
	1	0
1	Complete observability	Partial observability
0	Complete observability	Partial observability

7.3.3 *A Bivariate Model for Bias Correction*

To improve the efficiency of bias correction, it is necessary to add a formal representation of the credit-granting procedure to the model.

7.3.3.1 *Partial Observability*

In practice, an applicant has to provide information on his/her exogenous characteristics by filling out a credit application form. Therefore, the exogenous covariates in vector x are observed once the answers to all questions are given. Next, the decision variable y_1 is observed, and the groups of accepted and denied applicants are separated. The risk variable y_2 is observed only among the accepted credit applicants, because default on a loan can occur only if a loan is granted in the first place. There is partial observability since we do not observe the risk variable in the group of rejected credit applicants. The observability of endogenous variables is summarized in Table 7.1 above.

7.3.3.2 *Latent Model*

Let us formalize the observability by providing a specification of the conditional probabilities of the two endogenous variables. To do this, we introduce the following two latent (unobserved) quantitative variables that satisfy a linear model (Poirier 1980; Meng and Schmidt 1985):

$$y_{1,i}^* = z_{1i}' b_1 + u_{1i}, \qquad y_{2,i}^* = z_{2i}' b_2 + u_{2i}, \qquad (7.12)$$

where the bivariate errors $(u_{1i}, u_{2i})'$ are i.i.d. with the bivariate normal distribution

$$N \left[\begin{pmatrix} 0 \\ 0 \end{pmatrix}, \begin{pmatrix} 1 & \rho \\ \rho & 1 \end{pmatrix} \right].$$

z_{1i}' and z_{2i}' are observable vectors of transformed covariates of individual characteristics (which may have common elements), and b_1 and b_2 are vectors of unknown parameters. The dichotomous endogenous qualitative risk and decision variables are defined, respectively, by

$$y_{1,i} = \mathbf{1}_{y_{1,i}^* > 0}, \qquad y_{2,i} = \mathbf{1}_{y_{2,i}^* > 0}, \qquad (7.13)$$

where $\mathbf{1}_{y^* > 0} = 1$ if $y^* > 0$, and $\mathbf{1}_{y^* > 0} = 0$ otherwise. The distribution of Y_1 (respectively, Y_2) given the covariates corresponds to a probit model with explanatory variable z_1 (respectively, z_2).

We have

$$
\begin{aligned}
P[Y_{1,i} = 0 \mid x_i] &= P(Y_{1,i}^* < 0 \mid x_i) \\
&= P(z_{1i}' b_1 + u_{1i} < 0 \mid x_i) \\
&= P(u_{1i} < -z_{1i}' b_1 \mid x_i) \\
&= \Phi(-z_{1i}' b_1) = 1 - \Phi(z_{1i}' b_1),
\end{aligned}
$$

where Φ denotes the c.d.f. of the standard normal distribution. Similarly, we have

$$
\begin{aligned}
P[Y_{2,i} = 1, \ Y_{1,i} = 1 \mid x_i] &= P(Y_{2,i}^* \geqslant 0, \ Y_{1,i}^* \geqslant 0 \mid x_i) \\
&= P(u_{1i} \geqslant -z_{1i}' b_1, \ u_{2i} \geqslant -z_{2i}' b_2 \mid x_i) \\
&= P(-u_{1i} \leqslant z_{1i}' b_1, \ -u_{2i} \leqslant z_{2i}' b_2 \mid x_i) \\
&= F(z_{1i}' b_1, \ z_{2i}' b_2; \rho),
\end{aligned}
$$

where $F(\cdot, \cdot; \rho)$ denotes the c.d.f. of the bivariate Gaussian distribution

$$N \left[\begin{pmatrix} 0 \\ 0 \end{pmatrix}, \begin{pmatrix} 1 & \rho \\ \rho & 1 \end{pmatrix} \right].$$

7.3.3.3 Interpretation

The interpretation of the parameters is as follows.

$z_{1i}' b_1$ is the "objective" score of interest for risk assessment.

$z_{2i}' b_2$ is the "subjective" score, which underlies the credit-granting decision. It can be quite different from the score of interest, when the decision makers have additional information about the individual. In any case, it is interesting to compare the individual rankings determined by these two scores.

The parameter ρ measures the endogeneity of the selection procedure. It is the coefficient of correlation between Y_1 and Y_2. We saw earlier in the text that selectivity bias, due to endogenous selection, arises when Y_1 and Y_2 are (conditionally) correlated. There is no selectivity bias due to endogenous selection when variables Y_1 and Y_2 are conditionally independent, that is, if, and only if, $\rho = 0$. Thus, the test of the null hypothesis $\{\rho = 0\}$ allows us to check if it is necessary to correct for selectivity bias (see Proposition 7.4).

Note that the dependence (i.e., correlation) between Y_1 and Y_2 is conditional on the explanatory variables z_1, z_2. The dependence and therefore the need for bias correction may disappear under a finer stratification when the number of variables in the score is increased. This approach is pursued below.

7.3.3.4 The Log-Likelihood Function

When a sample of size n is drawn randomly from data on both granted and rejected credit applications, the log-likelihood becomes

$$\log L = \sum_{i=1}^{n} \log l_i$$

$$= \sum_{i=1}^{n} \{y_{1,i} y_{2,i} \log F(z'_{1i} b_1, z'_{2i} b_2; \rho) + (1 - y_{2,i}) y_{1,i} \log[\Phi(z'_{1i} b_1)$$

$$- F(z'_{1i} b_1, z'_{2i} b_2; \rho)] + (1 - y_{1,i}) \log[1 - \Phi(z'_{1i} b_1)]\}. \tag{7.14}$$

The log-likelihood function can be separated into two terms that pertain to complete observations on $y_{1,i}$ and partial observations on $y_{2,i}$.

We get

$$\log L = \log L_1 + \log L_{2|1},$$

where

$$\log L_1 = \sum_{i=1}^{n} \{y_{1,i} \log \Phi(z'_{1i} b_1) + (1 - y_{1,i}) \log[1 - \Phi(z'_{1i} b_1)]\},$$

$$\log L_{2|1} = \sum_{i=1}^{n} y_{1,i} \left\{ y_{2,i} \log \frac{F(z'_{1i} b_1, z'_{2i} b_2; \rho)}{\Phi(z'_{1i} b_1)} \right.$$

$$\left. + (1 - y_{2,i}) \log \left[1 - \frac{F(z'_{1i} b_1, z'_{2i} b_2; \rho)}{\Phi(z'_{1i} b_1)} \right] \right\}.$$

This log-likelihood function can be maximized with respect to all parameters b_1, b_2, ρ. Alternatively, we can consider a two-step estimation method in which each component of the additive formula of the log-likelihood function is maximized separately.

First step: maximization of $\log L_1(b_1)$ with respect to parameter b_1. The estimator is denoted by $\hat{b}_1$.

Second step: maximization of the second component $\log L_{2|1}$ after replacing b_1 by its first-step approximation. We get the estimators

$$(\hat{b}_2, \hat{\rho}) = \arg\max_{b_2, \rho} L_{2|1}(\hat{b}_1, b_2, \rho).$$

Note that the "subjective" score underlying the granting decision, $z'_{i2}b_2$, cannot be estimated without prior estimation of the "objective" score $z'_{i1}b_1$. The comparison of the objective and subjective scores can be interpreted as an audit of the credit officer.

7.3.3.5 Local Analysis

The maximum likelihood approach is rather difficult to implement since it involves multiple integrals due to the presence of the c.d.f. of a bivariate Gaussian distribution. For this reason, it may be interesting to consider some tractable approximations of $\log L_{2|1}$. A simple approximation formula is derived by considering the behavior of this function in a neighborhood of the null hypothesis of exogenous selection $\{\rho = 0\}$. It is based on the proposition below, which is proved in Appendix 7.5.

Proposition 7.5. $F(y_1, y_2; \rho) = \Phi(y_1)\Phi(y_2) + \rho\varphi(y_1)\varphi(y_2) + o(\rho)$, *where* $o(\rho)$ *is negligible with respect to* ρ.

Let us consider a local approximation of the term that appears in the expression of $L_{2|1}$; we get

$$P[Y_2 = 1 \mid Y_1 = 1, x_i] = \frac{F(z'_{1i}b_1, z'_{2i}b_2; \rho)}{\Phi(z'_{1i}b_2)}$$

$$\simeq \Phi(z'_{2i}b_1) + \rho\varphi(z'_{2i}b_2)\frac{\varphi(z'_{1i}b_1)}{\Phi(z'_{1i}b_1)}$$

$$\simeq \Phi\left[z'_{2i}b_2 + \rho\frac{\varphi(z'_{1i}b_1)}{\Phi(z'_{1i}b_1)}\right].$$

Introducing this approximation formula into the expression for $L_{2|1}$ simplifies the two-step estimation procedure. Indeed, in the second step we have to maximize

$$\tilde{L}_{2|1}(\hat{b}_1, b_2; \rho) = \sum_{n=1}^{n} y_{1,i}\left\{y_{2,i}\log\Phi\left[z'_{2i}b_2 + \rho\frac{\varphi(z'_{1i}\hat{b}_1)}{\Phi(z'_{1i}\hat{b}_1)}\right]\right.$$

$$\left. + (1 - y_{2,i})\log\left[1 - \varphi\left[z'_{2i}b_2 + \rho\frac{\varphi(z'_{1i}\hat{b}_1)}{\Phi(z'_{1i}\hat{b}_1)}\right]\right]\right\}.$$

This is a probit model with explanatory variables z_2 and $\varphi(z'_{1i}\hat{b}_1)/\Phi(z'_{1i}\hat{b}_1)$. The correction for endogenous selection is obtained by increasing the number of variables in the score and including the appropriate ratio $\varphi(z'_{1i}\hat{b}_1)/\Phi(z'_{1i}\hat{b}_1)$, called *the Mill ratio*.

7.4   Concluding Remarks

In empirical studies, the samples of individuals are often partitioned (stratified) with respect to some random variables. When the partitioning is performed with respect to an exogenous variable, the outcome is called exogenous stratification. In contrast, when the endogenous risk variable is used for assigning individuals to different risk categories, the outcome is called endogenous stratification. We saw that exogenous stratification does not cause any problems, but endogenous stratification entails biased risk estimators, due to the selectivity bias. There exist statistical methods of correction for selectivity bias that can be used for endogenously stratified samples. In risk analysis based on duration data, the common problem of partial observability is encountered, due to censoring or truncation. In competing risk models, the censoring is caused endogenously by individual behaviors.

7.5   Appendix: First-Order Expansion of the C.D.F. of a Bivariate Normal Distribution

We obtain

$$
\begin{aligned}
F(y_1, y_2; \rho) &= \int_{-\infty}^{y_1} \int_{-\infty}^{y_2} \frac{1}{2\pi(1-\rho^2)^{1/2}} \exp -\left[\frac{u^2 + v^2 - 2\rho uv}{2(1-\rho^2)}\right] du\, dv \\
&\sim \int_{-\infty}^{y_1} \int_{-\infty}^{y_2} \frac{1}{2\pi} \exp -\left[\frac{u^2 + v^2 - 2\rho uv}{2}\right] du\, dv \\
&\sim \int_{-\infty}^{y_1} \int_{-\infty}^{y_2} \frac{1}{\sqrt{2\pi}} \exp -\frac{u^2}{2} \frac{1}{\sqrt{2\pi}} \exp -\frac{v^2}{2}(1+\rho uv)\, du\, dv \\
&= \int_{-\infty}^{y_1} \int_{-\infty}^{y_2} \varphi(u)\varphi(v)(1+\rho uv)\, du\, dv \\
&= \Phi(y_1)\Phi(y_2) + \rho\varphi(y_1)\varphi(y_2).
\end{aligned}
$$

References

Afifi, A., and R. Elashoff. 1966a. Missing observations in multivariate statistics. I. Review of literature. *Journal of the American Statistical Association* 61:595–604.

Afifi, A., and R. Elashoff. 1966b. Missing observations in multivariate statistics. II. Review of literature. *Journal of the American Statistical Association* 62:10–29.

Altman, E. 1977. Predicting performance in the savings and loan association industry. *Journal of Monetary Economics* 3:443–66.

Altman, E., and R. Eisenbeis. 1978. Financial applications of discriminant analysis: a clarification. *Journal of Financial and Quantitative Analysis* March:185–205.

Amemiya, T., and Q. Vuong. 1987. A comparison of two consistent estimators in the choice based sampling qualitative response model. *Econometrica* 55:699–702.

Boyes, W., D. Hoffman, and S. Low. 1989. An econometric analysis of the bank credit scoring problem. *Journal of Econometrics* 40:3–14.

Cosslett, S. 1981. Maximum likelihood estimation for choice based samples. *Econometrica* 49:1289–316.

Gumbel, E. 1960. Bivariate logistic distributions. *Journal of the American Statistical Association* 55:698–707.

Hartman, R. 1991. A Monte-Carlo analysis of alternative estimators in models involving selectivity. *Journal of Business and Economic Statistics* 9:41–50.

Hsieh, D., C. Manski, and D. McFadden. 1985. Estimation of response probabilities from augmented retrospective observations. *Journal of the American Statistical Association* 80:651–62.

Joy, O., and J. Toffelson. 1975. On the financial applications of discriminant analysis. *Journal of Financial and Quantitative Analysis* December:723–39.

King, G., and L. Zeng. 1999. Logistic regression in rare events data. *Political Analysis* 9:137–63.

Lancaster, T., and G. Imbens. 1990. Choice based sampling of dynamic populations. In *Panel Data and Labor Market Studies* (ed. J. Hartog, G. Ridder, and J. Theeuwes), pp. 21–44. Amsterdam: North-Holland.

Manski, C. 1989. Anatomy of the selection problem. *Journal of Human Resources* 24:343–60.

Manski, C. 1994. The selection problem. In *Advances in Econometrics, Sixth World Congress* (ed. C. Sims), pp. 143–70. Cambridge University Press.

Manski, C., and S. Lerman. 1987. The estimation of choice probabilities from choice based samples. *Econometrica* 45:1977–88.

Manski, C., and D. McFadden. 1991. Alternative estimation and sample designs for discrete choice analysis. In *Structural Analysis of Discrete Data with Econometric Applications* (ed. C. Manski and D. McFadden). Cambridge, MA: MIT Press.

Meng, C., and P. Schmidt. 1985. On the cost of partial observability in the bivariate probit model. *International Economic Review* 26:71–86.

Newey, J. 1988. Two step series estimation of sample selection models. Massachusetts Institute of Technology, Department of Economics Working Paper, No. 99-04.

Palepu, K. 1986. Predicting takeover targets: a methodological and empirical analysis. *Journal of Accounting and Economics* 8:3–35.

Poirier, D. 1980. Partial observability in bivariate probit models. *Journal of Econometrics* 12:209–17.

Sawa, T. 1984. A generalization of the univariate logit model and its bivariate extension. London School of Economics Working Paper EM/1984/93.

Xie, Y., and C. Manski. 1989. The logit model and response based samples. *Sociological Methods and Research* 17(3):283–302.

8

Transition Models

In this chapter we study individual histories recorded in discrete time. For each individual i, $i = 1, \ldots, n$, the history is formed by a sequence of observations $Y_{i,t}$, $t = 0, 1, \ldots, T_i$ (say), with values in a finite state space. In general, the states are qualitative. To facilitate analytical computations we assign a dummy variable, whose values indicate one of the J qualitative states $j = 1, \ldots, J$ observed at a given time. For example, each firm among the corporate bonds issuers has an individual history formed by a sequence of credit quality ratings, provided by Moody's (see Section 8.3). In this particular case, the state space is defined by the following set: {Aaa, Aa, A, Baa, Ba, B, Caa, D}, and the associated dummy variable takes values $j = 1, \ldots, 8$.

In the first part of the chapter we focus on the time-series component, and suppose that individual histories are independent with identical distributions. Moreover, we assume that each individual history forms a homogeneous Markov chain of order one. This process has a particular type of temporal dependence; of all the states in the entire history, only the last contains all the information needed to help us predict the present state. Using the homogeneous Markov assumption, we simplify the dynamic structure of individual histories for feasibility of modeling and prediction. First we give the definitions of Markov chains and transition probabilities and discuss the parametrization and estimation methods. Next, we address the effects of individual characteristics. A Markov chain with time-invariant individual characteristics can be modeled by a polytomous logit model, which is easy to implement. An extension to this model can accommodate explanatory variables which vary across individuals as well as across time. The last effect arises, for example, when transition probabilities depend on time spent in the last occupied state (the so-called duration dependence). In the final part of the chapter we explain the role of transition probabilities in the analysis of migration of individuals between predetermined classes of risk. This is performed in the context of an empirical example of credit card usage. We conclude the chapter with comments on the dynamics of corporate credit ratings provided by the rating agencies, such as Moody's.

8.1 Homogeneous Markov Chains

In this section, we consider i.i.d. individual histories, that is, we assume that the history of individual i is independent of the history of individual j, while their distributions are identical. The individual can be a person, a firm, or an open account credit. Each history is a process with its own dynamics, defined by the form of serial dependence of the present state on the preceding ones. For convenience, we omit the individual index, and denote the history of a single individual by Y_t, $t = 0, 1, \ldots, T, \ldots$.

8.1.1 Distribution of the Markov Chain

The distribution of a process is characterized by the marginal distribution of Y_0, and the conditional distributions of Y_1 given Y_0, Y_2 given (Y_1, Y_0), $\ldots$, Y_t given $\underline{Y_{t-1}} = \{Y_{t-1}, \ldots, Y_0\}$. In a *homogeneous Markov chain of order one*, the past dependence of the conditional distributions is limited to the dependence on the most recent observation. (This is the so-called *Markov property*.) By the *homogeneity property*, the conditional distributions are time invariant.

Henceforth, we will refer to the "Markov chain of order one" as the "Markov chain," for ease of exposition.

Definition 8.1. The process Y_t, $t = 0, 1, \ldots, T$, with state space $\{1, \ldots, J\}$ is a homogeneous Markov chain if, and only if,

$$P_t[Y_t = j \mid Y_{t-1} = k_1, \ Y_{t-2} = k_2, \ \ldots, \ Y_0 = k_t] = P[Y_t = j \mid Y_{t-1} = k_1],$$
$$\text{independent of } t, \ \forall t = 1, \ldots, T, \ \forall j, \ k_1, k_2, \ldots, k_t = 1, \ldots, J.$$

The distribution of a homogeneous Markov chain is entirely characterized by

- the initial distribution,

$$\mu_j = P[Y_0 = j], \quad j = 1, \ldots, J;$$

and

- the transition matrix,

$$P = (p_{j,k}).$$

Each element of the transition matrix defines the probability of a one-step transition from state k, occupied at $t - 1$, to state j at time t:

$$p_{j,k} = P[Y_t = j \mid Y_{t-1} = k], \quad j, k = 1, \ldots, J. \tag{8.1}$$

By the property of homogeneity, all one-step transition probabilities are time invariant.

The initial distribution consists of J probabilities associated with each state in the state space. These probabilities tell us how likely it is that the chain originated from any of the J states at time 0. Obviously, the components of the initial distribution are nonnegative and sum up to one:

$$\mu_j \geqslant 0, \quad \forall j = 1, \ldots, J, \quad \text{and} \quad \sum_{j=1}^{J} \mu_j = 1. \tag{8.2}$$

The transition matrix is of dimension $J \times J$. Its elements are nonnegative and sum up to one, column by column:

$$p_{j,k} \geqslant 0, \quad \forall j, k = 1, \ldots, J, \quad \text{and} \quad \sum_{j=1}^{J} p_{j,k} = 1, \quad \forall k = 1, \ldots, J. \tag{8.3}$$

The probability of any finite history is equal to the joint probability of all states occupied in that history. By replacing the joint probability with the product of the conditional and marginal probabilities, we can rewrite the probability of any finite history of a homogeneous chain of order one in a more convenient form:

$$
\begin{aligned}
P[Y_t = j_t, \ Y_{t-1} = j_{t-1}, \ \ldots, \ Y_0 = j_0] \\
= P[Y_t = j_t \mid Y_{t-1} = j_{t-1}]P[Y_{t-1} = j_{t-1} \mid Y_{t-2} = j_{t-2}] \\
\cdots P[Y_1 = j_1 \mid Y_0 = j_0]P[Y_0 = j_0] \\
= p_{j_t, j_{t-1}} p_{j_{t-1}, j_{t-2}} \cdots p_{j_1, j_0} \mu_{j_0}.
\end{aligned}
\tag{8.4}
$$

The product of conditional probabilities in the second line is replaced by the product of one-step transition probabilities in the last line. The last component in each line is the initial probability, that is, the marginal probability of the very first state in the finite history.

The prediction at horizon h is obtained from the conditional distribution at horizon h. The conditional distribution at horizon h is a $J \times J$ matrix of probabilities of h-step transitions from state k at time t to state j at time $t + h$.

Proposition 8.2.

(i) *The conditional distribution at horizon h is*

$$P[Y_{t+h} = j \mid Y_t = k] = p_{j,k}^{(h)}, \quad \forall j, k = 1, \ldots, J,$$

where $p_{j,k}^{(h)}$ *is the generic element of the matrix P^h. The matrix of probabilities of transitions in h steps is equal to the power h of the matrix of one-step transition probabilities, that is, to the power h of the transition matrix P.*

(ii) *The marginal distribution of Y_t is*

$$\mu_j^{(t)} = P[Y_t = j] = \sum_{k=1}^{J} p_{j,k}^{(t)} \mu_k, \quad \forall j = 1, \ldots, J.$$

Proof. These results follow directly from formula (8.4). For instance, we obtain

$$P[Y_t = j_t, Y_0 = j_0] = \sum_{j_{t-1}} \cdots \sum_{j_1} P[Y_t = j_t, Y_{t-1} = j_{t-1}, \ldots, Y_0 = j_0]$$

$$= \sum_{j_{t-1}} \cdots \sum_{j_1} p_{j_t, j_{t-1}} p_{j_{t-1}, j_{t-2}} \cdots p_{j_1, j_0} \mu_{j_0}$$

$$= p_{j_t, j_0}^{(t)} \mu_{j_0}.$$

The marginal distribution of Y_t is the sum of probabilities that the chain was initiated in any of the J states at time 0, each multiplied by the probability of a t-step transition from the initial state to any state in the state-space at time t.   □

Proposition 8.2 emphasizes the importance of linear algebra in Markov chain analysis, since the power matrix P^h provides the probabilities of transitions h steps ahead, and $\mu^{(t)} = P^t \mu$.

The Markov chain has the property of time invariance (the *stationarity property*) if and only if the marginal distributions are identical at different dates. This arises when $\mu = P\mu$.

Proposition 8.3. *The homogeneous Markov chain is stationary if, and only if, the initial probability distribution is invariant with respect to multiplication by the transition matrix $\mu = P\mu$.*

The time invariance of marginal distributions implies that the moments including the marginal mean and variance (if these exist) are constant in time. Given the existence and time invariance of the mean and variance, the correlations between the realizations of the chain at time t and time $t + h$, called the autocorrelations, do not depend on time t, but only on the distance h between them. Stationarity is essential for identification and modeling of dynamic processes. In particular, stationarity in the sense of time-independent marginal means, variances, and autocovariances is required in the class of linear models of conditional means, called (V)ARMA models ((vector) autoregressive conditional moving average). The assumption of stationarity, in the broader sense of time-invariant marginal distributions, is common in nonlinear models.

8.1.2   *Alternative Parametrizations of a Markov Chain*

The transition matrix P depends on $J(J - 1)$ independent parameters due to the requirement that each column of a transition matrix sums up to one. Other parametrizations are linked to the spectral decomposition of the transition matrix. The proposition below is proved in Gantmacher (1959).

Proposition 8.4. *A transition matrix admits a spectral decomposition (in the complex domain), with at least one eigenvalue equal to one, and the other eigenvalues being of modulus less than or equal to one.*

Therefore, if $\lambda_1 = 1, \lambda_2, \ldots, \lambda_J$ are the eigenvalues of P, and if Q denotes a matrix of associated eigenvectors, we get

$$P = Q \wedge Q^{-1} = Q \operatorname{diag}(\lambda) Q^{-1}. \tag{8.5}$$

From the expression $P' = [Q']^{-1} \wedge Q' = (Q^{-1})' \wedge [(Q^{-1})']^{-1}$, it follows that Q^{-1} is the transpose of a matrix of eigenvectors of P'. The *singular value decomposition* of the transition matrix is given below.

Proposition 8.5. *A transition matrix can be written as*

$$P = \sum_{j=1}^{J} \lambda_j u_j v'_j,$$

where

- $u_j, j = 1, \ldots, n$, *is a basis of eigenvectors of* P,
- $v_j, j = 1, \ldots, n$ *is a basis of eigenvectors of* P'.

The two bases are related as follows:

$$u'_j v_k = \begin{cases} 1 & \text{if } j = k, \\ 0 & \text{otherwise.} \end{cases}$$

The last condition simply follows from the equality $Q^{-1} Q = \text{Id}$.

For illustration, Proposition 8.5 implies the following transition matrix decomposition for a stationary Markov chain with a single eigenvalue equal to one. From Proposition 8.3 it follows that the initial distribution μ is an eigenvector associated with $\lambda_1 = 1$. From (8.3) the vector $e = (1, \ldots, 1)'$ is an eigenvector of P' associated with $\lambda_1 = 1$. Moreover, $e'\mu = 1$, since μ is a probability distribution. We get

$$P = \mu e' + \sum_{j=2}^{J} \lambda_j u_j v'_j. \tag{8.6}$$

This expression provides a new parametrization of the transition matrix P, in terms of the elements of its singular value decomposition. This decomposition is well defined by the eigenvalues $\lambda_j, j = 2, \ldots, J$, and eigenvectors $v_j, j = 2, \ldots, J$. Under this approach, we end up with $J(J - 1)$ independent parameters, since the eigenvectors are defined up to a multiplicative scalar.

Formula (8.6) allows us to study the properties of the chain at long horizons (ergodicity properties).

Proposition 8.6. *Let us consider a stationary Markov chain with a single eigenvalue equal to 1, and the other eigenvalues being of modulus strictly less than 1. We then have*

$$\lim_{h \to \infty} P^h = \mu e'.$$

Proof. From (8.6) we get

$$P^h = \mu e' + \sum_{j=2}^{J} \lambda_j^h u_j v_j',$$

which tends to $\mu e'$ when h tends to infinity, since

$$\lim_{h \to \infty} \lambda_j^h = 0, \quad j = 2, \dots, J.$$

$\square$

Thus, at long horizons h the conditional distribution of Y_{t+h} given Y_t tends to the marginal distribution. In particular, the initial state has no effect in the long run.

The property described here is called ergodicity. Ergodicity is a useful condition for economic and statistical analysis. From the economic point of view, it allows for defining and studying the equilibrium (long-run) properties of a dynamic system. From the statistical point of view, ergodicity allows us to obtain the consistency of estimators based on a set of observations from a single realization of the process. Indeed, any estimator such as the sample mean or variance is based on averaging across a finite set of observations in time. Under ergodicity, the estimator will converge to the corresponding theoretical moment. Nevertheless, the statistical argument is not so important in a panel framework, where the number of observations in time is rather small, while the cross-sectional number of realizations of the process is large.

8.1.3 Two-State Space

For illustration of the results derived so far, let us consider the example of a Markov chain with a two-state space $j = 1, 2$. The transition matrix is

$$P = \begin{bmatrix} p_{11} & p_{12} \\ p_{21} & p_{22} \end{bmatrix}, \tag{8.7}$$

where $p_{11} + p_{21} = p_{12} + p_{22} = 1$, $p_{11} \geqslant 0$, $p_{12} \geqslant 0$, $p_{21} \geqslant 0$, $p_{22} \geqslant 0$.
    Therefore we obtain

$$P = \begin{bmatrix} p_{11} & 1 - p_{22} \\ 1 - p_{11} & p_{22} \end{bmatrix}, \quad p_{11}, p_{22} \in [0, 1]. \tag{8.8}$$

Since the trace of the matrix (that is, the sum of its diagonal elements) is equal to the sum of its eigenvalues, we have

$$\lambda_1 = 1, \quad \lambda_2 = p_{11} + p_{22} - 1. \tag{8.9}$$

The second eigenvalue is a measure of the stability of the chain within a given state. Its modulus is strictly less than one if p_{11} and p_{22} are not simultaneously equal to one.[1]

Let us examine the stationary distribution of the chain (under the assumption $p_{11} + p_{22} < 1$). The marginal distribution $\mu = (\mu_1, \mu_2)'$ is derived from the stationarity condition:

$$P\mu = \mu \iff p_{11}\mu_1 + (1 - p_{22})\mu_2 = \mu_1$$
$$\iff p_{11}\mu_1 + (1 - p_{22})(1 - \mu_1) = \mu_1$$
$$\iff (p_{11} + p_{22} - 2)\mu_1 + 1 - p_{22} = 0$$
$$\iff \mu_1 = \frac{1 - p_{22}}{2 - p_{11} - p_{22}} = \frac{p_{12}}{p_{12} + p_{21}}.$$

Then $\mu_2 = 1 - \mu_1$.

8.1.4 Qualitative Representation of the Process

Instead of describing the Markov chain as a unidimensional process with polytomous qualitative state space, we can introduce dichotomous qualitative processes which indicate the state occupied at each time t:

$$Z_{j,t} = \begin{cases} 1 & \text{if } Y_t = j, \\ 0 & \text{otherwise.} \end{cases} \tag{8.10}$$

Knowledge of the J qualitative processes $(Z_{j,t})$, $j = 1, \ldots, J$, is equivalent to knowledge of (Y_t). For instance, for a three-state space and an observed Markov chain,

$$(Y_t)\ 112331221123,$$

the three dichotomous qualitative processes are

$$(Z_{1t})\ 110001001100,$$
$$(Z_{2t})\ 001000110010,$$
$$(Z_{3t})\ 000110000001.$$

The following should be noted:

$$\sum_{j=1}^{J} Z_{j,t} = 1, \quad \forall t,$$

$$\sum_{j=1}^{J} j Z_{j,t} = Y_t, \quad \forall t.$$

---

[1] When $p_{11} = p_{22} = 1$, each of the two states is an absorbing state. The chain can enter an absorbing state, but can never quit that state. As a consequence, the initial state will be observed at each future point in time.

The qualitative representation of the process can simplify the formulas of predictors and estimators. Let us consider the prediction of $Z_{t+h} = [Z_{j,t+h}, \; j = 1, \ldots, J]'$ evaluated at date t. The prediction is given by the following conditional expectation:

$$E[Z_{j,t+h} \mid \underline{Y_t}] = P[Z_{j,t+h} = 1 \mid \underline{Y_t}]$$

$$= P[Y_{t+h} = j \mid Y_t]$$

$$= \sum_{k=1}^{J} p_{j,k}^{(h)} Z_{k,t}.$$

The conditional expectation (prediction) of Z_{t+h} given past Z_t is

$$E[Z_{t+h} \mid Z_t] = P^h Z_t, \tag{8.11}$$

which is a *vector autoregressive representation* (VAR) of the associated multivariate qualitative process.

Example 8.7. For the two-state-space chain, we get

$$E(Z_{1,t+1} \mid Z_t) = p_{11} Z_{1,t} + p_{12} Z_{2,t}$$

$$= p_{11} Z_{1,t} + p_{12}(1 - Z_{1,t})$$

$$= (p_{11} - p_{12}) Z_{1,t} + p_{12}.$$

Since $p_{11} - p_{12} = p_{11} + p_{22} - 1 = \lambda_2$ and $p_{12} = \mu_1(1 - \lambda_2)$, the autoregressive representation is

$$Z_{1,t+1} - \mu_1 = \lambda_2(Z_{1,t} - \mu_1) + \varepsilon_{1,t+1},$$

where $\varepsilon_{1,t+1}$ has conditional mean zero. The second eigenvalue can be interpreted as an autoregressive coefficient, which has to be of modulus less then one for stationarity. The marginal probability μ_1 is the long-term probability of state 1 (see also Proposition 8.6).

8.1.5 *Estimation*

Let us consider a set of observed individual histories $Y_{i,t}$, $t = 0, 1, \ldots, T_i$, $i = 1, \ldots, n$, or alternatively $Z_{i,t}$, $t = 0, 1, \ldots, T_i$, $i = 1, \ldots, n$. The log-likelihood function conditional on the initial states $Z_{i,0}$, $i = 1, \ldots, n$, is

$$\log l(z; P) = \sum_{i=1}^{n} \sum_{t=1}^{T_i} \sum_{j=1}^{J} \sum_{k=1}^{J} \{z_{i,j,t} z_{i,k,t-1} \log p_{j,k}\}. \tag{8.12}$$

The maximum likelihood estimator of transition probabilities maximizes the log-likelihood function under the constraints $p_{j,k} \geqslant 0, \forall j, k, \sum_{j=1}^{J} p_{j,k} = 1, \forall k$. Since the log-likelihood function has the additive form

$$\log l(z; P) = \sum_{k} \log l_k(z; P_k),$$

where $l_k(z; P_k)$ depends on the transition matrix through the elements of column k, independent maximizations column by column can be performed:

$$\max_{p_{j,k}, \, j \text{ varying}} \sum_{i=1}^{n} \sum_{t=1}^{T_i} \sum_{j=1}^{J} (z_{i,j,t} z_{i,k,t-1} \log p_{j,k})$$

$$\text{such that } \sum_{j=1}^{J} p_{j,k} = 1 \quad p_{j,k} \geqslant 0, \; \forall k.$$

The solutions are the following sample transition frequencies:

$$\hat{p}_{j,k} = \frac{\sum_{i=1}^{n} \sum_{t=1}^{T_i} z_{i,j,t} z_{i,k,t-1}}{\sum_{i=1}^{n} \sum_{t=1}^{T_i} z_{i,k,t-1}}, \quad j = 1, \ldots, J. \tag{8.13}$$

Proposition 8.8. *The maximum likelihood estimators of transition probabilities are equal to the sample transition frequencies.*

Equation (8.11) can also be estimated by least squares. We observe that (8.11) implies a set of seemingly unrelated regressions (SURs):

$$Z_{i,j,t} = \sum_{k=1}^{J} p_{j,k} Z_{i,k,t-1} + \varepsilon_{i,j,t}, \quad i, j, t \text{ varying}, \tag{8.14}$$

where $\varepsilon_{i,j,t}$ is a zero-mean error term. Since the explanatory variables are the same in all equations, the GLS estimator is equal to the set of OLS estimators of the parameters in each regression estimated one by one. Also, the explanatory variables $Z_{i,k,t-1}$, k varying, are orthogonal so that $Z_{i,k,t-1}^2 = Z_{i,k,t-1}$. Therefore, the OLS estimator of $p_{j,k}$ is given by

$$\tilde{p}_{j,k} = \frac{\sum_{i=1}^{n} \sum_{t=1}^{T_i} z_{i,j,t} z_{i,k,t-1}}{\sum_{i=1}^{n} \sum_{t=1}^{T_i} z_{i,k,t-1}}.$$

The following proposition summarizes the results.

Proposition 8.9. *The maximum likelihood (ML) estimator of transition probabilities coincides with the OLS estimator based on prediction formula (8.14) of the associated qualitative process.*

This property suggests the use of standard OLS software for computing the estimates and their standard errors.

8.2   Explanatory Variables

The effect of observed explanatory variables on the dynamics of a process can be modeled by using either the transition probabilities or the long-run and adjustment parameters. Both approaches are illustrated below for a two-state space. The transition matrix is given by

$$P = \begin{bmatrix} p_{11} & p_{12} \\ p_{21} & p_{22} \end{bmatrix}.$$

The marginal probability of state 1 is

$$\mu_1 = \frac{p_{12}}{p_{12} + p_{21}},$$

and the adjustment coefficient is

$$\lambda_2 = p_{11} + p_{22} - 1.$$

To satisfy the homogeneity property of the Markov chain, only time-invariant individual covariates x can be introduced into the model.

8.2.1 Specification of the Transition Probabilities

Each column of the transition matrix defines a probability distribution on a two-state space. Hence, we can consider a dichotomous qualitative model for each column (see Chapter 2 and McRae (1977)). For instance, a dichotomous logit is

$$p_{11} = \frac{1}{1 + \exp z_1' b_1} = 1 - p_{21},$$

$$p_{22} = \frac{1}{1 + \exp z_2' b_2} = 1 - p_{12},$$

where z_1 and z_2 are the transformations of time-independent individual covariates. $z_1' b_1$ and $z_2' b_2$ are the two scores associated with the model. The expressions for the long-run and adjustment coefficients are

$$\left.\begin{aligned} \mu_1 &= \frac{\exp z_1' b_1 (1 + \exp z_1' b_1)^{-1}}{\exp z_1' b_1 (1 + \exp z_1' b_1)^{-1} + \exp z_2' b_2 (1 + \exp z_2' b_2)^{-1}}, \\ \lambda_2 &= (1 + \exp z_1' b_1)^{-1} + (1 + \exp z_2' b_2)^{-1} - 1. \end{aligned}\right\} \quad (8.15)$$

The parameters b_1 and b_2 are easily estimated by the maximum likelihood method. For instance, b_1 is estimated by a logit maximum likelihood method applied to a set of observations with state 1 as the initial state.

8.2.2 Specification of the Adjustment and Long-Run Parameters

An alternative specification can be based on parameters μ_1 and λ_2, which vary between 0 and 1. We assume that

$$\left.\begin{aligned} \mu_1 &= \frac{1}{1 + \exp \tilde{z}_1' \tilde{b}_1} = 1 - \mu_2, \\ \lambda_2 &= \frac{1}{1 + \exp \tilde{z}_2' \tilde{b}_2}, \end{aligned}\right\} \quad (8.16)$$

where $\tilde{z}_1, \tilde{z}_2$ are transformations of the time-independent covariates x. We note that the expressions of μ_1, λ_2 in (8.15) and (8.16) are different. The choice of either one depends on the tractability and the purpose of study. The model constructed from transition probabilities is easier to estimate, while the model based on the adjustment and long-run parameters is more adequate for dynamic analysis. For instance, $\tilde{z}_1$ (respectively $\tilde{z}_2$) will include explanatory variables relevant for the long-run behaviour (respectively the short-run behaviour).

8.2.3 Time-Dependent Markov Chain

In panel data, which consist of a large number of individual histories of different lengths, various forms of nonstationarity can arise. The nonstationarities are caused by trends, seasonal effects, learning, and time-varying covariates. Technically, they are reflected by time-varying transition probabilities.

The logit models can be easily extended to accommodate time-dependent transition probabilities, and, in particular, the time-varying explanatory variables z_1, z_2. As an illustration, let us consider the two-state-space process of credit card use. The states are as follows: 1 if the card is used during a week, 0 otherwise. We are interested in predicting the future state of card use conditional on the current one. The transition probabilities from one state to another are likely to be influenced by a learning process, and are not the same for a new and an old cardholder. Therefore, we consider the following model, where

$$p_{11}(t) = (1 + \exp z_1' b_{11})^{-1}, \quad \text{if } t \leqslant 4, \tag{8.17}$$

$$= (1 + \exp z_1' b_{12})^{-1}, \quad \text{if } 5 \leqslant t \leqslant 8, \tag{8.18}$$

$$= (1 + \exp z_1' b_{13})^{-1}, \quad \text{if } 8 < t, \tag{8.19}$$

where t is the number of weeks since the opening of a credit card account (credit line). The differences between the transition probabilities at various points in time are due to different values of the parameters. Accordingly, b_{11} is the parameter that pertains to the first month of transactions on the credit card, b_{12} to the second month, and b_{13} is the parameter valid for all following transactions.

Expression (8.19) points out the differences between the scores in the first month, the second month, and in the "long term." The differences between scores are determined by parameters b_{11}, b_{12}, b_{13}.

The parameters of the model are unknown and need to be estimated. The estimation methods for a homogeneous and a time-dependent Markov chain are similar. However, the predictions may be different. Let us consider the prediction of a future state at horizon h. Prediction formula (8.11) is easily extended and becomes

$$E[Z_{t+h} \mid Z_t] = P(t + h - 1) \cdots P(t)Z_t, \tag{8.20}$$

where $P(t)$ denotes the transition matrix from the state occupied at t to the other state at $t + 1$. This formula can only be used at horizon $h \geqslant 2$, if $P(t+1), \ldots, P(t+$

Table 8.1.   Transition matrix, bank.

	1	2	3	4	5	6	7	8	9
1	0.84	0	0	0	0	0	0	0	0.06
2	0	0.87	0.18	0.07	0.01	0	0	0	0
3	0	0.07	0.63	0.20	0.03	0.01	0.28	0	0
4	0	0	0.11	0.56	0.20	0.01	0.20	0	0
5	0	0	0.04	0.15	0.62	0.13	0.26	0	0
6	0	0	0.03	0	0.13	0.84	0.26	0	0
7	0.04	0	0	0	0	0	0	0.99	0.03
8	0.10	0	0	0	0	0	0	0	0.21
9	0.02	0.06	0.01	0.02	0.01	0.01	0	0.01	0.70

$h - 1$) are known at date t. This condition is satisfied when the covariates include some deterministic functions of time. It does not hold if among the explanatory variables are time-varying individual covariates, whose values are unknown at time t (see Chapter 11). However, the prediction formula can still be used for comparing consequences of various future evolutions of covariates. This method is called the scenario analysis.

8.3   Transitions between Score Categories

Individual risk is not constant in time. Therefore an important application of transition models is the analysis of risk dynamics. In practice the set of admissible values of a canonical score is partitioned into different subsets. The probabilities of transitions between subsets are estimated by taking into account the individual and temporal heterogeneities, and are used to predict the future structure of risk with respect to the score, for a given pool of individual risks.

8.3.1   Revolving Consumer Credit

In this section we study a pool of revolving credits. Two types of (potential) customer are distinguished: the first type obtain their credit cards directly from the bank, while the second type obtain the cards indirectly from a supermarket, which acts as a financial intermediary. A dichotomous explanatory variable is introduced to indicate the issuer of each credit card. A score for the cardholders is established and the set of possible values of the score is partitioned into eight categories. An additional segment, denoted by 9, is added for new customers who do not have a credit account at the bank prior to the sampling period. The transitions concern exits and entries to score categories, related to the improvement or deterioration of the financial standing of cardholders. The estimated biannual transition matrices for the sample of cardholders are given in Tables 8.1 and 8.2. Tables 8.1 and 8.2 concern credit cards issued by the bank and the supermarket, respectively.

Table 8.2. Transition matrix, supermarket.

	1	2	3	4	5	6	7	8	9
1	0.94	0	0	0	0	0	0	0	0.21
2	0	0.89	0.22	0.07	0	0	0	0	0
3	0	0.05	0.65	0.22	0.03	0.01	0.43	0	0
4	0	0	0.09	0.58	0.26	0.01	0.18	0	0
5	0	0	0.02	0.11	0.59	0.17	0.20	0	0
6	0	0	0.01	0	0.01	0.80	0.19	0	0
7	0.01	0	0	0	0	0	0	0.99	0.01
8	0.04	0	0	0	0	0	0	0	0.09
9	0.01	0.06	0.01	0.02	0.01	0.01	0	0.01	0.69

Columns and rows 1–8 in Tables 8.1 and 8.2 give the probabilities that a cardholder who at the beginning of the sampling period belongs to a given credit score category either makes a transition to a higher score category by improving his credit history, remains in the same score category, or worsens his/her credit records and moves to a lower score category. The transitions are from a given column to a given row, so that each column sums up to one. The last column and row concern acquisition of new cards. In particular, column 9 gives the structure of new credit card buyers with respect to score.

Accordingly, a person who owns a credit card issued by the bank (Table 8.1) and belongs to score category 2 would remain in the same score category with probability 87%, move to score category 1 with probability 0%, and move to score category 3 with probability 7%. The same person can takes out a new card from the bank with probability 6%. We observe that most nonzero entries are clustered around the main diagonal. The largest probabilities lie exactly on the main diagonal. This means that in most cases the cardholders maintain their credit rating. They also have significant probabilities of changing the score category by moving away from the diagonal by up to two or three categories, in any direction. Further away from the diagonal, only very low probabilities and zero entries can be found. The zeros that appear in the top-right and bottom-left corners suggest that the cardholders change their score ratings gradually, and that changes of more than three categories are unlikely.

We wish to investigate whether the choice of the credit card issuer is economically relevant and has an impact on transitions of individuals between the eight score categories, including the entry into category 9 accomplished by purchasing a new card. This is equivalent to testing the significance of the dichotomous explanatory variable indicating the issuer. If the credit card issuer matters, the transitions in Tables 8.1 and 8.2 are different and these differences are statistically significant. Therefore, we proceed by comparing the matrices in Tables 8.1 and 8.2 (denoted P_1 and P_2, respectively) column by column. Next, we compute the values of a

Table 8.3.   Chi-squared statistics by column.

Segment	1	2	3	4	5	6	7	8	9
Chi-squared	0.088	0.011	0.042	0.013	0.026	0.013	0.103	0	0.933

chi-squared statistic:

$$\xi_j = \sum_{i=1}^{9} \frac{(p_{i,j}^1 - p_{i,j}^2)^2}{1/2(p_{i,j}^1 + p_{i,j}^2)}, \quad j = 1, \ldots, 9,$$

where the $p_{i,j}^1$ (respectively $p_{i,j}^2$) are the elements of P_1 (respectively P_2). The values of the test statistics are reported in Table 8.3.

The entry 0.088 in row 2, column 2 is the value of the test statistic for testing the null hypothesis "there is zero difference between column 1 of Table 8.1 and column 1 of Table 8.2" against the alternative "there is a difference." The entry 0.011 in row 2, column 3 is the value of the test statistic for testing the null hypothesis "there is zero difference between column 2 of Table 8.1 and column 2 of Table 8.2" against the alternative "there is a difference," and so on. In a large panel like this one, a test at level 5% will show the significance of differences for all segments; thus, it is preferable to consider the test statistics as measures of discrepancies between probability distributions and to compare their relative values. We observe the strongest impact in segment 9.

Before examining the dynamics of the population of cardholders, it is useful to partition the transition matrix in blocks, in order to distinguish the exit and entry effects of new cardholders depicted by segment 9. These blocks are defined by

$$P = \begin{bmatrix} Q & q_e \\ q_x' & q_{ex} \end{bmatrix},$$

where Q has dimension $(8, 8)$, q_e and q_x are of dimension $(8, 1)$, and q_{ex} is a scalar.

Let us denote by $N_t = (N_{1,t}, \ldots, N_{8,t})'$ the number of customers in each segment in period t, and by E_t^1, E_t^2 the number of new credit cards in period t issued by the bank and the supermarket, respectively. The dynamics of the rating structure is defined by the recursive equations

$$N_t = N_t^1 + N_t^2, \tag{8.21}$$

where

$$N_t^1 = Q^1 N_{t-1}^1 + q_e^1 E_t^1,$$
$$N_t^2 = Q^2 N_{t-1}^2 + q_e^2 E_t^2.$$

By recursive substitution we get

$$N_t = [Q^1]^t N_0^1 + [Q^2]^t N_0^2 + \sum_{j=0}^{t-1} \{ [Q^1]^j q_e^1 E_{t-j}^1 + [Q^2]^j q_e^2 E_{t-1}^2 \}. \tag{8.22}$$

Table 8.4. Changes between February and August 1993.

	Segment							
	1	2	3	4	5	6	7	8
Bank Variation	-3.9%	5.7%	-0.14%	-1.42%	-0.15%	-1.09%	-23.94%	4.49%
Supermarket Variation	11.9%	13.1%	7.61%	7.67%	5.10%	5.14%	-5.37%	25.11%

Therefore, the change in the rating structure can be predicted at horizon t (at date 0) only if the future number of new credit cards to be issued is known. Formula (8.22) can be used to compare different scenarios, such as a constant, an increasing, or a decreasing number of new credit cards, or substitution effects between both types of card issuers under the constraint $E_t^1 + E_t^2 = \text{const.}$ As an illustration, we report above the estimated changes $(N_{j,1} - N_{j,0})/N_{j,0}$, $j = 1, \ldots, 8$, of the numbers of customers in each score category at the horizon of one semester, when $E_1^1 = E_0^1$, $E_1^2 = E_0^2$. The first part of Table 8.4 concerns the credit cards issued by the banks, and the second part of Table 8.4 concerns the credit cards issued by the supermarket.

Among the customers of the bank (the top part of the table), we observe a decline in the number of cardholders in all score categories, except for category 8. A large decrease, of almost one-quarter, is detected in category 7. On the contrary, for the supermarket we report an increase in the number of cardholders across all score categories, except for category 7. The largest increase occurs in category 8, which rose by slightly more than one-quarter.

8.3.2 Corporate Rating Dynamics

Bond ratings play a key role in corporate financing and investment decisions. A firm that issues highly rated bonds usually receives better credit terms than a firm whose bonds are low rated. Note that the bond issuers are large corporates. Moody's, Standard & Poor's (S&P), and Fitch are the three major corporate credit-rating agencies. Many investors on the market rely exclusively on the credit quality ratings and the bond prices of various companies for predicting corporate defaults (see also Section 11.2). Accordingly, these investors see the credit-rating dynamics as a proxy of risk dynamics. Since credit ratings change in time, the matrices of probabilities of transitions of firms from one credit-rating category to another are recalculated by the rating agencies each year (or month), and then published. The historical transition matrices are sometimes presented in the P-Id form. P-Id is called the *generator matrix* and is more suitable for financial calculations in continuous time. Table 8.5 shows an estimator of the generator matrix. In the P-Id form the columns of the matrix sum up to zero, and therefore the diagonal elements may turn negative.

Table 8.5.　Historical generator matrix (Moody's data).

	Aaa	Aa	A	Baa	Ba	B	Caa	D
Aaa	−0.0683	0.0169	0.0007	0.0005	0.0002	0.0000	0.0000	0.0000
Aa	0.0615	−0.0993	0.0237	0.0028	0.0005	0.0004	0.0000	0.0000
A	0.0066	0.0784	−0.0786	0.0585	0.0045	0.0014	0.0000	0.0000
Baa	0.0000	0.0027	0.0481	−0.1224	0.0553	0.0059	0.0074	0.0000
Ba	0.0002	0.0009	0.0047	0.0506	−0.1403	0.0691	0.0245	0.0000
B	0.0000	0.0001	0.0012	0.0075	0.0633	−0.1717	0.0488	0.0000
Caa	0.0000	0.0000	0.0001	0.0008	0.0026	0.0208	−0.3683	0.0000
D	0.0000	0.0002	0.0000	0.0016	0.0138	0.0741	0.2876	0.0000

Table 8.6.　Distribution of S&P rating by year (U.S. companies).

Year	AAA	AA	A	BB
1978	8.2	28.9	47.1	15.8
1979	10.1	28.3	47.1	14.4
1980	9.3	27.0	47.3	16.5
1981	8.1	25.3	46.9	19.8
1982	6.6	27.1	42.6	23.7
1983	5.1	27.5	42.7	24.7
1984	3.7	28.8	47.1	20.4
1985	2.8	26.1	46.2	24.9
1986	2.5	26.6	45.7	25.1
1987	3.2	25.6	44.6	26.6
1988	3.4	22.9	47.2	26.5
1989	3.8	22.5	44.4	29.3
1990	3.2	20.7	41.8	34.3
1991	3.8	19.6	46.5	30.1
1992	4.0	18.9	46.5	16.5
1993	3.5	17.7	41.2	37.6
1994	3.1	17.3	39.0	40.6
1995	2.8	17.1	39.8	40.3

　　It has been empirically documented that both the transition and marginal probabilities vary in time. As an illustration, Table 8.6 provides the distribution of the S&P ratings between 1978 and 1995.[2]

　　If the transitions were time homogeneous, the marginal probabilities would be constant in time. In contrast, we note a trend in the marginal distributions of ratings. This stylized fact is also revealed in the Moody's rating. To cite Lucas and Lonski (1992), in 1970 Moody's downgraded 21 issues and upgraded 23 issues. In 1990,

---

[2] The plausible causes of time variation are outlined below.

Table 8.7. Year dummies.

Year	1978	1979	1980	1981	1982	1983	1984	1985	1986
α	0.000	0.007	−0.030	−0.036	−0.065	−0.127	−0.131	−0.288	−0.334

Year	1987	1988	1989	1990	1991	1992	1993	1994	1995
α	−0.328	−0.355	−0.408	−0.443	−0.434	−0.458	−0.567	−0.659	−0.760

Moody's downgraded 601 issues and upgraded only 301. The trend displayed by annual rating distributions is likely to be related to a trend in transition probabilities.

In several articles published by daily newspapers it was argued that U.S. corporate credit quality has declined in the last couple of decades. The decline was confirmed by some research studies that documented the trend (see, for example, Lucas and Lonski 1992; Grundy 1997). However, there are several possible explanations of the observed trend, such as

(i) the declined quality of corporate debt,

or else

(ii) the time variation of the structure of rated companies;

(iii) the rating rules implemented by Moody's and S&P becoming tougher in time (Pender 1992).

The distinction between hypotheses (i) and (iii) is of great importance since the law requires that some investors purchase only bonds with high ratings, such as AAA, AA, or A.

Blume et al. (1998) attempted to replicate the S&P score. They considered an *ordered probit model*, where the rating $Y_{i,t}$ of corporation i at t is based on a latent Gaussian variable $Y_{i,t}^*$:

$$Y_{i,t} = \begin{cases} \text{AAA} & \text{if } a_3 \leqslant Y_{i,t}^*, \\ \text{AA} & \text{if } a_2 \leqslant Y_{i,t}^* < a_3, \\ \text{A} & \text{if } a_1 \leqslant Y_{i,t}^* < a_2, \\ \text{BB} & \text{if } Y_{i,t}^* < a_1, \end{cases}$$

where

$$Y_{i,t}^* = \alpha_t + z_{i,t}'b + \varepsilon_{i,t},$$

and the $\varepsilon_{i,t}$ are Gaussian heteroskedastic error terms.

The explanatory variables z are selected financial ratios that belong to key ratios used in the S&P analysis. The intercept coefficient α was set to be time dependent. The estimated values of the α_t coefficients are given in Table 8.7.

The trend effect is depicted by the evolution of the α_t coefficient, and is present even after a (partial) correction for heterogeneity by means of explanatory variable

z. However, even if we assume that all relevant z variables are included, we cannot say which one of hypotheses (i) and (iii) is true. Indeed the results can be interpreted in the two following different ways:

(i) $Y_{i,t}^*$ measures the individual risk at time t, which is increasing due to declining credit quality;

(ii) $z_{it}'b$ measures the individual risk, which is constant for a given z structure, while the rating agencies keep changing the threshold $a_3 - \alpha_t, a_2 - \alpha_t, a_1 - \alpha_t$ to make the rating rules tougher.

This identification problem can only be solved if additional information becomes available. This may require a more detailed knowledge of the S&P rating procedure. However, as Standard & Poor's (1996) wrote about their own score, there are no fixed rules and "subjectivity is at the heart of every rating." An alternative solution would consist of observing defaults and recording the credit risk rating of companies who went out of business. In an old study, Ang and Patel (1975) found that the S&P ratings had little power for predicting "financial" distress in the following year. In conclusion, it may be necessary to audit the auditing companies.

8.4   Concluding Remarks

This chapter discussed data indexed by time t and individual i that display both variation in time (time series) and across individuals (cross-section). We considered processes that allow each individual at any point in time to occupy one of a finite number of states. The exits and entries from one state to another are called transitions and occur with a given probability. Under the time-homogeneous Markov chain assumption, the transition probabilities are time invariant and form a transition matrix. The purpose of many studies is to estimate the transition matrix in its natural form or under an alternative, more parsimonious parametrization, based on the singular value decomposition. The transition models are easily extended to account for observable individual or temporal heterogeneity. Among many applications (see, for example, Spilerman 1972; Bartholomew 1973; Pitacco 1995; Janssen and Manca 1977), an interesting study concerns credit-rating migrations of bond issuers between various risk categories. We refer interested readers to Chapter 11, in which advanced transition models are discussed.

References

Anderson, T., and L. Goodman. 1957. Statistical inference about Markov chains. *Journal of the American Mathematical Society* 28:89–109.

Ang, J., and K. Patel. 1975. Bond rating methods: comparison and validation. *Journal of Finance* 30:631–40.

Bartholomew, D. 1973. *Stochastic Models for Social Processes*. Wiley.

Billingsley, P. 1961. *Statistical Inference for Markov Processes*. Chicago University Press.

Blum, M., F. Lim, and C. McKinlay. 1998. The declining credit quality of U.S. corporate debt: myth or reality? *Journal of Finance* 53:1389–413.

Gantmacher, F. 1959. *The Theory of Matrices*. New York: Chelsea.

Grundy, B. 1997. Preferreds and taxes. The relative price of dividends and coupons. University of Pennsylvania Discussion Paper.

Hickman, W. 1958. *Corporate Bond Quality and Investor Experience*. Princeton University Press.

Janssen, J., and R. Manca. 1997. A realistic nonhomogeneous stochastic pension funds model on scenario basis. *Scandinavian Actuarial Journal* 2:113–37.

Lucas, D., and J. Lonski. 1992. Changes in corporate credit quality 1970–1990. *Journal of Fixed Income* 1:7–14.

McRae, E. 1977. Estimation of time varying Markov processes with aggregate data. *Econometrica* 45:183–98.

Pender, K. 1992. Demystifying the ratings game. *San Francisco Chronicle*, February 17.

Pitacco, E. 1995. Actuarial models for pricing disability benefits: towards a unifying approach. *Insurance: Mathematics and Economics* 16:39–62.

Spilerman, S. 1972. The analysis of mobility processes by the introduction of independent variables into a Markov chain. *American Sociological Review* 37:277–94.

Standard & Poor's. 1996. *Standard & Poor's Corporate Ratings Criteria*. New York: Standard & Poor's.

9
Multiple Scores

In basic models for qualitative, count, and duration data presented in Chapters 2–6, the impact of individual covariates on the distribution of risk is summarized by a unique score. The advantage of using a unique score is that it allows for ranking individuals without ambiguity. However, in the presence of multiple risks, it is preferable to consider a set of scores with different interpretations. This approach was already adopted in the section of Chapter 7 on partial observability, and in Chapter 8 on transition models. In this chapter, further insights on multi-score analysis will be provided.

The problems to which multi-score analysis applies are, naturally, described at the beginning of the chapter. In technical terms, using a set of scores results in assigning a set of ratings to each individual. This allows for establishing a set of individual rankings that are not necessarily consistent with one another. It is essential for the analysis of multiple risks to create a set of different orderings of individuals with respect to risk. For example, a lender who simultaneously faces the risk of prepayment and the risk of default is interested in assessing the probability of a loss event related to each of these risks. Another example is the analysis of consumer choices from a set of available alternatives. The polytomous logit model introduced in this chapter can accommodate more than two alternatives associated with more than one score. Multiple scores will also appear in the profit maximization for the banking sector and in the utility maximization for individual choices. The efficiency of a score in any of the aforementioned applications depends on the relevance of explanatory variables included in that score. The proper choice of demographic and behavioral individual covariates is vital, not only for risk assessment, but also for market segmentation performed routinely prior to advertisement campaigns or new product offerings.

In the presence of multiple scores, technical difficulties can be caused by an excessive number of scores. It is possible to eliminate all redundant scores and determine the minimum necessary number of scores to be used. A solution is provided by a score reduction technique, which is based on the singular value decomposition of a matrix. An empirical illustration of household portfolio allocation analysis appears at the end of the chapter.

Table 9.1.   Partial observability ("n.o." stands for "not observed").

Y_1	Y_2
1	1
1	0
0	n.o.

9.1   Examples

Multiple scores arise naturally when risk of default is classified with respect to timing. For example, one can distinguish between default that occurs early in the contractual term and default that occurs later, as their financial consequences are very different. By the same token, risks of losses from car collisions can be classified with respect to severity. Let us first examine default on personal loans.

9.1.1   Default Risk and Preselection

The credit-granting procedure is formalized as follows: there are two endogenous dichotomous variables Y_1 and Y_2. Y_1 is the decision variable, that is, the outcome of the selection procedure of credit applications:

$$Y_{1,i} = \begin{cases} 1 & \text{if credit is granted,} \\ 0 & \text{otherwise.} \end{cases}$$

Y_2 is the risk associated with individual i:

$$Y_{2,i} = \begin{cases} 1 & \text{for default,} \\ 0 & \text{otherwise.} \end{cases}$$

The endogenous variables are partly observed. In particular, Y_2 is observed only when Y_1 takes the value 1. This means that individual i can default on a loan only if he/she has been offered a loan in the first place. The observable set of values of Y_1 and Y_2 is given in Table 9.1.

In general, default is observed only among the bank customers whose credit applications were accepted in the first place. At this point, one might be tempted to estimate risk of default from the observations available on current borrowers. As pointed out in Chapter 7, such a risk estimate is not accurate and suffers from selectivity bias; the reason being that the true sample of all credit applicants has been endogenously reduced to a subsample of accepted credit applicants, which is not representative of the true risk that characterizes all credit applicants.

In order to correct the prediction of risk for selectivity bias, we introduced in Chapter 7 a bivariate probit model (7.12), (7.13). In this model, the outcomes of the observed endogenous variables Y_1 and Y_2 depend on two latent linear regressions with individual characteristics as explanatory variables, and with Gaussian error

Table 9.2. Default timing ("n.o." stands for "not observed").

Y_1	Y_2	Y_3	Y_4	Y_5	Y_6
0	n.o.	n.o.	n.o.	n.o.	n.o.
1	0	n.o.	n.o.	n.o.	n.o.
1	1	0	n.o.	n.o.	n.o.
1	1	1	0	n.o.	n.o.
1	1	1	1	0	n.o.
1	1	1	1	1	0
1	1	1	1	1	1

terms. Each regression includes a score, denoted by $z'b_1$ and $z'b_2$, respectively. Below, we discuss similar specifications for the analysis of competing risks arising from uncertainty involved in credit-granting decisions, default, prepayment, and customer response to direct marketing.

9.1.2 Term Structure of Default

A term structure of a random variable is a set of predictions of that variable at various horizons. In applications to individual risk we might, for example, be interested in predicting corporate failure at the horizons of one, two, or three years (see, for example, Dambolena and Khoury 1980), or in predicting separately early and late defaults on consumer credit.

Let us consider a credit with maturity six months. Within that period the borrower can default on the loan. We are interested in predicting the time-to-default, which is necessarily less than six months. Let us measure the time-to-default in one-month units of time and denote it by Y_j, $j = 1, \ldots, 6$. Y_j is an indicator variable equal to 0 if default occurs in month j, and equal to 1 otherwise.

All possible default timings are given in Table 9.2.

Table 9.2 reveals the possibility of interpreting the time-to-default as an outcome determined by six partially observed dichotomous variables, associated with each month. Suppose that each month is associated with a score $z'b_j$, $j = 1, \ldots, 6$. The parameters of the score vary across the maturities due to the variation in the risk of default during that period.

The model has an intrinsic sequential structure. We observe Y_2 only if $Y_1 = 1$ was previously observed; we observe Y_3 only if $Y_1 = 1$ and $Y_2 = 1$ were previously observed; and so on. The sequential structure is depicted by the conditional probabilities below.

- The probability of $Y_1 = 1$, that is, of no default in month 1 (conditional on the exogenous covariates), is

$$P[Y_1 = 1 \mid X] = F(z'b_1),$$

where F is a given cumulative distribution function.

Table 9.3.   Conditional survivor function.

Age of the contract	Probability of no default
0	$F(z'b_1)F(z'b_2)\cdots F(z'b_6)$
1	$F(z'b_2)\cdots F(z'b_6)$
2	$F(z'b_3)\cdots F(z'b_6)$
3	$F(z'b_4)\cdots F(z'b_6)$
4	$F(z'b_5)F(z'b_6)$
5	$F(z'b_6)$

- The probability of $Y_2 = 1$, i.e., no default in month 2, conditional on $Y_1 = 1$, i.e., no default in month 1 (and on the exogenous covariates), is

$$P[Y_2 = 1 \mid Y_1 = 1, \; X] = F(z'b_2).$$

- The probability of $Y_j = 1$, i.e., no default in month j, conditional on $Y_1 = \cdots = Y_{j-1} = 1$, i.e., no default in any of the previous months (and on the exogenous covariates), is

$$P[Y_j = 1 \mid Y_1 = \cdots = Y_{j-1} = 1, \; X] = F(z'b_j), \quad j = 2, \ldots, 6.$$

$1 - F(z'b_j)$, $j = 1, \ldots, 6$, is the default intensity of the loan in month j, that is, the probability that the loan soon terminates by default.[1]

Let us show how the probabilities of other events can be evaluated. For example, the probability of no default during the whole lifetime of the loan is

$$P[Y_j = 1, \; j = 1, \ldots, 6 \mid X] = F(z'b_1)F(z'b_2)\cdots F(z'b_6).$$

The probability of default in the third month is

$$P[Y_1 = Y_2 = 1, \; Y_3 = 0 \mid X] = F(z'b_1)F(z'b_2)[1 - F(z'b_3)].$$

The probability of no default during the residual life of the loan can be evaluated for each of the six months as shown in Table 9.3.

9.1.3   *Differentiated Incident Severity*

In the model of time-to-default, we distinguished between loss events that occurred early and late. By analogy, one can distinguish between loss events with different severities.[2] The severity model is comprised of

---

[1] By introducing a set of different scores, we avoid using the "proportional," or "accelerated," hazard models (see Section 6.3).

[2] Time-to-default is not necessarily positively correlated with severity, since the most severe default can arise early rather than late.

Table 9.4. Observed severity ("n.o." stands for "not observed").

	Y_1	Y_2
	1	n.o.
	0	h

- a dichotomous qualitative variable that indicates the occurrence of a loss event,

$$Y_1 = \begin{cases} 1 & \text{if no incident occurs,} \\ 0 & \text{otherwise;} \end{cases}$$

- an ordered variable, which is the severity measure on a scale from 0 to H,

$$Y_2 = h, \quad h = 1, \ldots, H,$$

where h denotes the realized severity.

The severity is observed only if default occurs in the first place. Therefore Y_2 is partially observed, as summarized in Table 9.4.

Let us consider two scores $z'b_1$ and $z'b_2$ that determine the observable outcomes of both variables. The probability of no default conditional on individual covariates is

$$P[Y_1 = 1 \mid X] = F(z'b_1),$$

Y_2 obeys an ordered qualitative model (see, for example, Gourieroux 1989, Chapter 2). It is assumed that the severity depends on the value of the latent variable Y_2^* that satisfies a linear regression model:

$$Y_2^* = z'b_2 + u_2,$$

where the error term u_2 has the cumulative distribution function G. The support of Y_2^* (that is, the set of all admissible values) is partitioned into $H - 1$ distinct segments by an increasing sequence of thresholds a_h, $h = 1, \ldots, H$. The observed severity $Y_2 = h$ if, and only if, $a_h \leqslant Y_2^* < a_{h+1}$.

The marginal probability of severity h is

$$
\begin{aligned}
P[Y_2 = h \mid X] &= P[a_h \leqslant Y_2^* < a_{h+1} \mid X] \\
&= G[-z'b_2 + a_{h+1}] - G[-z'b_2 + a_h].
\end{aligned}
$$

It is different from the probability of observing a loss event of severity h:

$$P[Y_1 = 0, \ Y_2 = h \mid X] = [1 - F(z'b_1)]\{G[-z'b_2 + a_{h+1}] - G[-z'b_2 + a_h]\},$$

which is the probability of joint occurrence of a loss event and severity h.

Table 9.5.   The possible outcomes of a loan agreement.

Y_1	Y_2
0	0
0	1
1	0

9.1.4   Default and Prepayment

Default and prepayment are two important risks on a loan that any lender has to consider. Let us comment on two relevant issues in this context. First, default and prepayment are competing risks, because a loss, if it occurs, can only be caused by one of these two risks, whichever comes first. Clearly, default can only be observed if it occurs before the potential prepayment and prior to the contractual term. On the other hand, prepayment can be observed only when it occurs before potential default and prior to the contractual term.

Second, default and prepayment imply different types of loss.

(i) As a consequence of default, the lender loses the entire remaining balance on the loan (if the recovery rate is zero).

(ii) As a consequence of a prepayment, the entire remaining balance is repaid early. However, the maturity of the contract becomes shorter than the one initially agreed upon. The shorter maturity term can cause financial losses for the following reason. The funds advanced in consumer loans by a bank can be borrowed from another financial institution (so-called refinancing). Very often banks refinance at a fixed interest rate and maturity equal to the maturity of the consumer loan. However, unlike the individual borrowers, banks have no option of prepayment. A loss results if a borrower prepays the loan while the lender has to continue to pay the interests on refinancing—in particular, in a period of falling interest rates.[3]

Let us use two latent dichotomous variables to formalize the competing risks of default and prepayment:

$$Y_1 = \begin{cases} 1 & \text{for default,} \\ 0 & \text{otherwise,} \end{cases}$$

$$Y_2 = \begin{cases} 1 & \text{for prepayment,} \\ 0 & \text{otherwise.} \end{cases}$$

All possible outcomes are listed in Table 9.5.

---

[3] This problem can be circumvented by using a more appropriate refinancing strategy, for instance by securitizing the pool of credits.

Therefore, at the contractual term of a credit agreement:

(i) there is neither default, nor prepayment;

(ii) there is prepayment—the credit agreement ends before the contractual term;

(iii) there is default—a recovery procedure is initiated.

Let us establish the relationship between the times to default and prepayment. For this purpose, the following latent durations are defined:

τ_1, time to potential prepayment,

τ_2, time to potential default,

T_0, contractual term.

The outcomes of a credit agreement can be formalized as follows:

$$Y_1 = Y_2 = 0, \qquad \text{if and only if } \tau_1 \geqslant T_0, \ \tau_2 \geqslant T_0,$$
$$Y_1 = 0, \ Y_2 = 1, \quad \text{if and only if } \tau_2 < \tau_1, \ \tau_2 < T_0,$$
$$Y_1 = 1, \ Y_2 = 0, \quad \text{if and only if } \tau_1 < \tau_2, \ \tau_1 < T_0.$$

The probabilities of various outcomes are easy to compute when the duration variables are log-normally distributed:

$$\log \tau_1 = z' b_1 + u_1,$$
$$\log \tau_2 = z' b_2 + u_2,$$

where u_1, u_2 are independent, zero-mean, normal error terms, with respective variances σ_1^2 and σ_2^2. Then the respective probabilities of the three outcomes depend on two scores $z' b_1$ and $z' b_2$ and are given by

$$P[Y_1 = Y_2 = 0 \mid X]$$
$$= P[\tau_1 \geqslant T_0, \ \tau_2 \geqslant T_0 \mid X]$$
$$= P[\tau_1 \geqslant T_0 \mid X] P[\tau_2 \geqslant T_0 \mid X]$$
$$= \Phi \left[\frac{z' b_1 - \log T_0}{\sigma_1} \right] \Phi \left[\frac{z' b_2 - \log T_0}{\sigma_2} \right],$$

$$P[Y_1 = 0, \ Y_2 = 1 \mid X]$$
$$= P[\tau_2 < \tau_1, \ \tau_2 < T_0 \mid X]$$
$$= P[z' b_1 + \sigma_1 v_1 < z' b_2 + \sigma_2 v_2, \ z' b_2 + \sigma_2 v_2 < \log T_0]$$
$$\quad \text{(where } v_1 \text{ and } v_2 \text{ are independent standard normal variables)}$$
$$= E\{ P[z' b_1 + \sigma_1 v_1 < z' b_2 + \sigma_2 v_2 \mid v_2] \mathbf{1}_{z' b_2 + \sigma_2 v_2 < \log T_0} \}$$
$$= E \left\{ \Phi \left(\frac{z' b_2 - z' b_1 + \sigma_2 v_2}{\sigma_1} \right) \mathbf{1}_{v_2 < (\log T_0 - z' b_2)/\sigma_2} \right\}.$$

This expression requires integrating the term between brackets with respect to the Gaussian distribution of v_2. It can be computed numerically. Similarly, we have

$$P[Y_1 = 1, \ Y_2 = 0 \mid X] = P[\tau_1 < \tau_2, \ \tau_1 < T_0 \mid X]$$

$$= E\left\{ \Phi\left(\frac{z'b_1 - z'b_2 + \sigma_1 v_1}{\sigma_2} \right) \mathbf{1}_{v_1 < (\log T_0 - z'b_1)/\sigma_1} \right\}.$$

9.1.5 Default and Credit Promotion

Direct mail is a powerful promotional technique that allows marketers to target individual customers with more precision than newspaper and broadcast advertising. Providers of financial services mail credit card and other personal loan offers to customers on a regular basis. A complete direct mailing strategy begins with targeting a market niche and ends with response analysis. Its success depends on reaching the right individuals and properly selecting the recipients. Therefore, market segmentation, with respect to some demographic or behavioral individual characteristics, is essential in the first phase. The objective of direct mail is to stimulate individuals to apply for credit, which is *a priori* approved. Therefore, the response analysis is equivalent to processing the new loans. However, if too many individuals are targeted or these are not properly selected, direct mail may unnecessarily increase the risk exposure, by increasing the amount of credit issued to risky individuals.

Direct mail can be formalized and examined in a joint study of the mailing decision, customer response, and default. Let us consider a single individual on the mailing list. The actions involved in direct marketing are represented by the following three latent dichotomous variables:

$$Y_1 = \begin{cases} 1 & \text{for direct mail,} \\ 0 & \text{otherwise;} \end{cases}$$

$$Y_2 = \begin{cases} 1 & \text{for loan request,} \\ 0 & \text{otherwise;} \end{cases}$$

$$Y_3 = \begin{cases} 1 & \text{for default,} \\ 0 & \text{otherwise.} \end{cases}$$

The credit-granting decision is not included in the model because the loan is implicitly approved. There is partial observability in the sense that default can be observed provided that a loan is granted, and this occurs provided that the individual responds to the mail. The observable outcomes are listed in Table 9.6.

Note that the direct-mail variable Y_1 is controlled by the lender and does not depend on the endogenous behavior of the borrower. The borrower controls variables Y_2, Y_3. The probability distributions of these variables are conditional on $Y_1 = 1$. Therefore, according to the response scheme, it is not possible to identify the effect of mailing on default, for example. To solve this identification problem, it is necessary

Table 9.6. Credit promotion by direct mail ("n.o." stands for "not observed").

Y_1	Y_2	Y_3
1	0	n.o.
1	1	1
1	1	0

to compare the subsample of individuals who receive a credit offer with a benchmark sample of individuals who are not targeted by direct mail and apply for credit on their own initiative.

9.1.6 *Polytomous Logit Model*

The *polytomous logit model* describes individual choices among more than two mutually exclusive alternatives. Let individual i make a choice among $l = 1, \ldots, L$ alternatives and let Y_i be the polytomous qualitative variable of individual choice. Formally, we have

$$Y_i = l, \quad l = 1, \ldots, L,$$

if alternative l is selected by individual i.

In the polytomous logit model the elementary probabilities of each alternative choice conditional on covariates are

$$P[Y = l \mid X] = \frac{\exp(z'b_l)}{\sum_{k=1}^{L} \exp(z'b_k)},$$

where $b_l, l = 1, \ldots, L$, are parameter vectors and z is a vector of transformations of individual covariates. Hence, the model includes a set of scores $z'b_k, k = 1, \ldots, L$. Since

$$P[Y = l \mid X] = \frac{\exp(z'(b_l - b_1))}{\sum_{k=1}^{L} \exp(z'(b_k - b_1))},$$

the parameter vectors are identifiable up to a vector of constants. The multiplicity of solutions is eliminated by introducing the identifying restriction $b_1 = 0$.

For example, for $L = 2$ alternatives, the logit elementary probabilities are

$$P[Y = 1 \mid X] = \frac{1}{1 + \exp(z'b_2)}$$

and

$$P[Y = 0 \mid X] = 1 - P[Y = 1 \mid X].$$

This is the standard dichotomous logit model examined in Chapter 2. For $L = 3$ alternatives, the elementary probabilities are

$$P[Y = 1 \mid X] = \frac{1}{1 + \exp(z'b_2) + \exp(z'b_3)},$$

$$P[Y = 2 \mid X] = \frac{\exp(z'b_2)}{1 + \exp(z'b_2) + \exp(z'b_3)},$$

$$P[Y = 3 \mid X] = \frac{\exp(z'b_3)}{1 + \exp(z'b_2) + \exp(z'b_3)}.$$

Due to the identification problem, the parameter values are not directly interpretable, while their differences are. More precisely, let us consider two alternatives k and l among the L alternatives, and consider the choices made by individuals in the endogenous subpopulation $\mathcal{P}_{k,l}$, who retain either k or l. We obtain

$$P[Y = k \mid Y = k \text{ or } l, \ X] = \frac{\exp(z'b_k)}{\exp(z'b_k) + \exp(z'b_l)}$$

$$= \frac{1}{1 + \exp z'(b_k - b_l)}.$$

The differences $(b_k - b_l)$ represent the sensitivities of the conditional probabilities of individual choices in $\mathcal{P}_{k,l}$, with respect to the explanatory variables.

9.1.7   *The Hypothesis of Irrelevant Alternatives*

The polytomous logit model allows for detecting how individual choices change when an additional alternative is offered. A typical example, often considered in consumer behavioral studies, is the offering of a new product on the market. Most companies that sell products make a new-product development process part of their ongoing operations. The new product is successful if the consumers modify their behavior and begin to buy the new product instead of old ones. To assess this effect, we have to compare the individual consumer choices made before and after the new product became available. Let us consider two logit models and denote by Y^b, Y^a the indicators of consumer choices made before and after. We have

$$P[Y^b = l \mid X] = \frac{\exp(z'b_l)}{\sum_{k=1}^{L} \exp(z'b_k)}, \quad l = 1, \ldots, L,$$

$$P[Y^a = l \mid X] = \frac{\exp(z'\gamma_l)}{\sum_{k=1}^{L+1} \exp(z'\gamma_k)}, \quad l = 1, \ldots, L + 1.$$

The two expressions above define the probabilities of choosing product l among the L alternatives before the new product is added (superscript "b") and of choosing product l among $L + 1$ alternatives after the new product is added. Note the multiplicity of scores for choices made before the new product offering; a score with a different parameter b_k, $k = 1, \ldots, L$, is associated with each product. The set of scores for choices made after the new product offering differs from the set of scores for choices made before. This effect is emphasized by different notations (γ instead of b). In particular, a score with a different parameter $\gamma_k, k = 1, \ldots, L$, is associated with each product in the enlarged market.

In the closed set of alternatives, the new product is considered successful if it modifies the relative market shares of the other products. The relative market shares of products $k, l = 1, \ldots, L$ are

(i) $P[Y^{\mathrm{b}} = k \mid X]/P[Y^{\mathrm{b}} = l \mid X] = \exp z'(b_k - b_l)$ before the new product offering; and

(ii) $P[Y^{\mathrm{a}} = k \mid X]/P[Y^{\mathrm{a}} = l \mid X] = \exp z'(\gamma_k - \gamma_l)$ after the new product offering.

The relative market shares are not modified if, and only if,

$$b_k - b_l = \gamma_k - \gamma_l.$$

We say that the new alternative (product) $L + 1$ is irrelevant with respect to other existing alternatives (products) and has no impact on consumer behavior if, and only if,

$$b_k - b_l = \gamma_k - \gamma_l, \quad \forall k, l = 1, \ldots, L.$$

9.2 Profit- (Utility-) Optimizing Decisions

Multiple scores appeared in all examples examined so far. They determined the probabilities of simultaneous risks, as well as the observability of risk and other related variables, such as severity. Let us now investigate the impact of multiple scores on the profit maximization and utility maximization of banks, insurers, and marketers who operate in a competitive environment.

9.2.1 *Promotional Mailing Decisions*

Direct mail is known to marketers as the promotional technique that provides the best return on investment. This is in part due to the very low cost of acquisition of new customers. Formally, the acquisition cost is the total cost of mailing divided by the number of new customers that came from that mailing. A profit-optimizing company needs to be able to manage the costs of the campaign so that the cost of acquisition remains in proper relation to the sales generated from advertising.

Our analysis concerns the direct-mail strategy of a consumer credit provider. The bank or financial institution has to manage the following three types of costs: the cost of loan servicing, the cost of default on a loan, and the acquisition cost. Let us consider the model introduced in Section 9.1.5, and introduce the following notation:

γ, the (expected) gain, when credit is granted and no default occurs;

c_1, the (expected) cost, when credit is granted and default occurs;

c_0, the acquisition cost.

The direct-mail campaign generates profits if the (expected) gain per loan to be achieved in the presence of promotion exceeds the (expected) gain per loan to be achieved in the absence of promotion. The computation of expected gains is conditioned on the exogenous covariates of recipients included in the mailing list. More precisely, the expected gain per loan without credit promotion is

$$G_0(X) = \gamma P[Y_2 = 1, \ Y_3 = 0 \mid Y_1 = 0, \ X]$$
$$- c_1 P[Y_2 = 1, \ Y_3 = 1 \mid Y_1 = 0, \ X],$$

and the expected gain per loan with credit promotion is

$$G_1(X) = \gamma P[Y_2 = 1, \ Y_3 = 0 \mid Y_1 = 1, \ X]$$
$$- c_1 P[Y_2 = 1, \ Y_3 = 1 \mid Y_1 = 1, \ X] - c_0.$$

As mentioned earlier in the text, the crucial factor for the success of direct mail is targeting the proper market segment (niche), that is, reaching the right people. Therefore, the recipients of direct mail need to be carefully selected. The individuals on the mailing list are distinguished with respect to some exogenous covariates. Ideally, these covariates are such that the following inequality is satisfied:

$$G_1(X) \geqslant G_0(X)$$
$$\Longleftrightarrow \gamma\{P[Y_2 = 1, \ Y_3 = 0 \mid Y_1 = 1, \ X] - P[Y_2 = 1, \ Y_3 = 0 \mid Y_1 = 0, \ X]\}$$
$$- c_1\{P[Y_2 = 1, \ Y_3 = 1 \mid Y_1 = 1, \ X] - P[Y_2 = 1, \ Y_3 = 1 \mid Y_1 = 0, \ X]\}$$
$$\geqslant c_0,$$

that is, the expected gain from promotion per borrower exceeds the acquisition cost.

The above comparison of expected gains suggests that the profit depends on the distribution of three variables: Y_1, Y_2, Y_3. In other words, more information is required in addition to the probability of default (i.e., $P[Y_3 = 0 \mid X]$) and the impact of direct mail on total amount of credits granted (i.e., $P[Y_2 = 1 \mid Y_1 = 1, \ X] - P[Y_2 = 1 \mid Y_1 = 0, \ X]$).

In the special case where default is independent of Y_1 and Y_2, the expected gain criterion is simplified:

$$G_1(X) \geqslant G_0(X)$$
$$\Longleftrightarrow [P[Y_2 = 1 \mid Y_1 = 1, \ X] - P[Y_2 = 1 \mid Y_1 = 0, \ X]]$$
$$\times [\gamma P[Y_3 = 0 \mid X] - c_1 P[Y_3 = 1 \mid X]] - c_0 \geqslant 0.$$

The decision to implement the direct-mail campaign depends jointly on the probability of default and on the effect of direct mail on the number of credit contracts. The optimization criterion is a nonlinear function of (a) underlying scores associated with default probabilities and (b) the effects of direct mail. Moreover, the nonlinear criterion function depends on various costs.

9.2.2 Time-to-Default

Let us now consider the profit-maximizing behavior of a bank regarding consumer credit. Default on a loan is the only source of risk incorporated in the analysis, but the emphasis is on the timing.

The time-to-default is specified as in Section 9.1.2. In addition, we introduce

c_0, the fixed cost of collecting information about a potential customer (the cost of a credit check on the applicant);

γ, the expected gain from a credit contract with no default;

c_j, $j = 1, \ldots, 6$, the cost of credit granted with default in month j.

The optimal credit-granting decision is based on a comparison of expected gains from both a rejected and a granted credit application. The expected gain on a rejected credit application is negative and is given by

$$G_0(X) = -c_0.$$

The expected gain on a granted credit application is

$$G_1(X) = -c_0 - c_1 P[Y_1 = 0 \mid X] - c_2 P[Y_1 = 1, \ Y_2 = 0 \mid X]$$
$$- \cdots - c_6 P[Y_1 = \cdots = Y_5 = 1, \ Y_6 = 0 \mid X]$$
$$+ \gamma P[Y_1 = \cdots = Y_6 = 1 \mid X].$$

Under a risk-neutral selection of applicants, credit is granted if

$$G_1(X) \geqslant G_0(X)$$
$$\iff \gamma P[Y_1 = \cdots = Y_6 = 1 \mid X]$$
$$- c_1 P[Y_1 = 0 \mid X] - \cdots - c_6 P[Y_1 = \cdots = Y_5 = 1, \ Y_6 = 0 \mid X] \geqslant 0.$$

Let us disregard the time variation of the score, that is, assume that the individual is characterized by one value of a score, constant during the six months of a contractual term. Formally, we set $z'b_j = z'b$ independent of j, $j = 1, \ldots, 6$ (see Section 9.1.2). We obtain

$$G_1(X) \geqslant G_0(X)$$
$$\iff \gamma F(z'b)^6 - c_1[1 - F(z'b)] - \cdots - c_6 F(z'b)^5[1 - F(z'b)] \geqslant 0$$
$$\iff g[F(z'b)] \geqslant 0,$$
$$\text{where } g(p) = \gamma p^6 - c_1(1 - p) - c_2 p(1 - p) - \cdots - c_6 p^5(1 - p),$$

where $g(p)$ is the expected profit from offering the loan. When the costs are constant in time, we obtain

$$g(p) = \gamma p^6 + c(p^6 - -1) = (\gamma + c)p^6 - c;$$

the expected profit from offering the loan is an increasing function of the probability of no default.

Therefore, credit is granted if the probability of default is sufficiently small. However, when costs are time varying, the g function may be nonmonotone. The nonmonotonicity would imply, for example, that granting credit to a customer who is expected to default early is not profitable, while granting credit to a customer who is expected to default late is profitable. This effect is quite common. Credit granted to a customer with late default may indeed be profitable, as the lost remaining balance will be small. By the time of default, the borrower would have already repaid a large portion of the principal and interest.

9.2.3 Utility-Maximizing Behavior

Individual choices among alternatives can be examined in the structural framework of utility-maximizing individual behavior.

For ease of exposition, we consider $L = 3$ alternatives and denote by $V_{l,i}$, $l = 1, \ldots, 3, i = 1, \ldots, n$, the utility levels associated with alternative l and individual i. The utility levels are represented by latent variables and are used to define individual choices. More precisely, under utility-maximizing behavior, we have

$$Y_i = 1, \quad \text{if } V_{1,i} > V_{2,i}, \ V_{1,i} > V_{3,i},$$
$$Y_i = 2, \quad \text{if } V_{2,i} > V_{1,i}, \ V_{2,i} > V_{3,i},$$
$$Y_i = 3, \quad \text{if } V_{3,i} > V_{1,i}, \ V_{3,i} > V_{2,i},$$

where $Y_i, i = 1, \ldots, 3$, is the variable of individual choice among three alternatives. The utility maximization can be formalized using the polytomous logit choice model. Let us assume that individual utility provided by choice l is a linear function of individual covariates. More precisely, the utility levels depend on scores, which vary across individuals (subscript "i") and across the alternative choices (subscript "l"):

$$V_{l,i} = z_i' b_l + v_{l,i}, \quad l = 1, 2, 3,$$

where the error terms $v_{l,i}, l = 1, 2, 3, i = 1, \ldots, n$, are independent with a Gompertz distribution. The Gompertz distribution has the c.d.f. $F(v) = \exp(-\exp(-v))$. An individual chooses alternative 1 if the utility provided by alternative 1 exceeds the utility levels of alternative 2 and alternative 3. The probability that an individual chooses alternative 1 conditional on her covariates is

$$
\begin{aligned}
P[Y = 1 \mid X] \\
&= P[V_1 > V_2, \ V_1 > V_3 \mid X] \\
&= P[z'b_1 + v_1 > z'b_2 + v_2, \ z'b_1 + v_1 > z'b_3 + v_3 \mid X] \\
&= P[v_2 < v_1 + z'b_1 - z'b_2, \ v_3 < v_1 + z'b_1 - z'b_3 \mid X] \\
&= \int \exp[-\exp[-(v + z'b_1 - z'b_2)]] \\
&\qquad \times \exp[-\exp[-(v + z'b_1 - z'b_3)]] \, d[\exp[-\exp(-v)]]
\end{aligned}
$$

$$= \int \exp[-(\exp-v)\{\exp(z'b_2 - z'b_1) + \exp(z'b_3 - z'b_1) + 1\}]\,d(\exp(-v))$$

$$= \frac{1}{\exp(z'b_2 - z'b_1) + \exp(z'b_3 - z'b_1) + 1}$$

$$= \frac{\exp z'b_1}{\sum_{l=1}^{3} \exp(z'b_l)}.$$

By substituting the utility levels with the linear functions of individual covariates we end up with the expression of the elementary probability of a polytomous logit model. The identifiability condition required in logit models has a structural interpretation. The utility levels are identifiable up to an increasing affine transformation. Thus, the conditional mean of V_1 can be set equal to zero as the identifying constraint.

9.3 Multi-Score Reduction Technique

So far we have considered models with a set of linearly independent scores, on which no constraints were imposed. In some applications, however, the scores may feature linear dependence (collinearity). This means that one or more scores are linear functions of the remaining ones, and can be deleted from the system. Below, we show that by imposing proper constraints the total number of scores can be reduced to the number of linearly independent scores. This, in turn, eliminates redundant information and can significantly improve the efficiency of the analysis. In this section, we describe a general technique which allows for reduction of the number of scores.

9.3.1 Basic Notions

Let the output of a model with multiple scores be a set of estimates $z'\hat{b}_1, \ldots, z'\hat{b}_J$, say, which approximate the true unknown scores $z'b_1, \ldots, z'b_J$. The unknown scores may display some linear dependence, and for this reason we wish to determine the minimum number of scores which are linearly independent and to find their expressions.

When all scores depend on the same (set of) transformed explanatory variables z, the approach consists of examining the rank of the following matrix of coefficients: $B = (b_1, \ldots, b_J)$, of size (K, J), where K is the number of explanatory variables included in the scores.

The rank of the B matrix is equal to $r \leqslant \min(K, J)$ if, and only if, this matrix can be decomposed into

$$B = \beta\alpha', \tag{9.1}$$

where β and α are of dimensions (K, r) and (J, r), respectively. If $\beta_1, \ldots, \beta_r$ denote the columns of matrix β, and the α_{ij} denote the elements of matrix α, formula (9.1) implies that

$$z'b_k = \sum_{l=1}^{r} \alpha_{l,k} z'\beta_l, \quad k = 1, \ldots, K. \tag{9.2}$$

Thus, any score $z'b_k$ can be obtained by adding up the latent scores $z'\beta_l$, $l = 1, \ldots, L$. The coefficients $\alpha_{l,k}$ represent the sensitivities of the initial score with respect to the latent ones.

The latent scores are not uniquely defined. Indeed, if we consider a square invertible matrix Q of dimension (r, r), we get

$$B = \beta \alpha'$$
$$= \beta Q Q^{-1} \alpha'$$
$$= \beta Q [\alpha Q'^{-1}]'$$
$$= \tilde{\beta} \tilde{\alpha}',$$

where $\tilde{\beta} = \beta Q$, $\tilde{\alpha} = \alpha Q'^{-1}$. Therefore the latent scores are defined up to an invertible linear transformation.

9.3.2 Singular Value Decomposition (SVD)

If the matrix B were perfectly known, the rank $r = \text{rk } B$ and the matrices β, α could be found by performing the *singular value decomposition* of matrix B. Indeed, any rectangular matrix B with rank r can be written as

$$B = \gamma \, \text{diag}(\lambda) \delta', \tag{9.3}$$

where

- γ is a (K, r) matrix such that $\gamma' \gamma = \text{Id}_r$,
- δ is a (J, r) matrix such that $\delta' \delta = \text{Id}_r$,
- $\text{diag}(\lambda)$ is a diagonal matrix of size (r, r) and with positive elements λ_j, $j = 1, \ldots, r$.

From spectral decomposition of formula (9.3), it follows that

$$BB' = \gamma \, \text{diag}(\lambda) \delta' \delta \, \text{diag}(\lambda) \gamma'$$
$$= \gamma \, \text{diag}(\lambda^2) \gamma', \tag{9.4}$$

$$B'B = \delta \, \text{diag}(\lambda^2) \delta'. \tag{9.5}$$

The two matrices BB' and $B'B$ are nonnegative and symmetric, with respective dimensions (K, K) and (J, J). They admit r strictly positive eigenvalues $\mu_1 \geqslant \cdots \geqslant \mu_r > 0$, while their remaining eigenvalues are equal to zero. Expressions (9.4), (9.5) show how the elements of spectral decomposition in (9.3) can be derived from joint spectral decomposition of BB' and $B'B$.

We have

- $\lambda_j = \mu_j^{1/2}$, $j = 1, \ldots, r$,
- γ is a set of orthonormal eigenvectors of BB' associated with eigenvalues μ_j, $j = 1, \ldots, r$,
- δ is a set of orthonormal eigenvectors of $B'B$ associated with eigenvalues μ_j, $j = 1, \ldots, r$.

The technique for reducing the number of scores consists of the following steps.

Step 1: unconstrained estimation of the multi-score model, which provides an approximation $\hat{B}$ of B.

Step 2: Spectral decomposition of $\hat{B}\hat{B}'$ and $\hat{B}'\hat{B}$. It is important to note that even if $r = \text{rk } B < \min(J, K)$, the estimated rank $\hat{r} = \text{rk } \hat{B}$ is, in general, equal to $\min(J, K)$, that is, different from the true value of r. However, we expect that there is a cutoff point in the eigenvalues $\hat{\mu}_j$, j varying, ranked in descending order, which separates the nonzero eigenvalues from those that are arbitrarily close to zero. The order $\hat{r}$ of the eigenvalue associated with that cutoff point approximates r. Then the associated eigenvectors provide the approximations $\hat{\delta}$, $\hat{\gamma}$ of δ and γ. Finally, we compute $\hat{\lambda}_j = (\hat{\mu}_j)^{1/2}$, $\hat{\beta} = \hat{\gamma}$, $\hat{\alpha} = \hat{\delta} \, \text{diag}(\hat{\lambda})$.

9.3.3 Statistical Inference

In empirical research, collinearity has to be eliminated either for the feasibility of estimation (perfect collinearity) or for the validity of statistical inference.

The SVD approach described in the previous subsection provides consistent estimators of α, β, but is not always sufficiently accurate. Its efficiency can be improved in the following way (Gill and Lewbel 1992; Gourieroux et al. 1995): let us denote by vec $\hat{B}$ the vector obtained by stacking the columns of $\hat{B}$, and by $\hat{\Sigma}$ the estimated variance–covariance matrix of vec $\hat{B}$. More accurate estimators of β, α can be derived by minimizing the criterion

$$\xi(\alpha, \beta) = [\text{vec } \hat{B} - \text{vec}(\beta\alpha')]' \hat{\Sigma}^{-1} [\text{vec } \hat{B} - \text{vec}(\beta\alpha')] \tag{9.6}$$

with respect to α, β. Intuitively, minimizing the criterion above is equivalent to minimizing the distance between the estimated matrix $\hat{B}$ of coefficients that appear in the scores and the true value of matrix B written in the form of a product $\beta\alpha'$ (9.1). The presence of the inverse of $\hat{\Sigma}$ in the criterion function means that each estimator is weighted with respect to its estimated variance, that is, is assigned a weight proportional to its precision.[4]

Simple algebra leads to

$$\xi(\alpha, \beta) = [\text{vec } \hat{B} - (\text{Id}_J \otimes \beta) \, \text{vec } \alpha']' \hat{\Sigma}^{-1} [\text{vec } \hat{B} - (\text{Id}_J \otimes \beta) \, \text{vec } \alpha']$$

$$= [\text{vec } \hat{B} - (\text{Id}_K \otimes \alpha) \, \text{vec } \beta']' \hat{\Sigma}^{*-1} [\text{vec } \hat{B} - (\text{Id}_K \otimes \alpha) \, \text{vec } \beta'],$$

where $\hat{\Sigma}^* = Q\hat{\Sigma}Q'$, "$\otimes$" denotes the tensor product of matrices, and Q is the permutation matrix such that vec $\hat{B}' = Q$ vec $\hat{B}$.

The minimization can be performed sequentially, first with respect to α, then with respect to β, and so on. These step-by-step minimizations are equivalent to solving a set of generalized linear regressions. More precisely, let us consider the

---

[4] The role of the weighting matrix is analogous to the role of the estimated variance matrix in the feasible "generalized least squares" estimator.

expressions of the generalized least squares estimators of functions G and H of α and β, respectively:

$$G(\beta) = [(\mathrm{Id}_J \otimes \beta') \hat{\Sigma}^{-1} (\mathrm{Id}_J \otimes \beta)]^{-1} (\mathrm{Id}_j \otimes \beta') \hat{\Sigma}^{-1} \operatorname{vec} \hat{B},$$

$$H(\alpha) = [(\mathrm{Id}_K \otimes \alpha') \hat{\Sigma}^{*-1} (\mathrm{Id}_K \otimes \alpha)]^{-1} (\mathrm{Id}_K \otimes \alpha') \hat{\Sigma}^{*-1} \operatorname{vec} \hat{B}'.$$

The algorithm for computing $\hat{\alpha}$, $\hat{\beta}$ is based on recursively solving the following system of equations:

$$\operatorname{vec} \alpha'_{p+1} = G(\beta_p),$$

$$\operatorname{vec} \beta'_{p+1} = H(\alpha_{p+1}).$$

The recursions are run until the numerical convergence is reached. Next, the elements of $\hat{\alpha}$, $\hat{\beta}$ can be used to find the linearly independent scores, according to formula (9.2).

9.4   Household Portfolio Allocation

In the analytical examples, we emphasized the role of scores and the importance of individual characteristics in the profit- and utility-maximizing behaviors of bank, marketers, and other companies. In the following empirical example, we study the relationship between individual characteristics, such as income, wealth, and other socioeconomic and demographic variables, and the household choices of asset portfolios and asset allocations. The data come from a panel sample of 9530 French households observed in the sampling period 1991–92. In those years, many households did not invest on the stock market at all. Also, the portfolios owned by the households were little diversified.[5] An important factor and potential reason for weak diversification is that mutual funds were not available in France in the sampling period. There are other plausible arguments put forward, such as trading costs (Brennan 1975; Goldsmith 1976; Dumas and Luciano 1991; Hess 1991), the no-short-sell constraint (Lintner 1971; Paxson 1990; Amemiya et al. 1993), and the lack of liquidity of some financial assets (Guiso et al. 1994; Caroll and Samwick 1998; Domowitz 1998).

9.4.1   Description of the Data Set

Surveys conducted routinely by the French National Statistical Institute (INSEE) provide information on the financial standing of households. The survey concerns 25 types of financial assets, classified in the following four groups.

Group 1. Savings Account (SA).

Group 2. Home Buying Plan (HBP).

Group 3. Stocks and Shares (SS) (including bonds and mutual funds).

Group 4. Life Insurance (LI) (which is considered a financial asset due to low taxation).

---

[5] Recently, the situation has changed due to privatizations of public firms and distribution of shares to individual shareholders, such as private investors or employees.

Table 9.7. Asset holding rates and wealth.

Type of asset	Wealth				Total
	< 100	$100 \leqslant \cdots < 500$	$500 \leqslant \cdots < 1000$	> 1000	
Savings account	73.0	89.4	92.2	86.4	76.0
HBP	26.8	50.2	55.4	53.5	44.0
Stocks and shares	9.8	64.0	86.6	92.3	20.2
Life insurance	26.3	68.5	84.5	90.9	34.2

These four groups of assets are not distinguished with respect to financial returns. Indeed, assets within each group can generate very different returns. Instead, the above classification is based on the costs of assets, tax rates, and the way French households perceive the assets in the economy.

The explanatory variables are both quantitative and qualitative. Among the quantitative variables we have the age and squared age,[6] the income (INC), and the household total wealth (W). The qualitative characteristics are represented by the associated indicators. Accordingly, we have the indicator of gender (equal to 1 if the head of household is female, 0 otherwise), the indicator of family structure (FAM = 1 if there are more than three people in the household, 0 otherwise), the indicator of marital status (MAR = 1 if the head of the household is married, 0 otherwise), the indicator of education (ACAD = 1 if the head of the household has a university degree, 0 otherwise), the indicator of retirement (RETR = 1 if the head of the household is retired, 0 otherwise), the indicator of the city size (CITY = 1 if the household is in a city of more than 100 000 inhabitants, 0 otherwise), and the indicator of ownership (OWN = 1 if the household owns a house, 0 otherwise).

Table 9.7 reports the rates of various types of assets held by households as a function of wealth.

The proportion of households that invest in stocks and bonds in the whole sample is rather small ($\simeq 20\%$). This tendency is not only observed in France, but also in the United States, the United Kingdom, and Japan (see, for example, Shorrocks 1982; Bertaut 1992; Haliassos and Bertaut 1995; Amemiya et al. 1993).[7] When the wealth effect is considered we see that the least wealthy households prefer secure investments, such as the savings account. Very few of these households hold bonds and stocks. The distribution of wealth among various assets changes as we move towards the more wealthy households. These households are capable of bearing more financial risk. The most wealthy households invest the greatest portion of their wealth in stocks and bonds and are likely to be less averse to risk than other household categories.

---

[6] Squared age is used to accommodate the life cycle effect

[7] The lack of diversification contradicts the prediction of the optimal portfolio theory (Markowitz 1992).

Table 9.8.   Asset holding rates and diversification.

Diversification	Frequency	Holding rate	Asset bundle	Conditional holding rate
No asset	938	12.0		100.0
One asset	2737	35.0	SA	78.8
			HBP	11.9
			SS	7.3
			LI	2.0
				100.0
Two assets	2143	27.4	SA & HBP	48.1
			SA & LI	28.2
			SA & SS	10.5
			HBP & LI	8.9
			HBP & SS	2.9
			SS & LI	1.4
				100.0
Three assets	1384	17.7	SA & HBP & LI	57.2
			SA & HBP & SS	25.2
			SA & SS & LI	12.4
			HBP & SS & LI	5.2
				100.0
Four assets	613	7.9		100.0

Table 9.8 shows the diversity of assets in the portfolios of single assets and in the bundles of two, three, and four.

Table 9.8 shows the portfolio allocation of households. In terms of asset diversification, most households hold one or two assets. A savings account is the predominant asset in any bundle.

The data on asset diversification suggest using a sequential logit to model the discrete choices of portfolio allocations. Sequential logit differs from the traditional logit in that choices are not made simultaneously, but with a clear time ordering instead. Suppose that the choice decisions are made in the following order.

First choice: the number of assets, i.e., the diversification level (four alternatives: single asset or bundles of two, three, or four).

Second choice: the portfolio allocation conditional on the diversification level (four alternatives: SA, HBP, SS, LI).

Third choice: the money invested in each asset conditional on the number of assets held and the portfolio allocation (not a discrete choice: logit not applicable).

9.4.2 Model Estimation

The model is estimated in three steps. In the first step, the households choose the number of assets by deciding on one among four alternatives. The probabilities of all outcomes are obtained by estimating the polytomous logit model from the whole sample.

In the second step, the sample of households is divided into four subsamples, depending on the choice concerning the number of assets made in step 1. A set of four polytomous logit models is estimated separately from the four subsamples to accommodate the household's decision on the type of asset(s) included in the portfolio, which is a choice from the set of four (SA, HBP, SS, LI).

In the third step, the sample is classified with respect to the number of assets (step 1) and type of assets (step 2) held by the households. A linear regression run for each category of households approximates the size of investment in each asset.

9.4.2.1 Diversification

Let us denote by $j = 0, \ldots, 4$ the number of assets in the portfolio and by $p_{j,i}$ the probability that household i chooses alternative j. Let us consider a *polytomous logit model* (see Section 9.1.5) with selection probabilities specified as

$$p_{j,i}(\beta) = \frac{\exp(z_i' \beta_j)}{\sum_{j=0}^{4} \exp(z_i' \beta_j)}, \quad j = 0, \ldots, 4, \tag{9.7}$$

with the identifying constraint $\beta_0 = 0$. $y_{j,i}$ is the indicator function of the choice decision by the household, i.e., $y_{j,i} = 1$, if household i includes j assets in the portfolio. The unknown parameters β_j, $j = 1, \ldots, 4$, are estimated by the maximum likelihood estimator. The estimators $\hat{\beta}_j$, $j = 1, \ldots, 4$, are solutions of the following optimization:

$$\max_{\beta_1, \ldots, \beta_4} \sum_{i=1}^{n} \sum_{j=0}^{4} y_{j,i} \log p_{j,i}(\beta). \tag{9.8}$$

The estimated parameters and their standard errors are given in Table 9.9.

As expected, the probability of holding multiple assets increases with income and wealth. This finding is consistent with economic theory.

The households of age 75 have the greatest probability of holding one asset; the households of age 34 (respectively, 45 and 48) have the greatest probability of holding two assets (respectively, three and four assets).

This result is consistent with the life cycle theory. During its lifetime, a household acquires the assets gradually; first it holds only one asset, then two, three, and four. Later in life, the level of diversification diminishes before retirement.

We also observe the significant and positive effect of education. The highly educated households have a better understanding of market mechanisms and finance. Among other relevant characteristics are the size of family and home ownership.

Table 9.9. Choice of diversification level.

Explanatory variables	One asset	Two assets	Three assets	Four assets
Constant	9.94	−11.42	−34.58	−67.94
	(3.11)	(3.46)	(4.07)	(5.91)
AGE	−0.28	0.25	0.87	1.39
	(0.14)	(0.15)	(0.18)	(0.25)
AGE^2 10^{-2}	0.19	−0.36	−0.98	−1.46
	(0.15)	(0.17)	(0.19)	(0.26)
INC 10^{-5}	0.90	1.62	3.70	5.74
	(0.62)	(0.64)	(0.67)	(0.74)
W 10^{-5}	4.21	5.28	5.55	5.92
	(0.33)	(3.29)	(3.30)	(3.31)
GENDER	1.96	2.68	0.41	−2.11
	(0.84)	(0.90)	(1.00)	(1.28)
FAM	0.17	0.24	0.85	1.67
	(1.03)	(1.10)	(1.22)	(1.59)
MAR	0.60	3.24	2.47	0.17
	(0.94)	(1.01)	(1.13)	(1.49)
ACAD	−2.22	−0.15	−0.62	−3.27
	(1.07)	(1.13)	(1.24)	(1.53)
RETR	2.39	1.42	1.95	2.42
	(1.61)	(1.73)	(1.91)	(2.31)
CITY	0.74	0.51	0.04	2.11
	(0.86)	(0.93)	(1.03)	(1.31)
OWN	0.92	2.30	4.28	9.02
	(1.02)	(1.08)	(1.17)	(1.51)

Table 9.10. Number of combinations.

j	one asset	two assets	three assets	four assets
K_j	4	6	4	1

Large families and homeowners feel the need for security, which increases their probability of holding life insurance.

9.4.2.2 *Portfolio Allocation*

To each diversification level $j = 1, \ldots, 4$ correspond various bundles of four available assets (SA, HBP, SS, LI), denoted by K, $K = 1, \ldots, K_j$. From Table 9.8 we know that in practice the bundles of assets shown in Table 9.10 are held.

Table 9.11. Choice of asset (one asset).

Explanatory variables	HBP	SS	LI
Constant	−48.92	−55.85	−59.41
	(5.80)	(11.62)	(7.27)
AGE	1.24	0.29	1.57
	(0.28)	(0.52)	(0.34)
AGE^2 ($\times 10^{-2}$)	−1.50	−0.26	−1.75
	(0.33)	(0.56)	(0.37)
INC ($\times 10^{-5}$)	2.42	3.65	2.01
	(0.77)	(1.43)	(1.02)
W ($\times 10^{-5}$)	6.46	9.79	7.27
	(1.25)	(1.46)	(1.28)
GENDER	−1.55	−4.51	−1.88
	(1.30)	(2.99)	(1.62)
FAM	3.17	4.51	−1.39
	(1.55)	(3.93)	(1.91)
MAR	3.28	3.62	4.09
	(1.45)	(3.31)	(1.91)
ACAD	2.80	10.04	−1.34
	(1.56)	(3.42)	(2.21)
RETR	−3.50	−2.89	3.09
	(2.81)	(5.73)	(2.95)
CITY	0.17	−5.95	−1.37
	(1.34)	(3.21)	(1.68)
OWN	−0.04	−0.32	−1.26
	(1.53)	(3.45)	(1.83)

For instance, households with three assets hold the following bundles: SA & HBP & LI; SA & HBP & SS; SA & SS & LI; HBP & SS & LI.

For $j = 1, 2, 3$—that is, for portfolios of one, two, and three assets—the polytomous logit models represent the choices of portfolio allocations conditional on the diversification level. The choice probabilities are

$$\Pi_{K|j;i}(\alpha) = \frac{\exp(z_i'\alpha_{K,j})}{\sum_{K=1}^{K_j}\exp(z_i'\alpha_{K,j})}, \quad K = 1, \ldots, K_j, \quad (9.9)$$

with the identifying constraints $\alpha_{0,j} = 0$, $j = 1, 2, 3$. The estimation results (parameter estimates and t-ratios) are given in Tables 9.11–9.13.

Let us interpret the effects of some selected exogenous variables. The "large-city" indicator is a significant characteristic of households who own stocks and shares; the coefficient on the city variable is negative when stocks and shares are included in the household's portfolio, and positive otherwise. The fact that inhabitants of large

Table 9.12.   Portfolio allocation (two assets).

Explanatory variables	SA & SS	HBP & SS	SA & LI	HBP & LI	SS & LI
Constant	−24.13	−48.03	−24.17	−46.17	−85.62
	(6.83)	(13.14)	(4.94)	(8.61)	(19.98)
AGE	−0.01	0.65	0.86	1.29	1.92
	(0.29)	(0.61)	(0.21)	(0.41)	(0.84)
AGE^2 ($\times 10^{-2}$)	0.23	−0.64	−0.58	−1.29	−1.64
	(0.29)	(0.67)	(0.22)	(0.45)	(0.85)
INC ($\times 10^{-5}$)	0.56	1.44	−0.83	2.24	3.36
	(1.05)	(1.47)	(0.82)	(1.01)	(1.82)
W ($\times 10^{-5}$)	1.84	3.66	−1.48	0.72	3.62
	(0.69)	(0.93)	(0.72)	(0.85)	(1.06)
GENDER	−0.34	−2.68	−2.12	−2.47	−2.01
	(1.67)	(2.82)	(1.15)	(1.71)	(3.79)
FAM	−0.20	2.77	−3.44	−1.83	−1.67
	(2.21)	(3.61)	(1.41)	(1.97)	(4.86)
MAR	−1.00	−4.21	−0.71	0.32	−5.91
	(1.91)	(3.22)	(1.36)	(2.12)	(4.46)
ACAD	2.25	7.27	−4.76	−3.56	2.37
	(2.00)	(3.11)	(1.49)	(2.08)	(4.38)
RETR	4.98	−3.38	0.66	−0.99	2.55
	(2.88)	(6.03)	(2.11)	(3.62)	(6.37)
CITY	−2.81	−1.07	0.32	0.12	−4.99
	(1.68)	(2.88)	(1.17)	(1.75)	(3.91)
OWN	1.81	−0.13	0.79	0.57	0.25
	(1.82)	(3.25)	(1.26)	(1.91)	(4.14)

cities own stocks is probably due to the larger amount of information available to them from advertisements, compared with the inhabitants of rural areas. We also find that households that consist of married parents with children prefer less risky assets such as savings accounts and home-buying plans.

Let us consider the age variable and study its effect on the probability of holding life insurance. The probability of holding life insurance, regardless of the number of assets held, is a product of the conditional probability of holding life insurance given the number of assets (estimated by logit in step 2) times the marginal probability of holding that number of assets (estimated by logit in step 1). Therefore, if the age of interest is 45, we substitute 45 for age and evaluate the following expression:

$$p_{\text{LI},i}(\text{age}) = \sum_{j=1}^{4} p_{j,i}(\text{age}) \sum_{k \in \tilde{K}_j} \Pi_{k|j;i}(\text{age}), \qquad (9.10)$$

Table 9.13. Portfolio allocation (three assets).

Explanatory variables	SA & HBP & LI	SA & SS & LI	HBP & SS & LI
Constant	4.74	−40.5	−33.27
	(6.98)	(11.58)	(15.04)
AGE	0.43	0.74	0.56
	(0.31)	(0.45)	(0.66)
AGE^2 ($\times 10^{-2}$)	−0.51	−0.38	−0.78
	(0.32)	(0.41)	(0.71)
INC ($\times 10^{-5}$)	−0.11	1.01	1.80
	(0.75)	(0.99)	(1.21)
W ($\times 10^{-5}$)	−3.09	0.82	0.39
	(0.58)	(0.61)	(0.87)
GENDER	1.58	−0.01	−5.68
	(1.45)	(2.15)	(3.03)
FAM	−0.11	−3.47	−2.76
	(1.82)	(2.89)	(3.43)
MAR	1.77	0.96	2.56
	(1.67)	(2.46)	(3.59)
ACAD	−7.82	−1.57	2.00
	(1.64)	(2.42)	(3.27)
RETR	−0.89	1.89	5.41
	(2.76)	(3.49)	(5.62)
CITY	3.58	2.38	3.51
	(1.49)	(2.15)	(2.96)
OWN	−2.72	5.39	5.57
	(1.64)	(2.53)	(3.46)

where $\tilde{K}_j$ denotes the portfolios that include life insurance at the degree of diversification j.

We can also distinguish the marginal effect of age on the probability of holding life insurance. Intuitively, the marginal effect tells us by how much the probability of holding life insurance will change if the household members grow one year older. The marginal effect of age has a quite complicated form:

$$\frac{\partial p_{LI,i}(\text{age})}{\partial(\text{age})} = \sum_{j=1}^{4} \frac{\partial p_{j,i}(\text{age})}{\partial(\text{age})} \sum_{k \in \tilde{K}_j} \Pi_{k|j,i}(\text{age})$$

$$+ \sum_{j=1}^{4} p_{j,i}(\text{age}) \sum_{k \in \tilde{K}_j} \frac{\partial \Pi_{k|j;i}(\text{age})}{\partial(\text{age})}.$$

Table 9.14.   Asset quantity (one asset).

Explanatory variables	log(SA)	log(HBP)
Constant	2.79	3.76
	(0.75)	(2.74)
AGE	0.009	0.02
	(0.01)	(0.05)
AGE^2 ($\times 10^{-2}$)	0.019	-0.05
	(0.01)	(0.06)
log INC	0.38	0.34
	(0.06)	(0.22)
GENDER	-0.11	0.03
	(0.07)	(0.24)
FAM	0.26	0.07
	(0.09)	(0.29)
MAR	0.07	0.06
	(0.08)	(0.28)
ACAD	0.22	0.43
	(0.09)	(0.29)
RETR	0.28	0.68
	(0.13)	(0.66)
CITY	0.05	0.31
	(0.07)	(0.26)
OWN	0.16	0.15
	(0.16)	(0.28)

9.4.2.3   *Quantity of Assets in a Portfolio*

Finally, let us estimate how much money a household invests in each asset. We refer to this variable as the "quantity" of French francs (FF) invested in each asset. We use the following log-normal linear models of asset quantity conditional on the diversification j and portfolio composition K:

$$\log Q_{k|K,j;i} = z_i' \gamma_{k|K,j} + \varepsilon_{k|K,j}, \quad k \in K, \tag{9.11}$$

where Q denotes the quantity of FF, and the error terms are independent and normally distributed. The estimation results (parameter estimates and standard errors) are given in in Tables 9.14–9.17.

The quantities of FF invested in each asset are conditional on the type and total number of assets held by a household. Therefore, the coefficients have to be interpreted with caution. Let us consider Table 9.14. If the household holds only a savings account, the conditional effects of each explanatory variable on the quantity of FF deposited on the savings account owned by a household can be found in column 2.

Table 9.15.   Asset quantities (two assets).

Explanatory variables	log(SA)	log(HBP)	log(LI)
Constant	2.74	0.86	5.55
	(0.86)	(1.41)	(2.12)
AGE	0.016	−0.02	0.08
	(0.01)	(0.02)	(0.03)
AGE^2 ($\times 10^{-2}$)	0.002	0.001	−0.07
	(0.01)	(0.03)	(0.03)
log(INC)	0.43	0.61	0.05
	(0.07)	(0.11)	(0.17)
GENDER	−0.08	0.47	−0.32
	(0.07)	(0.12)	(0.18)
FAM	0.27	0.36	0.11
	(0.09)	(0.15)	(0.21)
MAR	−0.15	0.26	0.28
	(0.09)	(0.14)	(0.22)
ACAD	0.01	0.30	0.22
	(0.09)	(0.14)	(0.23)
RETR	0.26	0.27	−0.12
	(0.14)	(0.26)	(0.32)
CITY	0.10	0.07	−0.53
	(0.07)	(0.12)	(0.18)
OWN	0.24	0.14	0.48
	(0.08)	(0.13)	(0.18)

It is easy to see that the statistically significant coefficients are those associated with (a) the life cycle (age squared), (b) income, (c) family size, (d) high education, and (e) retirement. The more income a family generates, the more members it consists of, and the more educated the head of household is, the more funds the household will invest in the savings account. Let us trace the effect of retirement on asset quantities in the bundles of two (Table 9.15). If the household holds a savings account plus either a life insurance or a home-buying plan, then the money held on the account is conditionally positively correlated with the fact that the head of household is retired. If the household holds a home-buying plan plus either a savings account or life insurance, then in statistical terms there is no (significant) relationship between the money invested in the home-buying plan and the retirement of the head of household. Surprisingly, there is no significant statistical relationship between the variable "retirement" and the variable "life insurance" in the two-asset case. There is a significant link between the money invested in life insurance and retirement in the bundle of three (Table 9.16), which becomes statistically insignificant when one more asset is held (Table 9.17).

Table 9.16.   Asset quantities (three assets).

Explanatory variables	log(SA)	log(HBP)	log(SS)	log(LI)
Constant	5.45	2.54	4.12	−0.63
	(1.02)	(1.69)	(1.59)	(2.00)
AGE	0.044	−0.03	−0.01	0.02
	(0.016)	(0.03)	(0.02)	(0.03)
AGE^2 ($\times 10^{-2}$)	−0.012	0.02	0.04	0.02
	(0.016)	(0.03)	(0.02)	(0.03)
log(INC)	0.16	0.56	0.47	0.61
	(0.09)	(0.14)	(0.12)	(0.17)
GENDER	0.08	0.03	−0.16	0.26
	(0.08)	(0.13)	(0.12)	(0.16)
FAM	0.27	0.02	0.12	0.20
	(0.09)	(0.16)	(0.15)	(0.19)
MAR	0.05	−0.12	−0.12	0.32
	(0.09)	(0.16)	(0.15)	(0.19)
ACAD	0.13	0.48	0.39	0.04
	(0.09)	(0.16)	(0.14)	(0.19)
RETR	−0.04	−0.03	−0.06	−0.65
	(0.15)	(0.26)	(0.21)	(0.30)
CITY	0.07	−0.15	0.04	−0.06
	(0.08)	(0.14)	(0.13)	(0.16)
OWN	0.18	0.12	0.51	0.23
	(0.09)	(0.15)	(0.14)	(0.18)

9.4.3   *Reduction of the Number of Scores*

Let us now illustrate the technique, presented in Section 9.3, for reducing the score number by an application to the empirical example of household choices. In the estimation discussed above, we can distinguish 15 scores: 4 scores for the diversification level and 11 scores for the portfolio allocation choices. Therefore, the $\hat{B}$ matrix has dimension 11×15, where 11 is the number of explanatory variables (not including the intercept). By applying the singular value decomposition of matrix $\hat{B}$, we get the sequence of eigenvalues reported in Table 9.18.

Each eigenvalue is associated with an eigenvector, called a factor for brevity. We observe that there is a big difference between the first six eigenvalues and the following ones as these taper off. The first six eigenvalues are numerically different from zero. Therefore, we can assume that the 15 initial scores are determined by six latent scores. These latent scores are equal to the six eigenvectors (factors) in Table 9.19 obtained from the SVD.

Table 9.17. Asset quantities (four assets).

Explanatory variables	log(SA)	log(HBP)	log(SS)	log(LI)
Constant	3.89	6.97	1.09	−2.46
	(1.49)	(2.59)	(1.81)	(2.69)
AGE	0.03	−0.02	0.10	0.13
	(0.03)	(0.04)	(0.03)	(0.04)
AGE^2 ($\times 10^{-2}$)	−0.005	−0.02	−0.09	−0.10
	(0.03)	(0.04)	(0.03)	(0.04)
log(INC)	0.39	0.18	0.55	0.64
	(0.12)	(0.20)	(0.14)	(0.21)
GENDER	0.012	0.31	−0.35	0.06
	(0.11)	(0.19)	(0.14)	(0.20)
FAM	0.16	0.22	0.17	0.03
	(0.14)	(0.29)	(0.17)	(0.25)
MAR	−0.16	0.27	−0.34	0.12
	(0.14)	(0.24)	(0.17)	(0.25)
ACAD	−0.09	0.35	0.37	0.37
	(0.13)	(0.22)	(0.15)	(0.22)
RETR	0.22	0.24	0.38	0.18
	(0.19)	(0.34)	(0.23)	(0.35)
CITY	0.03	0.21	−0.06	−0.10
	(0.11)	(0.19)	(0.14)	(0.20)
OWN	0.19	−0.11	0.27	0.17
	(0.14)	(0.24)	(0.17)	(0.25)

Table 9.18. Eigenvalues from SVD.

Factor	Eigenvalue	Difference between consecutive eigenvalues	%	Cumulated %
Factor 1	6.96	4.27	63	63
Factor 2	2.69	1.87	24	87
Factor 3	0.82	0.59	7	94
Factor 4	0.22	0.04	2	96
Factor 5	0.18	0.06	2	98
Factor 6	0.12	0.114	1	99
Factor 7	0.006	0.0045	0.05	99.5
Factor 8	0.0015	0.0012	0.01	—
Factor 9	0.0003	0.0002	0.00	—
Factor 10	0.0001	0.0001	0.00	—
Factor 11	0.0000	—	—	—

Table 9.19. Latent scores.

Explanatory variables	Factor 1	Factor 2	Factor 3	Factor 4	Factor 5	Factor 6
AGE	0.352	0.166	−0.095	−0.491	−0.015	0.146
AGE^2 ($\times 10^{-2}$)	−0.356	−0.159	−0.001	0.455	0.045	−0.143
INC ($\times 10^{-5}$)	0.376	0.044	0.007	−0.005	0.008	0.260
W ($\times 10^{-5}$)	0.372	−0.070	0.118	0.011	0.246	0.124
GENDER	−0.349	0.051	0.240	0.015	0.534	0.633
FAM	0.219	−0.463	0.279	0.232	−0.041	0.329
MAR	0.207	0.223	0.814	0.068	0.135	−0.421
ACAD	0.310	−0.320	−0.126	0.418	−0.123	−0.051
RETR	0.126	0.524	0.308	0.371	0.459	−0.139
CITY	−0.227	0.436	0.246	0.122	−0.603	0.290
OWN	0.306	0.326	−0.084	0.407	−0.205	0.290

Each column of Table 9.19 provides the coefficients of individual covariates in the expressions of each of the six factors. For example, column 1 shows that factor 1 defines the first latent score as

$$S_1 = 0.352\text{AGE} - 0.356\text{AGE}^2 \times 10^{-2} + 0.376\text{INC} \times 10^{-5}$$
$$+ 0.372\text{W} \times 10^{-5} - 0.349\text{GENDER} + 0.219\text{FAM} + 0.207\text{MAR}$$
$$+ 0.310\text{ACAD} + 0.126\text{RETR} - 0.227\text{CITY} + 0.306\text{OWN}.$$

Accordingly, column 2 corresponds to score S_2, and so on up to column 6, which corresponds to score S_6. The estimates of latent scores can be used to make the estimated model more robust. One can reestimate the whole model in three steps using only seven explanatory variables: the constant and the six latent scores $S_1, \ldots, S_6$. This yields a new estimated score of the type $S = \hat{\gamma}_1 S_1 + \cdots + \hat{\gamma}_6 S_6$, which can be reinterpreted in terms of the initial covariates: age, income, and so on. For example, the coefficient on variable AGE in score S will be equal to

$$0.352\hat{\gamma}_1 + 0.166\hat{\gamma}_2 - 0.095\hat{\gamma}_3 - 0.491\hat{\gamma}_4 - 0.015\hat{\gamma}_5 + 0.146\hat{\gamma}_6.$$

In this expression, each $\hat{\gamma}_i$, $i = 1, \ldots, 6$, is multiplied by the set of coefficients of variable AGE in each latent score $S_1, \ldots, S_6$ reported in the first row of Table 9.19.

9.5 Concluding Remarks

There exist various criteria for ranking individuals, depending on the purpose of analysis. On the credit market, multiple scores may be used to assess and compare the probabilities of various risks, such as default or prepayment on a loan, as well as their timing with respect to maturity. The time at which default occurs, called the time-to-default, is a variable which allows the bank to make a very fine distinction between credit contracts that entail small losses and those that are marginally profitable.

Multiple scores can also be associated with choices made by individuals among many mutually exclusive alternatives. Formally, individual choices can be modeled using the polytomous logit model. An important choice criterion is maximization of individual utility, which underlies rational decisions. In the empirical example of asset choices we saw the effect of various explanatory variables on the outcomes of household decisions. In practice, one prefers to avoid handling too many different scores and wishes to use the smallest possible number of scores while still preserving all necessary information. We saw in this chapter a technique for determining the minimum necessary number of scores based on the singular value decomposition.

References

Allenby, G., and P. Lenk. 1994. Modeling household purchase behavior with logistic normal regression. *Journal of the American Statistical Association* 89:1218–31.

Amemiya, T., M. Saito, and K. Shimono. 1993. A study of household investment patterns in Japan: an application of generalized tobit models. *The Economic Studies Quarterly* 44:13–28.

Bertaut, C. 1992. Who holds stocks in the US? An empirical investigation. University of Maryland Discussion Paper (December).

Brennan, M. 1975. The optimal number of securities in a risky asset portfolio when there are fixed costs of transacting: theory and some empirical evidence. *Journal of Financial and Quantitative Analysis* 10:483–96.

Caroll, D., and A. Samwick. 1998. How important is precautionary saving? *Review of Economics and Statistics* 98:410–19.

Dambolena, I., and S. Khoury. 1980. Ratio stability and corporate failure. *Journal of Finance* 35:1017–26.

Domowitz, J. 1996. Empirical models of income uncertainty and precautionary saving. University of Michigan Discussion Paper.

Dumas, B., and E. Luciano. 1991. An exact solution to a dynamic portfolio choice problem under transaction costs. *The Journal of Finance* 46:577–95.

Gill, L., and A. Lewbel. 1992. Testing the rank and definiteness of estimated matrices with applications to factors, state space and ARMA models. *Journal of the American Statistical Association* 87:766–76.

Goldsmith, D. 1976. Transaction costs and the theory of portfolio selection. *Journal of Finance* 31:1127–39.

Gourieroux, C. 1989. *Econométrie des Variables Qualitatives*, 2nd edn. Paris: Economica.

Gourieroux, C., A. Monfort, and E. Renault. 1995. Inference in factor models. In *Advances in Econometrics and Quantitative Economics* (ed. G. Maddala, P. C. B. Phillips, and T. Srinivasan), pp. 311–53. Oxford: Blackwell.

Guiso, L., T. Japelli, and D. Terlitzzese. 1996. Income risk, borrowing constraints and portfolio choice. *American Economic Review* 86:158–72.

Haliassos, M., and C. Bertaut. 1995. Why do so few hold stocks? The view from asset pricing theory. *Economic Journal* 105:1110–29.

Hess, A. 1991. The effects of transaction costs on households financial asset demand. *Journal of Money, Credit and Banking* 23:383–409.

Hsu, P. 1991. Canonical reduction of the general regression problem. *Annals of Eugenics* 11:42–46.

Kimball, M. 1990. Precautionary saving in the small and in the large. *Econometrica* 58:53–73.

Koo, H. 1991. Consumption and portfolio choice with uninsurable income risk. Princeton University Discussion Paper.

Lintner, J. 1971. The effect of short selling and margin requirements in perfect capital markets. *Journal of Financial and Quantitative Analysis* 5:1173–95.

Markowitz, H. 1992. *Portfolio Selection: Efficient Diversification of Investment*, 2nd edn. Wiley.

Paxson, C. 1990. Borrowing constraints and portfolio choice. *Quarterly Journal of Economics* 105:535–43.

Shorrocks, A. 1982. The composition of asset holdings in the United Kingdom. *The Economic Journal* 92:268–84.

Uhler, R., and J. Cragg. 1971. The structure of the asset portfolios of households. *Review of Economic Studies* 42:341–57.

10

Serial Dependence in Longitudinal Data

This chapter is concerned with an intersection between the topics of time-series and panel-data econometrics. Each of these is a wide and quickly growing field, described in a number of monographs. Therefore, thorough coverage of the related econometric methodology is beyond the scope of this book. Instead, we focus our attention on a few selected models for a specific class of stochastic processes. A stochastic process (also called a time series) is a sequence of realizations of a random variable in time. The realizations can be independent[1] or serially correlated (autocorrelated). An example of a class of stochastic processes is the Markov chain discussed in Chapter 8. In this chapter, we examine the marked-point processes formed by sequences of events indexed by time. The events are observed along with the *marks*, that is, qualitative or quantitative variables characterizing each event. For example, a mark of a loss event is severity or a mark of any purchase or sell event is the price. More examples of marked events are given in Table 10.1 below.

The objective of this chapter is to introduce models for serially correlated marked events concerning a group of individuals (longitudinal data). Therefore, we will study processes indexed both by time and by individual, which form a panel. In panel data, the number of individuals is usually very large, while the number of observations in time is rather small. This is the opposite of time-series data, where n is small while the number of observations in time is quite large.

The basic model for marked-point processes relies on the assumption of time-independent events and marks. This is the so-called *compound Poisson process* discussed earlier. Later in the text, our attention will turn to serial dependence in the linear autoregressive model for continuous variables, the autoregressive conditional duration (ACD) model, and the integer autoregressive (INAR) model for counts. An extension to panel data will be discussed in regard to each of these specifications. We will also address serial correlation in marked-point processes due to time-varying unobserved heterogeneity. As an example, we describe a simulation study of a Poisson–gamma model investigating the cost of claim sensitivity with respect to transitory shocks. An empirical illustration of estimation and inference

---

[1] The realizations are independent in time if $f(Y_t)f(Y_\tau) = f(Y_t, Y_\tau) \; \forall t, \tau$, and are uncorrelated if the covariance between Y_t and Y_τ is zero.

Table 10.1.   Marked processes.

Individual	Event	Mark
Credit contract	Default of payment	Recovery rate and remaining balance
Insurance holder	Car accident	Cost of car repair
Car dealer	Sale of car	Make and model, price and markup

on a panel extension of the ACD model in application to credit card use appears at the end of the chapter.

10.1   Poisson and Compound Poisson Processes

For clarity of exposition, let us focus on one selected individual sequence of events, disregarding the individual characteristics. The Poisson model is a formal representation of a sequence of events, while the compound Poisson process is a formal representation of a sequence of marked events. Both models belong to continuous-time models.

10.1.1   Poisson Process

Any sequence of events generates the following auxiliary processes.

(1) The sequence of durations $D_1, \ldots, D_n$ generated by times to consecutive events measured with respect to a fixed point of origin (by convention equal to zero).

(2) The sequence of durations $Y_1, \ldots, Y_n$ between the consecutive events generated by inter-event times $Y_1 = D_1, Y_2 = D_2 - D_1, \ldots, Y_n = D_n - D_{n-1}$.

(3) The *counting process* $N(t)$, t varying (see Chapter 4), which counts the number of events observed between 0 and t. The counting process is a jump process. This means that a jump of size one is associated with each event time.

As illustrated in Figure 10.1, knowledge of any of the two duration processes and knowledge of the count process are equivalent.

Formally, the relationship between the counting process and the two sequences of durations is as follows:

$$N(t) = \text{number}\{n : D_n < t\}, \tag{10.1}$$

$$D_n = \inf\{t : N(t) = n\}, \tag{10.2}$$

$$Y_n = \inf\{t : N(t) = n\} - \inf\{t : N(t) = n - 1\}, \tag{10.3}$$

where, by convention, $\inf\{t : N(t) = 0\} = 0$.

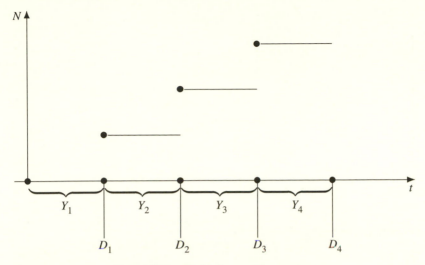

Figure 10.1. Path of a counting process.

The *Poisson process* is a count process that satisfies the following two conditions.

(A1) The increments are independent: that is, the differences $N(t_n) - N(t_{n-1})$, $N(t_{n-1}) - N(t_{n-2}), \ldots, N(t_1) - N(t_0)$ are independent for any $t_0 < t_1 < t_2 < \cdots < t_n$, and any n.

(A2) The intensity of events is constant and no more than one event can occur in a short time interval dt:

$$P[N(t + dt) - N(t) = 1] = \lambda \, dt + o(dt), \tag{10.4}$$

$$P[N(t + dt) - N(t) = 0] = 1 - \lambda \, dt + o(dt), \tag{10.5}$$

where the term $o(dt)$ is a function of dt such that $\lim_{dt \to 0} o(dt)/dt = 0$.

Given assumptions (A1), (A2) on the Poisson process, the properties of the associated inter-event times and count increments can be derived (see Appendix 10.5).

(i) In a Poisson process, the inter-event times Y_i, $i = 1, \ldots, n$, are independent and identically exponentially distributed with parameter λ.

(ii) In a Poisson process, the increments $N(t_2) - N(t_1)$, with $t_2 > t_1$, follow Poisson distributions with parameters $\lambda(t_2 - t_1)$.

This result highlights the relationship between the exponential model of durations (see Chapter 6) and the Poisson count model (see Chapter 5). The independence of events in a Poisson process implies the independence of its increments. It also implies that the inter-event durations are independent and feature the memoryless property characteristic of exponentially distributed durations.

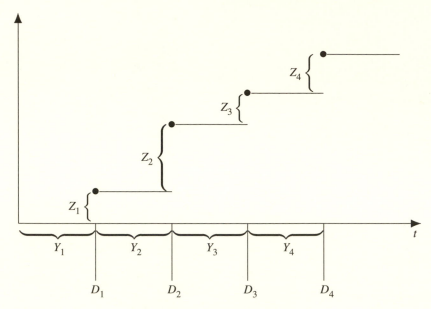

Figure 10.2.   Path of aggregate loss.

10.1.2   Compound Poisson Process

Let us now assume that we observe the events along with marks. The marks associated with the consecutive events form a process Z_j, $j = 1, \ldots$. For example, if the event is a car accident, the mark can represent the amount of money paid by the insurance company to settle the claim.

It is often insightful to aggregate the mark process in a fixed period of time. Regarding the automobile insurance, the aggregation would yield the total amount of money paid by the insurance company on all claims in a fixed period of time. The aggregate mark at time t, defined by

$$(N * Z)(t) = \sum_{j=1}^{N(t)} Z_j, \tag{10.6}$$

can then be interpreted as aggregate loss. The path of aggregate loss is a stepwise function, with jumps of size Z_j at each date of a new event (see Figure 10.2).

The basic model of aggregate loss is a compound Poisson process. The *compound Poisson process* satisfies assumptions (A1) and (A2) and the following additional assumption.

(A3) The marks Z_j, $j = 1, \ldots$, are independent and identically distributed with the cumulative distribution function G. The marks are also independent of the counting process ($N(t)$, t varying).

The probability distribution of the compound Poisson process of aggregate loss at time t is given by

$$P[(N * Z)(t) \leqslant z] = P\left[\sum_{j=1}^{N(t)} Z_j \leqslant z\right]$$

$$= \sum_{n=0}^{\infty} P[N(t) = n]P\left[\sum_{j=1}^{N(t)} Z_j \leqslant z \,\bigg|\, N(t) = n\right]$$

$$= \sum_{n=0}^{\infty} P[N(t) = n]P\left[\sum_{j=1}^{n} Z_j \leqslant z\right]$$

$$= \sum_{n=0}^{\infty} \exp(-\lambda)\frac{\lambda^n}{n!}G^{*n}(z),$$

where G^{*n} is the nth convolution of G. In one particular case, when the mark is a dichotomous qualitative variable that takes the values 0 and 1, the cumulative distribution G is Bernoulli $\mathcal{B}(1, p)$, and its n-convolution is a binomial distribution $\mathcal{B}(n, p)$. Substituting the binomial distribution for G^{*n} in the last expression yields

$$P[(N * Z)(t) \leqslant z] = \sum_{n \geqslant z}\left[\exp(-\lambda)\frac{\lambda^n}{n!}\frac{n!}{z!(n-z)!}p^z(1-p)^{n-z}\right]$$

$$= \frac{\exp(-\lambda)\lambda^z p^z}{z!}\sum_{n \geqslant z}\left(\frac{[\lambda(1-p)]^{n-z}}{(n-z)!}\right)$$

$$= \frac{\exp(-\lambda)\lambda^z p^z}{z!}\exp[\lambda(1-p)]$$

$$= \frac{\exp(\lambda p)(\lambda p)^z}{z!}.$$

We conclude that, when the mark is a simple 0–1 indicator function, the aggregate loss process follows a Poisson distribution with parameter λp.

In general, the compound Poisson process of aggregate loss involves two types of parameter, λ and G, where the first is a scalar, and the second is a function. In the analysis of aggregate losses, it is preferable to use two scores to rank the individuals with respect to the probabilities of a loss event and of the associated mark (for example, severity).

10.1.3 From Discrete Time to Continuous Time

As previously mentioned, the Poisson and compound Poisson are continuous-time models. In reality, data on loss events and claims are recorded in discrete time. Therefore, for feasibility of statistical analysis, we are interested in finding their discrete-time analogues. The analogues of the Poisson and compound Poisson models in discrete time exist and can be compared. Let us assume that some events occur

Table 10.2.   Comparison of discrete- and continuous-time representations.

	Distribution of inter-event duration	Distribution of the counting variable	Intensity
Discrete time	Geometric	Binomial	p_δ/δ
Continuous time	Exponential	Poisson	λ

at discrete dates $k\delta$, $k = 1, \ldots$, which are integer multiples of a very small fixed time unit δ. The following assumptions underlying the discrete-time representation are similar to (A1), (A2).

(A1*) The events at different dates are independent.

(A2*) The probability of an event occurring at date $k\delta$, $k = 1, \ldots$, is p_δ. No event occurs with probability $1 - p_\delta$.

It is easy to see that the durations between consecutive events—that is, the inter-event times—are independent, with identical distribution:

$$P[Y_1 \geqslant k\delta] = (1 - p_\delta)^{k-1}, \quad k = 1, \ldots. \tag{10.7}$$

We conclude that the inter-event times follow a geometric distribution. The distribution of the total number (count) of events between 0 and $k\delta$ is binomial $\mathcal{B}(k, p_\delta)$.

The discrete-time specification based on (A1*), (A2*) is an approximation of the continuous-time model. In order to observe this, let the time unit δ tend to zero, and let the intensity p_δ/δ tend to λ (say). We can rewrite (10.7) as follows:

$$\begin{aligned}
P[Y_1 \geqslant t] &= P[Y_1 \geqslant [t/\delta]\delta] \quad \text{(where } [\cdot] \text{ denotes the integer part)} \\
&= (1 - p_\delta)^{[t/\delta]-1} \\
&\sim \exp([t/\delta]\log(1 - p_\delta)) \\
&\sim \exp(-(t/\delta)p_\delta) \\
&\sim \exp(-\lambda t).
\end{aligned}$$

As the time unit shrinks to zero, the geometric distribution tends to the exponential distribution. Additionally, the binomial distribution of counts in discrete time tends to the Poisson distribution of counts in continuous time. The links between the discrete- and continuous-time models are given in Table 10.2.

10.2   Models with Serial Dependence

Serial correlation refers to the dependence of a process on its past realizations. In general, it means that the present value is influenced by past realizations. In Chapter 8 we saw a simple form of serial correlation in Markov chains of order 1, where the present value is determined by the last preceding realization.

Independence of realizations in time is the opposite of serial correlation. This assumption underlies the Poisson and compound Poisson processes (conditional on the individual characteristics), but is generally not fulfilled in practice, due to the effects of monitoring, individual learning, or moral hazard. The following examples should help clarify this issue.

(i) The premiums on automobile insurances are routinely updated depending on individual experience of the insurance holder. Typically a new claim causes an increase in the premium (called a malus). In order to reduce the probability of premium increase, the driver can make efforts to drive more safely. Then the driver is said to have adjusted her behavior according to the expected premium modification.

(ii) When a new product is introduced in the supermarket the individual consumption patterns are examined. Usually, the product is first purchased by a group of individuals, called early adopters. These consumers are curious and innovative, and are more likely to lead the majority of consumers, who are more conservative. They are particularly important to the success of new products because they tend to popularize products through their acceptance. Once early adopters learn to buy the new product, and their behavior is imitated by the majority of consumers, the product moves from birth to maturity in its life cycle.

(iii) In revolving credit, such as a credit card, an unpaid balance on a monthly statement leads to interest rates being added. This in turn results in an increase in the outstanding balance and minimum payment in the next monthly statement.

A natural way to model serial dependence in marked events is to consider a *path-dependent intensity* λ_t of the associated mark. Under this approach, at date t, λ_t depends on the history formed by the previous events and their marks. Formally, we have

$$\lambda_t = \lambda[(N * Z)(\tau), \ \tau < t]. \tag{10.8}$$

In general, this approach leads to untractable expressions of distributions for durations and counts, and is very difficult to implement.

Alternatively, one can model separately the path-dependent durations and path-dependent count data. A fair number of models are available from the time-series literature, but in most cases the extensions to panel data do not exist.

In this chapter we will pursue the separate representations. The panel versions of models will be either reviewed, or developed if necessary.

The first class of models is conceptually related to the linear autoregressive model. Obviously, the linear autoregressive model in its traditional form is not adequate for duration or count variables, because the distributions of durations and counts are not Gaussian.

The second class of models is based on the compound Poisson model with time-varying unobservable heterogeneity. In this setup, the dynamics of the heterogeneity factor induces serial dependence of events and marks.

Before describing the two classes of models, let us comment on the differences between sample sizes (numbers of observations) encountered in applied time-series and panel-data analysis. In applied time series, the samples comprise a fairly large number of observations in time. The time dimension can vary from 100 in macro-economic applications to several million in high-frequency financial data sets. Thus, the time-series literature focuses on stationary time series, which are observed for a time long enough that the effect of initial observations is disregarded. In panel data, the cross-sectional dimension (that is, the number of individuals in a sample) is often large, between 100 and several hundred thousand, while the time dimension is quite small, and can vary between 1 and 20, depending on the individual. In this case, the initial conditions matter, especially as they often contain important information (on learning, for example). In particular, in panel data, the initial conditions may depend on individual characteristics.

10.2.1 Autoregressive Models

10.2.1.1 Autoregressive Linear Model for Panel Data

For clarity of exposition, let us first consider the following linear regression model for panel data: $Y_{i,t} = z'_{i,t}b + u_{i,t}$, $i = 1, \ldots, n$, $t = 1, \ldots, T_i$, and discuss serial dependence in each individual history. The serial dependence can characterize either (a) the endogenous variable or (b) the error term.

(a) The linear autoregressive panel-data model with serially correlated endogenous variable is

$$Y_{i,t} = Y_{i,t-1}c + z'_{i,t}b + u_{i,t}, \quad i = 1, \ldots, n, \ t = 0, \ldots, T_i, \tag{10.9}$$

where the errors are i.i.d. The dependent variable associated with individual i (risk, say) depends on its last realizations and the current value of individual covariates $z'_{i,t}$. By recursive substitution, we get

$$Y_{i,t} = c^t Y_{i,0} + \sum_{j=0}^{t-1} c^j (z'_{i,t-j}b + u_{i,t-j}). \tag{10.10}$$

This current risk associated with individual i is written as a function of initial condition $Y_{i,0}$ and of error terms $u_{i,t-j}$, accumulated in the past. c is the autoregressive coefficient, which has to be less than 1 in absolute value, $|c| < 1$, for stationarity of the model. However, even when the model is stationary, the effect of the initial condition cannot be disregarded if, for a fair number of individuals i in the sample, only few observations in time are available.

The standard method of estimating parameters c and b consists of regressing $Y_{i,t}$ on $Y_{i,t-1}, z_{i,t}$ for $t \geqslant 1$. This practice eliminates all information contained in the n

initial observations $Y_{i,0}$, $i = 1, \ldots, n$. To avoid loss of information, an additional regression model for the initial values $Y_{i,0}$, $i = 1, \ldots, n$, can be incorporated:

$$Y_{i,0} = z'_{i,0}d + v_i, \quad i = 1, \ldots, n, \tag{10.11}$$

The extended approach consists of jointly estimating model (10.9) for $t \geqslant 1$ and model (10.11).

(b) The linear panel-data model with serially correlated error terms is

$$Y_{i,t} = z'_{i,t}b + v_{i,t}, \quad i = 1, \ldots, n, \ t = 1, \ldots, T_i, \tag{10.12}$$

where $v_{i,t} = cv_{i,t-1} + u_{i,t}$, $u_{i,t}$ are i.i.d. variables, and c is the autoregressive coefficient that satisfies the stationarity condition. By recursive substitution, we get

$$Y_{i,t} = z'_{i,t}b + \sum_{j=0}^{t-1} c^j u_{i,t-j} + c^t v_{i,0}. \tag{10.13}$$

This representation separates the effects of initial condition $v_{i,0}$ from the effect of past errors $u_{i,t-j}$. Note that the initial condition $v_{i,0}$ is unobserved and can be handled as follows.

When T_i is large, the initial condition can be set equal to zero, or, alternatively, $v_{i,0}$ can be replaced by a random draw from the marginal distribution of the autoregressive process.

When time dimension T_i is small, it is preferable to include an auxiliary model for $v_{i,0}$:

$$v_{i,0} = z'_{i,0}d + v_i, \quad i = 1, \ldots, n, \tag{10.14}$$

and to jointly estimate models (10.12) and (10.14).

A similar approach can be conceived for modelling durations or counts as endogenous variables. However, due to the properties of these variables, linear models are no longer available and nonlinear models are used instead.

10.2.1.2 *Autoregressive Conditional Duration (ACD) Model*

The ACD models were introduced for modelling the series of daily durations between consecutive trades of assets on financial markets (Engle and Russell 1997, 1998).[2] Let the duration between trades numbered $t - 1$ and t be denoted by (Y_t).[3] The ACD(1,1) model is a nonlinear model defined by the following two equations

$$Y_t = \psi_t \varepsilon_t, \quad t = 1, \ldots, T, \tag{10.15}$$

where the (ε_t) are i.i.d. variables, and the variable ψ_t satisfies the recursive equation

$$\psi_t = w + \alpha y_{t-1} + \beta \psi_{t-1}, \quad t = 1, \ldots, T. \tag{10.16}$$

---

[2] For example, trades of stocks and shares, such as IBM, Nortel, Alcatel, etc.

[3] The subscript t does not pertain to time, but instead to a deterministic consecutive trade numbering with respect to the market opening on a given day.

The acronym ACD(1,1) means that one lag of Y and one lag of ψ are included in the specification. Since $E(Y_t \mid Y_{t-1}) = \psi_t E\varepsilon_t$, ψ_t is interpreted as the conditional expected duration. Thus, the essential feature of the ACD model is the path dependence of the conditional first moment.

(i) The ACD(1,1) is stationary when $\alpha + \beta < 0$.

(ii) For positivity of the conditional expected duration, the following restrictions are imposed on the parameters: $w > 0, \alpha \geqslant 0, \beta \geqslant 0$.

When $\alpha = \beta = 0$, the serial dependence in durations is eliminated: $Y_t = w\varepsilon_t$.

The parameters of the ACD(1,1) model can be estimated by the maximum likelihood method. For example, if durations are assumed to be conditionally exponentially distributed, the parameter estimates are obtained by maximizing numerically the following criterion function:

$$(\alpha, \beta)' = \operatorname*{argmax}_{\alpha, \beta} \left\{ -\sum_{t=2}^{T} \log(w + \alpha y_{t-1} + \beta \psi_{t-1}) + (w + \alpha y_{t-1} + \beta \psi_{t-1})^{-1} y_t \right\}.$$

It is easy to derive the log-likelihood function based on the exponential distribution by replacing the intensity parameter by the reciprocal of expectation ψ_t.

The ACD(1,1) model is easily adjustable to panel data on borrowers, insureds or consumers. Let us propose the following approach:

$$Y_{i,t} = \psi_{i,t}\varepsilon_{i,t}, \quad i = 1, \ldots, n, \ t = 1, \ldots, T_i, \tag{10.17}$$

where the error terms are exponential i.i.d., and the subscripts i and t refer to the individual and the consecutive events, respectively. Suppose that the conditional expected duration satisfies the dynamic equation with a set of individual characteristics as additional explanatory variables,

$$\psi_{i,t} = \exp(z_i'b) + \alpha Y_{i,t-1} + \beta \psi_{i,t-1}, \quad t \geqslant 1, \tag{10.18}$$

and the initial conditions are such that

$$\psi_{i,1} = \exp(z_i'd). \tag{10.19}$$

By recursive substitution, $\psi_{i,t}$ can be expressed in terms of the initial conditions, lagged durations, and explanatory variables:

$$\psi_{i,1} = \exp(z_i'd),$$
$$\psi_{i,2} = \exp(z_i'b) + \alpha Y_{i,1} + \beta \exp(z_i'd),$$
$$\psi_{i,3} = \exp(z_i'b) + \alpha Y_{i,2} + \beta[\exp(z_i'b) + \alpha Y_{i,1} + \beta \exp(z_i'd)],$$

$$\vdots$$

The model can be extended by allowing α and β to depend on individual characteristics. This method would entail the use of three types of score: one for the marginal expected value of individual durations ($\exp(z_i'b)$), the second for the initial conditions ($\exp(z_i'd)$), and the third for the parameters.

10.2.1.3 Autoregressive Model for Count Data

In the literature, there exist a variety of autoregressive models for counts, which arise as extensions of the basic Poisson model. We restrict our attention to two specifications. Let Y_t, $t = 1, \ldots, T$, denote the integer-valued time series, such as counts of trades or claims in insurance.

(a) The most straightforward approach consists in including the lagged count among the explanatory variables of a Poisson regression model. The conditional distribution of Y_t given Y_{t-1} is then

$$Y_t \mid Y_{t-1} \sim \mathcal{P}[\exp(a + bY_{t-1})],$$

where the intensity depends on the lagged number of events. This model is easy to estimate, but the stationarity conditions are hard to derive and to verify.

(b) A more convenient specification is an analogue of the Gaussian autoregressive model for count data (see, for example, Campbell 1934; Al-Osh and Alzaid 1987, 1990; Zeger 1988; McKenzie 1988; Bockenholt 1999; Brannas and Hellstrom 2001). The process, called INAR(1), which stands for *integer autoregressive* of order 1, is written as

$$Y_t = \sum_{i=1}^{Y_{t-1}} Z_{i,t} + \varepsilon_t, \tag{10.20}$$

where the variables ε_t, $Z_{1,t}$, $Z_{2,t}$, ... are independent, with distributions: $\varepsilon_t \sim \mathcal{P}[\lambda(1 - \alpha)]$, $Z_{i,t} \sim \mathcal{B}(1, \alpha)$, where $\lambda > 0$, $1 > \alpha > 0$. By convention, $\sum_{i=1}^{0} Z_{i,t} = 0$. The acronym INAR(1) indicates that the first lag of Y appears as the upper bound on the sum. The model contains Poisson distributed error terms and features past dependence. The number of variables that determine the present count is stochastic, due to the binomial thinning operator.[4]

(i) The conditional distribution of Y_t given $Y_{t-1} = y_{t-1}$ is

$$\mathcal{B}(y_{t-1}; \alpha) * \mathcal{P}[\lambda(1 - \alpha)],$$

where "$*$" denotes the convolution.

(ii) The conditional distribution of Y_t given $Y_{t-h} = y_{t-h}$ is

$$\mathcal{B}(y_{t-h}; \alpha^h) * \mathcal{P}[\lambda(1 - \alpha^h)].$$

(iii) The process is strongly stationary for $0 < \alpha < 1$ and the marginal distribution of Y_t is $\mathcal{P}(\lambda)$.

The INAR(1)-based nonlinear forecasting is straightforward. The forecast formula at horizon h has the same form as the forecast at horizon h for a Gaussian AR(1) model, with the autoregressive coefficient α replaced by α^h.

---

[4] For more details concerning the properties of the model, we refer to Gourieroux and Jasiak (2006).

The first- and second-order conditional moments of an INAR(1) model are

$$E(Y_t \mid Y_{t-1}) = \alpha Y_{t-1} + \lambda(1 - \alpha),$$
$$V(Y_t \mid Y_{t-1}) = \alpha(1 - \alpha)Y_{t-1} + \lambda(1 - \alpha) \leqslant E(Y_t \mid Y_{t-1}).$$

The conditional mean is an affine function of the lagged count with autoregressive coefficient α. The fact that the conditional variance is less than or at most equal to the conditional mean indicates that the INAR(1) model features conditional underdispersion. In addition, the INAR(1) model features conditional heteroskedasticity (time-varying conditional variance). The conditional variance is an increasing function of lagged counts.

The INAR(1) model can be extended to panel data by introducing parameters λ and α written as functions of individual characteristics:

$$\lambda_i = \exp(z_i'a),$$
$$\alpha_i = [1 + \exp(-z_i'b)]^{-1}.$$

10.2.2   Time-Dependent Heterogeneity

Omitted individual heterogeneity, modeled by a latent variable and discussed in previous chapters, was assumed to be constant in time and varying across individuals in a sample. As mentioned earlier, serial dependence in the endogenous variable of risk can be modeled by including dynamic individual heterogeneity. This approach seems natural in moral hazard, where the individual knows and controls her own heterogeneity variable, while the econometrician does not.[5] In this framework, latent individual heterogeneity is often interpreted as an unobservable effort of the individual, whose objective is to avoid losses. The effort depends on past individual records, and is adjusted in time accordingly. For example, the effort variable can represent safe driving in order to reduce the number of accidents, or debt management in order to avoid default.

A simple, dynamic specification for heterogeneity without serial correlation is obtained by assuming that unpredictable shocks hit the dynamic latent individual heterogeneity factor at each date. This renders accurate prediction of future heterogeneity impossible, even when many records of individual history are available. As a consequence, in the presence of dynamic heterogeneity, an automobile insurer needs to increase the premium to hedge against the lack of knowledge about the future driving of an insured. We prefer to focus on an alternative model of serially correlated latent individual heterogeneity that is more predictable.

10.2.2.1   Static Individual Heterogeneity

Let us first recall the model with individual heterogeneity in a static framework without covariates. The risk variable associated with individual i at time t is denoted

---

[5] However, the credit institutions and insurance companies will partly control the individual effort by means of premium updating.

by $Y_{i,t}$. The individual heterogeneity is assumed to be constant in time and is denoted by u_i. It can be univariate or multivariate, that is, it can consist of several components. The model is based on the following set of assumptions

(i) Individual risks $Y_{i,t}$ are independent, conditional on individual heterogeneity.

(ii) Individual risk $Y_{i,t}$ depends on u_i only (and not on the heterogeneity of other individuals). The conditional distribution of risk given heterogeneity u_i belongs to a given parametric class of distributions: $f(y \mid u_i; \theta)$ (say), where θ is a p-dimensional parameter.

(iii) The individual heterogeneities u_i, $i = 1, \ldots, n$, are independent and identically distributed across individuals.

(iv) The distribution of u_i is Gaussian, with zero mean and an identity variance–covariance matrix.

Under assumptions (i)–(iii), individual heterogeneity can be a vector, but its components are not uniquely defined unless assumption (iv) is imposed. When heterogeneity u_i has a distribution that belongs to a parametric family $g(u; \alpha)$ (say) that is not Gaussian, there exists a method that allows us to transform u_i into a Gaussian variable. Indeed, u_i can be written as $u_i = G(\Phi(u_i^*); \alpha)$, where $u_i^* \sim N(0, \mathrm{Id})$ and G is the quantile function (that is, the inverse of the distribution function) associated with the distribution of u_i, and Φ is the standard Gaussian cumulative distribution (the transformation to Gaussianity is illustrated in Example 10.1 below).

Assumption (iv) is then satisfied with u_i^* as the new heterogeneity factor. Under the change of variables, the set of parameters includes the parameter (vector) θ of the conditional distribution of $Y_{i,t}$ given u_i and the parameter (vector) α of the heterogeneity distribution.

10.2.2.2 Dynamic Individual Heterogeneity

Let us assume that individual heterogeneity $u_{i,t}$ is Gaussian. Then, a natural representation of serial correlation in individual heterogeneity is provided by the *vector autoregressive* (VAR) model, which is a linear, dynamic model. The use of a vector representation indicates that, as in the static approach, individual heterogeneity is allowed to be multivariate and to consist of several components. The set of assumptions has to be modified to accommodate the following dynamics.

(i) Individual risks $Y_{i,t}$ are independent, conditional on individual heterogeneity $u_{i,t}$, i, t varying.

(ii) The conditional distribution of $Y_{i,t}$ depends on individual heterogeneity $u_{i,t}$ only, and belongs to a given parametric class of distributions: $f(y \mid u_{i,t}; \theta)$.

(iii) The individual processes of heterogeneity $(u_{i,t}, \ t \geqslant 0)$, i varying, are independent and identically distributed across individuals.

(iv) The heterogeneity of each individual i is a process that satisfies a Gaussian autoregressive model:

$$u_{i,t} = \psi u_{i,t-1} + (\text{Id} - \psi\psi')^{1/2}\varepsilon_{i,t}, \quad t \leqslant 1,$$

where $u_{i,0}, \varepsilon_{i,t}, t \geqslant 1$, are independent Gaussian variables $N(0, \text{Id})$.

The form of variance–covariance matrix $\text{Id} - \psi\psi'$ ensures that the marginal distribution of $u_{i,t}$ is standard normal. Therefore, the marginal distribution of $Y_{i,t}$ is the same in both the static and dynamic frameworks.

The likelihood function of the dynamic heterogeneity model (conditional on the initial heterogeneity) is

$$\prod_{i=1}^{n} \int \cdots \int \prod_{t=1}^{T_i} \left\{ f(y_{i,t} \mid u_{i,t}; \theta) \right.$$
$$\left. \times \frac{\exp -\frac{1}{2}(u_{i,t} - \psi u_{i,t-1})'(\text{Id} - \psi\psi)^{-1}(u_{i,t} - \psi u_{i,t-1})}{(2\pi)^{k/2} \det(\text{Id} - \psi\psi')^{1/2}} \, du_{it} \right\},$$

where k denotes the dimension of heterogeneity, that is, the number of components in the vector. The likelihood function involves multiple integrals, which render the traditional estimation method untractable. However, the model is easy to simulate, which allows for using the simulation-based estimation methods (Gourieroux and Monfort 1996; Gourieroux and Jasiak 1999).

For an illustration of the transformation to Gaussianity discussed earlier in the text, let us consider the following example.

Example 10.1 (Poisson–gamma model with dynamic heterogeneity). Consider two risk variables $Y_{i,t}^1$ and $Y_{i,t}^2$ that represent the counts of the claims filed in a fixed period of time and the cost of claims, respectively. Suppose that both risks are influenced by unobservable individual heterogeneity. Accordingly, there are two unobservable heterogeneity factors denoted by $u_{i,t}^{*1}$ and $u_{i,t}^{*2}$, respectively. The assumptions are as follows:

(i) $Y_{i,t}^1$ and $Y_{i,t}^2$ are independent, conditional on $u_{i,t}^{*1}, u_{i,t}^{*2}$.

(ii) The heterogeneity components are independent.

(iii) The conditional distribution of count variables $Y_{i,t}^1$ given heterogeneity is Poisson $\mathcal{P}[u_{i,t}^{*1}\theta_1]$.

(iv) The conditional distribution of total cost given the count variable and heterogeneity is gamma distributed $\gamma[\theta_3 Y_{i,t}^1, \theta_2 u_{i,t}^{*2}]$.

(v) The marginal distributions of heterogeneity components are

$$u_{i,t}^{*1} \sim \gamma[\theta_4, \theta_4],$$
$$u_{i,t}^{*2} \sim \gamma[\theta_5, \theta_5].$$

We see that individual heterogeneity is gamma distributed. Therefore, in the first step, $u_{i,t}^{*1}$ and $u_{i,t}^{*2}$ need to be transformed into Gaussian variables. Let $G(\cdot\,;\theta)$ denote the c.d.f. of the gamma $\gamma(\theta,\theta)$ distribution and Φ the c.d.f. of the standard normal. The transformed heterogeneity components are:

$$u_{i,t}^1 = \Phi^{-1}[G(u_{i,t}^{*1};\theta_4)],$$
$$u_{i,t}^2 = \Phi^{-1}[G(u_{i,t}^{*2};\theta_5)].$$

Heterogeneities $u_{i,t}^1$ and $u_{i,t}^2$ are Gaussian and can be interpreted as follows: the variance of u^1 (respectively, u^2) represents the unexplained (and unexpected) variation in the number of claims (respectively, the total cost of claims), conditional on the average behavior of individuals in a given population of insureds. Additional complications can arise from contemporaneous and/or lagged correlation between the two heterogeneity factors.

10.3 Applications

Example 10.1 is explored further in a simulation study that illustrates the effects of dynamic heterogeneity on the cost of a claim.

10.3.1 Cost Sensitivity with Respect to Transitory Shocks

Let us consider the Poisson–gamma model with dynamic heterogeneity as described in Example 10.1. The parameters θ_1 and θ_4 are set equal to 0.2 and 0.1, respectively. This implies that the expected number of accidents is $EY^1 = \theta_1 = 20\%$, and its variance is $V(Y^1) = V(\theta_1 u^{*1}) + E(\theta_1 u^{*1}) = \theta_1[1 + \theta_1/\theta_4]$. The model features marginal overdispersion as the variance exceeds the mean by $\theta_1/\theta_4 = 2$. The parameters θ_3 and θ_2 are set equal to 100 and 0.1, respectively. Without heterogeneity (that is, when $u^{*2} = 1 \iff \theta_5 = +\infty$), the variance of cost per claim is $\theta_3/\theta_2 = 1000$. The expected cost per claim is $\theta_3/\theta_2^2 = 10\,000$. Moreover, we set $\theta_5 = 0.1$. For simplicity, it is assumed that the two heterogeneity processes are independent (no contemporaneous or lagged correlation of heterogeneity):

$$\left.\begin{aligned}u_{i,t}^1 &= 0.8u_{i,t-1}^1 + \sqrt{1 - 0.8^2}\,\varepsilon_{i,t}^1,\\ u_{i,t}^2 &= 0.5u_{i,t-1}^2 + \sqrt{1 - 0.5^2}\,\varepsilon_{i,t}^2,\end{aligned}\right\}$$

with initial conditions $u_{i,0}^1 = u_{i,0}^2 = 0$.

The model is used to simulate and predict the cost of a claim up to horizon H using the following steps.

Step 1: perform H independent draws $\varepsilon_{i,t}^{1,s}$, $\varepsilon_{i,t}^{2,s}$, $t = 1,\ldots,H$, in the standard normal distribution.

Step 2: apply equations (10.21) recursively to get simulated values $u_{i,t}^{1,s}$, $u_{i,t}^{2,s}$, $t = 1,\ldots,H$, of heterogeneity components.

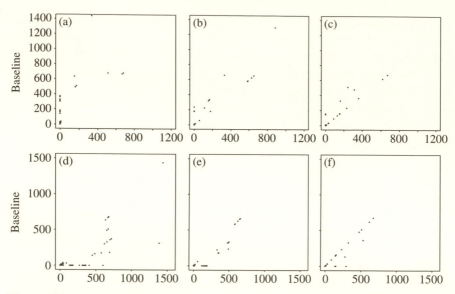

Figure 10.3. Costs and perturbed costs: (a) $H = 1$, negative shock; (b) $H = 5$, negative shock; (c) $H = 10$, negative shock; (d) $H = 1$, positive shock; (e) $H = 5$, positive shock; (f) $H = 10$, positive shock.

Step 3: for each date t, $t = 1, \ldots, H$, draw a value $Y_{i,t}^{1,s}$ of the count variable in the Poisson distribution $\mathcal{P}[u_{i,t}^{*1,s} \theta_1]$, where $u_{i,t}^{*1,s} = G^{-1}[\Phi(u_{i,t}^{1,s}), \theta_4]$.

Step 4: for each date t, $t = 1, \ldots, H$, draw a value $Y_{i,t}^{2,s}$ of the cost variable in the gamma distribution $\gamma[\theta_3 Y_{i,t}^{1,s}, \theta_2 u_{i,t}^{*2,s}]$, where $u_{i,t}^{*2,s} = G^{-1}[\Phi(u_{i,t}^{2,s}), \theta_5]$.

To study the shock effect, retain $\varepsilon_{i,t}^{1,s}$ and $u_{i,t}^{2s}$ and consider a positive or negative perturbation δ to heterogeneity $u_{i,t}^1$. Repeat the procedure by using the same set of $u_{i,t}^2$ and generating the new set of $u_{i,t}^1(\delta)$ as follows: add δ to the initial $\varepsilon_{i,1}^{1,s}$, that is, replace $\varepsilon_{i,1}^{1,s}$ by $\varepsilon_{i,1}^{1,s} + \delta$, for a given δ and apply the recursive equation of step 2 to get a set of new draws of $u_{i,t}^{1s}(\delta)$. Follow with steps 3 and 4. As the outcome of step 4 you get a new set of draws of the cost variable. It is then possible to compare the first set of cost draws $Y_{i,t}^{1,s}$ with the new cost draws $Y_{i,t}^{1,s}(\delta)$, modified by the transitory shock δ to heterogeneity error $\varepsilon_{i,1}^1$ at date 1. Such a comparison can be used to study the sensitivity of the cost of the claim to transitory shocks (due, for example to natural disasters, such as floods) in order to determine the amount of capital required to be held on reserve to cover the costs of future claims.

Figure 10.3 displays scatterplots, representing bivariate sample densities of the cost and perturbed cost variables predicted at horizons $H = 1, 5, 10$. Scatterplots (a)–(c) show the effects of a negative shock $\delta = -1$. Scatterplots (d)–(f) concern the positive shock $\delta = +1$. The baseline, that is, the predicted unperturbed cost, is measured on the y-axis. The perturbed costs are measured on the x-axis.

Under a negative (respectively, positive) shock, the observations tend to cluster above (respectively, below) the 45° line. They approach the 45° line when the horizon increases and the shock effect diminishes. This means that the perturbed costs converge to the unperturbed cost levels as the shock effects taper off. Since the dynamics is nonlinear, we observe asymmetric effects of positive and negative shocks of the same magnitude. In particular, cost responses to positive shocks are more persistent than cost responses to negative shocks. Thus, the consequences of positive shocks last longer.

10.3.2 *Learning in Revolving Credit*

The most common type of credit is open account (revolving) credit. It is a form of credit extended to the consumer in advance of any transaction. Typically a lender, such as a bank or a retail outlet, agrees to let the consumer buy up to a specified amount on open account. The consumer's obligation is to make payments in accordance with the specified terms. Many people have one or more bank credit cards, such as MasterCard or Visa. Very often the same bank or institution offers several types of credit card. They differ in terms of the annual fee, the interest rate charged on unpaid balances, and additional features, such as travel insurances and air miles.

In the following example, we study the dynamics of individual debt. The database contains records on about 5 000 000 credit cards. A sample of 15 637 individual credit histories has been drawn from this population. The individual histories are right censored due either to the end of the sampling period, or customer default. The variables observed for each individual i are

- the number of charges to the credit card, N_i;
- the durations between consecutive charges to the credit card, $D_{1,i}, \ldots, D_{N_i,i}$;
- the last right censored duration, $D^*_{N_i+1,i}$;
- the amounts charged to the card, $Y_{1,i}, \ldots, Y_{N_i,i}$.

The individual data can be used to trace out the evolution of individual debt in time. The total amount charged to the card is plotted for three customers in Figure 10.4.

The trajectory of debt in time is a piecewise linear function with a kink at each payment or repayment date. The downward sloping segments correspond to repayments of outstanding balances, while the upward jumps indicate subsequent amounts charged on the card. We observe that none of the three individuals has entirely repaid the initial balance in the sampling period. It seems that the repayments concern only the minimum amounts required in monthly statements. Two individuals make big purchases in the middle of the sampling period. The third individual is more cautious and only slightly increases her outstanding debt. The illustrated debt dynamic is consistent with the pattern of credit card use in practice. On average, the unpaid balance on an American credit card is $10 000.

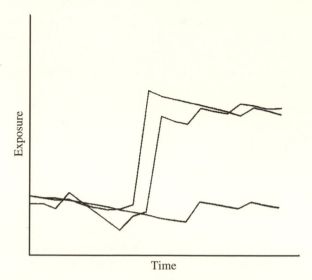

Figure 10.4.   Evolution of individual debt.

Table 10.3.   Distribution of charges to credit card ("NI" stands for
the number of individuals who used the card N_i times).

N_i	1	2	3	4	5	6	7	8	9	10
NI	15 637	10 617	8014	6354	5130	4258	3565	3035	2580	2246

N_i	11	12	13	14	15	16	17	18	19	20
NI	1974	1743	1529	1347	1191	1060	939	834	724	638

The individual histories in the sample are of different lengths, both in terms of calendar time and the number of recorded charges to the card. Table 10.3 describes the survivor function of N_i in the sample.

The entries in Table 10.3 can be interpreted as follows. All individuals in the sample, that is, 15 637 persons, used the card at least one time, 10 617 persons used the card at least two times, and so on. There is a sudden drop in the number of credit card users who used the card at least three times compared with the number of those who used the card at least once. Only about 50% of the individuals under study used the card three or more times.

10.3.2.1   Duration Analysis

The time to first transaction depends on the institution that issued the credit card. If the card was issued by a retail outlet, such as a supermarket or a department store, it is close to zero. It is also quite short if the card was requested by the consumer at a local bank agency. In contrast, it can be quite long if the credit card was offered by a

Table 10.4. Autocorrelogram of the duration process.

lag h	1	2	3	4	5	6	7	8	9	10
$\rho(h)$	0.20	0.16	0.10	0.09	0.06	0.06	0.02	0.04	0.02	0.02

lag h	11	12	13	14	15	16	17	18	19	20
$\rho(h)$	−0.03	−0.03	−0.02	−0.04	−0.02	−0.04	−0.03	0.00	−0.002	−0.02

credit institution via a direct-mail promotion. For this reason, data on first durations are treated separately.

The duration data are first examined to check for evidence of serial correlation. The serial correlation in duration dynamics can be detected by plotting an autocorrelogram computed by averaging across both individuals and events. The estimated correlation of order 1 is $\hat{\rho}(1) = \hat{\gamma}(1)/\hat{\gamma}(0)$, where

$$\hat{\gamma}(1) = \frac{1}{n} \sum_{i=1}^{n} \frac{1}{N_i - 3} \sum_{t=3}^{N_i} D_{t,i} D_{t-1,i} - \left(\frac{1}{n} \sum_{i=1}^{n} \frac{1}{N_i - 3} \sum_{t=3}^{N_i} D_{t,i} \right)^2,$$

$$\hat{\gamma}(0) = \frac{1}{n} \sum_{i=1}^{n} \frac{1}{N_i - 2} \sum_{t=2}^{N_i} D_{t,i}^2 - \left(\frac{1}{n} \sum_{i=1}^{n} \frac{1}{N_i - 2} \sum_{t=2}^{N_i} D_{t,i} \right)^2.$$

One should proceed with caution in interpreting the autocorrelogram as it disregards individual heterogeneity.

Due to the large number of individual observations, the autocorrelations are significant and the hypothesis of independent (uncorrelated) durations is rejected. Therefore, a compound Poisson model is not adequate.

10.3.2.2 Dormancy

The individual histories of charges to a credit card may feature a transition to an inactive status, called a *dormancy* (see, for example, Carling et al. 1998). The probability p_n that a credit card becomes dormant after the nth transaction can be approximated by the difference between the survivor function computed from the series of complete durations, $D_{n,i}$, and the survivor function computed from the joint set of complete and right censored durations, $D_{n,i}$, $D_{n,i}^*$.

Figure 10.5 displays the probability of dormancy with respect to times between consecutive charges to the credit card. p_n is equal to the vertical distance between the two curves representing the two aforementioned survivor functions, evaluated at $1, 2, \ldots,$ up to 5 months. The probability of dormancy is an increasing function of inter-transaction times.

The dormancy probabilities computed with respect to the count of transactions charged to the card are shown in Table 10.5.

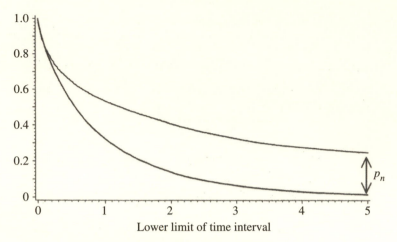

Figure 10.5. The dormancy.

Table 10.5. Dormancy probabilities.

n	2	3	4	5	6	7	8	9	10
p_n	0.13	0.09	0.08	0.07	0.06	0.06	0.05	0.05	0.04

n	11	12	13	14	15	16	17	18	19
p_n	0.03	0.03	0.03	0.04	0.03	0.05	0.03	0.04	0.04

The dormancy probability is high when the card is used up to five times. When the credit card is used more frequently, that is, to make more than six charges, $n = 6$, the dormancy probability drops and remains stable in the interval (3%,5%).

10.3.2.3 The ACD(1,1) Model

Given the empirical evidence on serial correlation in inter-transaction durations, one can proceed directly to dynamic modelling. Let us consider the panel extension of the ACD(1,1) model proposed earlier. The time to first transaction is deleted from the sample. Two separate specifications for the duration between the first and the second charge to a credit card and all the following intercharge durations are considered:

$$D_{2,i} = (Z_i'd)\varepsilon_{2i} = \psi_{1,i}\varepsilon_{2,i}, \tag{10.22}$$

$$D_{n+1,i} = \psi_{n,i}\varepsilon_{n+1,i}, \quad n \geqslant 2, \tag{10.23}$$

where

$$\psi_{n,i} = (Z_i'c) + (Z_i'a)D_{n,i} + (Z_i'b)\psi_{n-1,i}, \tag{10.24}$$

where innovations $(\varepsilon_{n,i})$ are independent and Weibull distributed, $P[\varepsilon_{n,i} > \varepsilon] = \exp(-\varepsilon^{\tau})$. The model includes observable heterogeneity, introduced in the form of individual dependent parameters of the model. These can be summarized by the

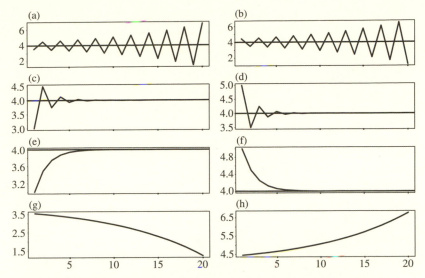

Figure 10.6. The admissible patterns: (a) reg(1, 1); (b) reg(1, 2); (c) reg(2, 1); (d) reg(2, 2); (e) reg(3, 1); (f) reg(3, 2); (g) reg(4, 1); (h) reg(4, 2).

following four scores:

$$S_i(d) = Z_i'd, \qquad S_i(a) = Z_i'a, \qquad S_i(b) = Z_i'b, \qquad S_i(c) = Z_i'c,$$

which accommodate cross-sectional variation of the parameters of the model. The values of scores can be used for segmentation of the population of customers. In particular, the scores would allow us to distinguish between different types of behavior concerning credit card use. For example, after the first charge to the card is recorded, the expectations of times to future charges satisfy

$$_1\hat{D}_{n+1} = S_i(c) + (S_i(a) + S_i(b))\,_1\hat{D}_n, \quad n \geqslant 2, \tag{10.25}$$

with $_1\hat{D}_2 = S_i(d)$, or equivalently are given by

$$_1\hat{D}_n = \frac{S_i(c)}{1 - S_i(a) - S_i(b)} + (S_i(a) + S_i(b))^{n-2}\left(S_i(d) - \frac{S_i(c)}{1 - S_i(a) - S_i(b)}\right),$$
$$n \geqslant 2. \tag{10.26}$$

We obtain various patterns of times to charges to the card, depending on the values of the "regression coefficient" $S_i(a) + S_i(b)$, and on the difference between the initial value $S_i(d)$ and the long-run duration limit $S_i(c)/[1 - S_i(a) - S_i(b)]$.

Whenever $|S_i(a) + S_i(b)| < 1$, there is convergence towards a steady-state equilibrium at $S_i(c)/(1 - S_i(a) - S_i(b))$. The convergence pattern can be smooth (decreasing or increasing), or can have oscillations (decreasing or increasing). Some regimes indicate an infinite expected time to the next charge to a credit card in the long run, which is a steady state.

Table 10.6.   The learning regimes.

	$S_i(d) < \dfrac{S_i(c)}{1 - S_i(a) - S_i(b)}$	$S_i(d) > \dfrac{S_i(c)}{1 - S_i(a) - S_i(b)}$
$S_i(a) + S_i(b) < -1$	reg(1, 1)	reg(1, 2)
$-1 < S_i(a) + S_i(b) < 0$	reg(2, 1)	reg(2, 2)
$0 < S_i(a) + S_i(b) < 1$	reg(3, 1)	reg(3, 2)
$1 < S_i(a) + S_i(b)$	reg(4, 1)	reg(4, 2)

Figure 10.6 illustrates the convergence patterns corresponding to each cell in Table 10.6. It is easy to distinguish between cases associated with convergence (growth or oscillations) and divergence, that is, no use of the credit card in the future.

The four scores associated with the ACD(1,1) model can be computed for any new holder of a credit card. The learning regime of the new customer can then be predicted and, if it is convergent, the steady state of credit card use can be assessed.

10.3.2.4   Estimation Results

Table 10.7 contains a list of the significant explanatory variables included in the scores associated with the panel ACD model.

Unfortunately, most estimation results cannot be disclosed as the data are highly confidential. The following information on coefficient estimates is available.

- Score = coefficient on the lagged duration:

Number of years at same address	<2	0.03
	2–5	0.02
Number of years in current job	12–19	−0.025
Initial score	<3000	0.088
	3000–4000	0.103
	>5000	0.064

- Score = initial condition: 17 significant variables.

- Score = coefficient on ψ_{n-1}: 25 significant variables.

- Score = coefficient on the constant: 27 significant variables.

The last step of dynamic modelling is diagnostic checking. The goodness-of-fit of the Weibull distribution to the data is assessed by plotting the logarithm of the estimated survivor function of residual $\hat{\varepsilon}_{i,t}^{\hat{\tau}}$.

If the fit is good, then the log-survivor is a linear function of time (which is the power exponent on the error in a Weibull distribution). Figure 10.7 reveals a linear form that confirms the good fit of the panel ACD(1,1) model.

Table 10.7. List of explanatory variables.

Variable	Class	Identification number
Constant		0
Age	<18	1
	18–27	2
	38–43	3
	>43	4
Number of years in current job	<5	5
	5–8	6
	8–10	7
	12–17	8
	>17	9
Number of years at same address	<2	10
	2–5	11
	>9	12
Number of years as bank customer	<2	13
	2–4	14
	4–5	15
	12–17	16
	>17	17
Monthly income	<6 000	18
	6 000–6 500	19
	6 500–8 000	20
	11 500–13 000	21
	13 000–16 000	22
	>16 000	23
Home ownership	Homeowner	24
	Lives with parents	25
	Unknown	26
Nationality	EEC (except France)	27
	Non-EEC	28
Marital status × number of children	Single	29
	Divorced	30
	Co-tenant without children	31
	Married, at most one child	32
	Married more than two children	33

Table 10.7.   (*Continued.*)

Variable	Class	Identification number
Occupation	Temporary employment	34
	Executive	35
	Worker	36
	Salesman	37
	Retired	38
Initial score	<3000	39
	3000–4000	40
	>5000	41
Bank	No bank account	42
	BNP	43
	CCP	44
	Crédit Agricole	45
	Crédit Mutuel	46
	Post	47
Credit card issuer	Furniture store	48
	Hypermarket	49
	DIY superstore	50
	"Blanc–brun" card	51
	Travel agency	52
	Car seller	53

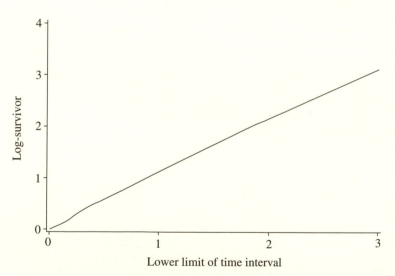

Figure 10.7.   Logarithm of the estimated survivor function of ϵ_τ.

10.4 Concluding Remarks

In this chapter we stressed the importance of serial correlation in marked-point processes of events generated by learning or moral hazard phenomena. The applied and theoretical literature offers a variety of models for durations and count variables. Our discussion was limited to the most popular models in their basic representations. Recently, several extensions to the ACD model have emerged, such as the stochastic volatility duration (SVD) model (Ghysels et al. 2003), or the autoregressive gamma model (Gourieroux and Jasiak 2006). In regard to count data, the most commonly used models are the integer autoregressive (INAR) model and its extensions. In marketing, the INAR models are used for the assessment of the effects of new product arrivals or promotions (see, for example, Henderson and Quelch 1985; Ehrenberg 1988; Alawadi and Neslin 1996). In credit and insurance, the INAR-based applications concern dynamic analysis of contract prices (see, for example, Gourieroux and Jasiak 1999, 2004).

10.5 Appendix: Distributions of the Duration and Count Variables

10.5.1 Distribution of the First Duration

We have

$$
\begin{aligned}
P[Y_1 > t + \mathrm{d}t \mid Y_1 > t] &= P[N(t + \mathrm{d}t) - N(t) = 0 \mid N(t) - N(0) = 0] \\
&= P[N(t + \mathrm{d}t) - N(t) = 0] \quad \text{(from (A1))} \\
&= 1 - \lambda \, \mathrm{d}t + o(\mathrm{d}t).
\end{aligned}
$$

Since

$$
\begin{aligned}
P[Y_1 > t + \mathrm{d}t \mid Y_1 > t] &= \frac{P[Y_1 > t + \mathrm{d}t]}{P[Y_1 > t]} \\
&= \frac{\bar{F}(t + \mathrm{d}t)}{\bar{F}(t)},
\end{aligned}
$$

where $\bar{F}$ is the survivor function of Y_1, we deduce that

$$
\frac{\bar{F}(t + \mathrm{d}t)}{\bar{F}(t)} = 1 - \lambda \, \mathrm{d}t + o(\mathrm{d}t) \iff \frac{\bar{F}(t + \mathrm{d}t) - \bar{F}(t)}{\bar{F}(t)} = -\lambda \, \mathrm{d}t + o(\mathrm{d}t)
$$

$$
\iff \frac{\mathrm{d} \log \bar{F}(t)}{\mathrm{d}t} = -\lambda
$$

$$
\iff \bar{F}(t) = \exp(-\lambda t).
$$

Therefore, Y_1 admits an exponential distribution with parameter λ.

10.5.2   Independence of Durations

Let us consider the first two durations, for instance. We have that

$P[Y_2 > y \mid Y_1 = y_1]$

$\quad = P[N[y_1 + y] - N(y_1) = 0 \mid N(y_1) - N(y_1^-) = 1, \ N(y_1^-) - N(0) = 0]$

$\qquad$ (where $N(y^-)$ denotes the limit of $N(z)$ when z tends to y from below)

$\quad = P[N[y_1 + y] - N(y_1) = 0] \quad$ (from (A1))

$\quad = P[N(y) - N(0) = 0]$

$\qquad$ (due to the stationarity of increments, implied by (A2))

$\quad = P[Y_1 > y]$

$\quad = \exp(-\lambda y).$

Therefore, this conditional distribution is independent of y_1 and identical to the distribution of Y_2. Similar arguments apply for checking that $Y_1, \ldots, Y_n$ are i.i.d. exponential variables.

10.5.3   Distribution of the Count Variable

We have

$$P[N(t) = n] = P[Y_1 + \cdots + Y_n < t < Y_1 + \cdots + Y_{n+1}]$$

$$= P[Y_1 + \cdots + Y_{n+1} > t] - P[Y_1 + \cdots + Y_n > t]$$

$$= \int_0^t \frac{\lambda^{n+1} \exp(-\lambda y) y^n}{\Gamma(n+1)} \, dy - \int_0^t \frac{\lambda^n \exp(-\lambda y) y^{n-1}}{\Gamma(n)} \, dy$$

$$= \exp(-\lambda t) \frac{(\lambda t)^n}{n!},$$

where the last equality is obtained by integrating by parts and the previous one by noting that $Y_1 + \cdots + Y_n$ follows a $\gamma(n, \lambda)$ distribution.

References

Ailawadi, K., and S. Neslin. 1996. The effect of promotion on consumption: buying more and consuming it faster. Darmouth College Discussion Paper.

Al-Osh, M., and A. Alzaid. 1987. First order integer valued autoregressive (INAR(1)) process. *Journal of Time Series Analysis* 8:261–75.

Alzaid, A., and M. Al-Osh. 1990. An integer valued pth-order autoregressive structure (INAR(p)) process. *Journal of Applied Probability* 27:314–24.

Anderson, P., O. Borgan, R. Gill, and N. Keiding. 1993. *Statistical Models Based on Counting Processes*. Springer.

Baltagi, B. 2001. *Econometric Analysis of Panel Data*. Wiley.

Bauwens, L., and P. Giot. 2001. *Econometric Modelling of Stock Market Intraday Activity*. Amsterdam: Kluwer.

Blundell, R., R. Griffith, and J. Van Reenen. 1995. Dynamic count data models of technological innovation. *The Economic Journal* 105:333–44.

Bockenholt, U. 1999. Mixed INAR(1) Poisson regression models: analyzing heterogeneity and serial dependencies in longitudinal count data. *Journal of Econometrics* 89:317–38.

Brannas, K., and J. Hellstrom. 2001. Generalization to the integer valued AR(1) model. *Econometric Reviews* 20:425–43.

Bucklin, R., and J. Lattin. 1991. A two-state model of purchase incidence and brand choice. *Marketing Science* 19:24–39.

Campbell, J. 1934. The Poisson correlated function. *Proceedings of the Edinburgh Mathematical Society* 2:18–26.

Carling, K., T. Jacobson, and K. Roszbach. 1998. Duration of consumer loans and bank lending policy: dormancy versus default risk. Stockholm School of Economics, Working Paper 280.

Chintagunta, P. 1993. Investigating purchase incidence, brand choice and purchase quantity decisions of households. *Marketing Science* 12:184–208.

Gourieroux, C., and J. Jasiak. 2004. Heterogeneous INAR(1) model with application to car insurance. *Insurance: Mathematics and Economics* 34:177–92.

Dirickx, Y., and L. Wakeman. 1976. An extension of the Bierman–Hausman model for credit granting. *Management Science* 22:1229–37.

Ehrenberg, A. 1988. *Repeat Buying*. Oxford University Press.

Engle, R., and J. Russell. 1997. Forecasting the frequency of change in quoted foreign exchange prices with the autoregressive conditional duration model. *Journal of Empirical Finance* 4:187–212.

Engle, R., and J. Russell. 1998. The autoregressive conditional duration model. *Econometrica* 66:1127–63.

Fisher, R. 1938. The statistical utilization of multiple measurements. *Annals of Eugenics* VIII:376–86.

Ghysels, E., C. Gourieroux, and J. Jasiak. 2003. Stochastic volatility duration models. *Journal of Econometrics* 119:413–33.

Gourieroux, C. 1999. The econometrics of risk classification in insurance. *Geneva Papers for Risk and Insurance* 24(2):119–37.

Gourieroux, C., and J. Jasiak. 1999. Nonlinear panel data model with dynamic heterogeneity. In *Panel Data Econometrics: Future Directions* (ed. J. Krishnakumar and E. Ronchetti), pp. 127–48. Amsterdam: North-Holland.

Gourieroux, C., and J. Jasiak. 2004. Heterogeneous INAR(1) model with application to car insurance. *Insurance, Mathematics and Economics* 34:177–92.

Gourieroux, C., and J. Jasiak. 2006. Autoregressive gamma process. *Journal of Forecasting* 25:129–152.

Gourieroux, C., and A. Monfort. 1996. *Simulation Based Econometric Methods*. Oxford University Press.

Gross, D., and N. Souleles. 1999. How do people use credit cards? University of Pennsylvania Discussion Paper.

Hamdan, M. and H. Al-Bagyati. 1971. Canonical expansion of the compound correlated bivariate Poisson distribution. *Journal of the American Statistical Association* 66:390–93.

Harvey, A., and C. Fernandez. 1989. Time series models for count or qualitative observations. *Journal of Business and Economic Statistics* 7:407–22.

McKenzie, E. 1988. Some ARMA models for dependent sequences of Poisson counts. *Advances in Applied Probability* 20:822–35.

Neslin, S., C. Henderson, and J. Quelch. 1985. Consumer promotions and the acceleration of product purchases. *Marketing Science* 4:147–65.

Roszbach, K. 1998. Bank lending policy, credit scoring and the survival of loans. Stockholm School of Economics, Working Paper 261.

Srinivasan, V., and Y. Kim. 1987. The Bierman–Hausman credit granting model: a note. *Management Science* 33:1361–62.

Zeger, S. 1988. A regression model for time series of counts. *Biometrika* 75:621–29.

11

Management of Credit Risk

In the last decade, the number and complexity of financial products has increased significantly. In response to this phenomenon, a banking supervisory committee was established in Basel (Basle), Switzerland. The objectives of the Basle Committee are the development and worldwide coordination of risk control and management methods. In 1995, the Basle Committee signed a document called the Basle Accord, in which it imposed mandatory rules for determining the amount of capital reserve as an instrument of market risk control. These rules are based on a risk measure, called the *Value-at-Risk* (VaR). The VaR is used to determine the minimum capital reserve required to be set aside by each bank for coverage of a potential loss on a portfolio of assets, which can occur with some small fixed probability in a fixed holding period. Initially, the VaR concerned only portfolios of liquid assets, such as stocks, currencies, and so on. Later, the Basle Committee extended the VaR to portfolios of derivatives and credits (see Basle Committee on Banking and Supervision 2003). The coverage of VaR methodology provided in this chapter is related to credit risk and is limited to some selected topics of interest. Comprehensive coverage of VaR is beyond the scope of this book. Interested readers can consult the references listed at the end of the chapter, which give suggestions for further reading. These include the main Basle documents and basic academic contributions in this field. The content of the chapter is as follows: Section 11.1 defines the VaR and shows how the VaR is computed from the *profit and loss* (P&L) distribution. Next, the desirable properties of a risk measure and the notion of *expected shortfall* are introduced. The implementation of risk control measures to credit risks is presented in Section 11.2. Two approaches to the determination of the P&L distribution, based on market data and individual data, respectively, are described. Section 11.3 presents risk analysis for portfolios of corporate bonds with an emphasis on default correlation and stochastic migration.

11.1 Measures of Risk and Capital Requirement

The central issue in risk control is the determination of the amount of a financial loss that may be incurred with a given probability. Given this amount, the bank has to assess how much capital is required to cover that loss. The capital will be set aside by the bank and held on reserve. In this section, we describe the general problem of determining the minimum capital requirement without any references

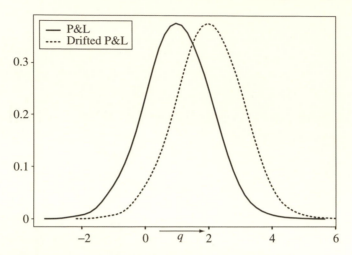

Figure 11.1. The effect of capital requirement on P&L distribution.

to portfolios of individual contracts. Let us introduce the P&L variable, denoted by $X_{t,H}$ at time t, which stands for profit or loss at horizon H. $X_{t,H}$ is the sum of the terminal value of the portfolio at $t + H$, and of the various payoffs, such as dividends, interest payments, margin requirements, and so on, between t and $t + H$. To simplify the presentation, we implicitly assume a zero risk-free interest rate during the holding period. At time t, the value of $X_{t,H}$ is unknown, while the distribution of $X_{t,H}$, called the P&L distribution, is available; it depends on date t, horizon H, and the portfolio structure. This distribution assigns probabilities of occurrence to all possible values of $X_{t,H}$, including the negative values, which are future losses. The aim of risk control is to reduce the probabilities associated with negative values of $X_{t,H}$ by keeping on reserve (not investing) an amount of money called the *required capital* and denoted by $q_{t,H}(X)$. Then, the total portfolio value at $t + H$ becomes $X_{t,H} + q_{t,H}(X)$. This means that the risk control results in a horizontal shift of the P&L distribution to the right, which reduces the probabilities of potential losses.

The crucial question is how and how often the required capital has to be updated. To answer it, we need to evaluate the amount q at some future fixed dates t of consecutive portfolio updatings, and at a fixed horizon H.

11.1.1 Value-at-Risk

A natural determinant of the minimum capital requirement is the probability of a loss. The minimum capital associated with loss probability α is

$$P_t[X_{t,H} + q < 0] = \alpha \iff P_t[X_{t+H} < -q] = \alpha$$
$$\iff q = -F_{t,H}^{-1}(\alpha), \tag{11.1}$$

where $F_{t,H}^{-1}(\alpha)$ is the α-quantile of the P&L distribution. This α-quantile is called the *Value-at-Risk* and is denoted by $\mathrm{VaR}_{t,H}(\alpha)$.

According to the definition given above, the VaR depends on the horizon, the loss probability α, and the selected P&L distribution. The official guidelines for determining these arguments can be criticized for suggesting

(a) the use of equal horizons for (i) liquid and illiquid assets, and (ii) credit (insurance) contracts with early and late potential default;

(b) computation of the P&L distribution either as the historical P&L, or the conditional P&L, that is, P&L conditional upon the available information; and

(c) the use of inputs provided by *internal models* (such as in Riskmetrics (JPMorgan 1996)) for VaR computation, which renders the VaR model-dependent. It is therefore computed in a different manner by different banks.

In practice, the arguments in the definition of VaR may be set equal to values that depend on the purpose, which can be the computation of minimum capital requirement imposed by the regulators, internal risk control, allocation of risk among trading tables, portfolio management and so on.

Remark 11.1. For coverage of market risk (that is, for portfolios of stocks and risk-free bonds) the regulators propose daily computation of the VaR at horizon $H = 10$ (corresponding to two weeks), with loss probability $\alpha = 1\%$, and based on the historical distribution computed from data collected in the previous year (approximately 250 days). The capital reserve (called the *market risk capital*) is then defined as

$$\mathrm{MRC}_t = \max\left[\mathrm{VaR}_{t-1}, k\frac{1}{60}\sum_{i=1}^{60} \mathrm{VaR}_{t-i} \right],$$

where the constant k is greater than 3 and typically varies between 3 and 4.

The MRC formula implies that risk is smoothed over 60 trading days, except when a sudden jump at $(t-1)$ is recorded. The constant k depends on the technological sophistication of a bank.[1]

Remark 11.2. Various models are used to specify the P&L distribution in the presence of market risk (see, for example, Gourieroux and Jasiak 2000, Chapter 16). These include the random walk model, implicitly proposed by the regulators, models with time dependence, such as discrete-time ARMA and ARCH models, or continuous-time factor models. Generally, the heterogeneity of assets in a portfolio is not taken into account, while it should be in portfolios of individual contracts. New modelling methodology needs to be developed to fill this gap.

---

[1] The Basle Committee distinguishes between so-called "standard" and "advanced" approaches.

Remark 11.3. Initially, the VaR was computed under the assumption of normality of the P&L distribution. Under the normality assumption, we get

$$P_t[X_{t,H} < -q] = \alpha \iff P_t\left[\frac{X_{t,H} - E_t X_{t,H}}{(V_t X_{t,H})^{1/2}} < \frac{-q - E_t X_{t,H}}{(V_t X_{t,H})^{1/2}}\right] = \alpha$$

$$\iff q = \text{VaR}_{t,H}(\alpha) = -(V_t X_{t,H})^{1/2}\Phi^{-1}(\alpha) - E_t X_{t,H},$$

where $\Phi^{-1}(\alpha)$ is the α-quantile of the standard normal distribution. The advantage of this approach is that it provides an expression of VaR as a function of the expected P&L and its volatility. However, the assumption of normality of the P&L distribution is not supported by the data. The empirical P&L distributions often feature fat tails or multiple modes. In such a case, the normality assumption leads to underestimation of risk and of the capital requirement.

11.1.2 Properties of a Risk Measure

In the insurance sector, VaR has not become a standard risk measure, despite being initially recommended as such by the regulators. The reason is that VaR disregards the severity of loss given default. Artzner et al. (1997, 1999) described a set of four desirable properties of a risk measure, in the context of capital requirement evaluation. Let us denote by $q(X)$ the required capital for X. The desirable properties are as follows.

(i) Monotonicity. If X is more risky than Y (stochastic dominance of order one),

$$q(X) \geqslant q(Y).$$

(ii) Invariance with respect to drift.

$$q(X + c) = q(X) - c, \quad \forall c, \ \forall X.$$

This condition means that the capital requirement needs to be included in the capital set aside by the firm.

(iii) Homogeneity.

$$q(\lambda X) = \lambda q(X), \quad \forall \lambda \geqslant 0, \ \forall X.$$

This is a kind of constant-return-to-scale condition. It seems natural for λ values close to 1, but may be questioned for illiquid assets, in particular. The selling price per share in a lot of 200 000 shares of such an asset may be much lower than the selling price per share in a lot of 1000 shares.

(iv) Subadditivity.

$$q(X + Y) \leqslant q(X) + q(Y), \quad \forall X, Y.$$

This condition favors corporate mergers and acquisitions, since the capital requirement on larger portfolios is smaller. It implies that large firms are subject to less control than small firms. Therefore, the relevance of the subadditivity condition seems questionable.

Conditions (iii) and (iv) imply the convexity of risk measure function q, that is, point out the advantage of diversification.[2] Concerning (iv), we can easily verify that the VaR measure does not satisfy the subadditivity property. Artzner et al. (1997, 1999) have introduced the *coherent risk measures*, which are functions q satisfying (i)–(iv). In particular, the expected shortfall (or *Tail VaR*) defined by

$$\text{TVaR}(\alpha) = -E_t[X_{t,H} \mid X_{t,H} + VaR_{t,H}(\alpha) < 0], \tag{11.2}$$

where

$$\text{VaR}_{t,H}(\alpha) = -F_{t,H}^{-1}(\alpha),$$

is a coherent risk measure. The Tail VaR is simply the price of a reinsurance contract for a risk-neutral investor. The associated capital requirement can be interpreted as the cost of self-reinsurance.

11.2 Credit Portfolio

In this section, we discuss the determination of capital requirement for portfolios of credits. The patterns of aggregate P&L distributions for credit portfolios share some specific characteristics discussed below. Since the aggregate P&L of a portfolio is a sum of P&Ls associated with each credit, it is necessarily influenced by the characteristics of each individual P&L. The following problems are often encountered.

  (i) The individual P&L distributions feature discontinuities due to dichotomous events, such as default or prepayment. For this reason, the individual P&L distributions need to be considered as mixtures of distributions.

 (ii) The portfolios may include heterogenous contracts (with different maturities, interest rates, monthly payments, and so on). Even when the contracts are of the same type, the risks associated with each of them are different, since default or prepayment rates depend on the characteristics of each borrower. Therefore, aggregation of individual risks is quite difficult.

(iii) The current P&L of a portfolio depends on future values of contracts up to $t + H$, say, if they are expected to terminate on that date or before. For credit contracts which can be traded on a secondary market, the future values may be determined by the market. This is the case for liquid corporate bonds. However, even the tradable contracts may become illiquid when the probability of default increases, and the market value fails to represent the underlying "fair value." The majority of credit contracts are not tradable on an organized market. From a theoretical point of view, this leads to an incomplete market framework, where the derivative prices, as well as the P&L variable, its distribution, and the capital requirement, are not unique.

---

[2] Note that the convexity condition can be satisfied even when the subadditivity and homogeneity conditions are not.

11.2.1   The P&L Distribution for a Credit Portfolio When the Horizon Is Equal To the Maturity

Let us explain the derivation of the P&L distribution for a portfolio of credits at a horizon equal to the maturity of loans in the portfolio. We will see that the form of the P&L distribution is quite complicated and non-Gaussian. In particular, it is a mixture of discrete and continuous distributions.

For convenience, let us assume a zero risk-free interest rate and consider a set of similar contracts with identical maturity H, identical interest rate γ, and identical constant monthly payment

$$m_i = B_{0,i} \frac{\gamma(1+\gamma)^H}{(1+\gamma)^H - 1} = B_{0,i} m$$

(say), where $B_{0,i}$ is the initial balance of the contract. The outstanding balance in month h is

$$B_{h,i} = B_{0,i} \frac{(1+\gamma)^H - (1+\gamma)^h}{(1+\gamma)^H - 1} = B_{0,i} c_h$$

(say). The P&L of an individual contract is given by

$$X_{i,H} = \begin{cases} B_{0,i} m H & \text{if there is neither default nor prepayment,} \\ B_{0,i}(mh + c_h) & \text{if there is a prepayment at } h, \\ B_{0,i}(mh + \alpha_{i,h} c_h) & \text{if there is a default at } h, \text{ where } \alpha_{i,h} \\ & \text{denotes the recovery rate, } \alpha_{i,h} \in (0,1). \end{cases}$$

Let us assume that the set of contracts can be partitioned into K homogeneous categories. The individual risks are independent with distributions depending on the category $k, k = 1, \ldots, K$, only, and the initial balances are equal in a given category. For the distribution of $X_{i,H}$, where i belongs to category k, denoted by f_k, and for the number of contracts of type k in the portfolio, denoted by $n_k, k = 1, \ldots, K$, the distribution of the aggregate P&L is

$$f = \underset{k=1}{\overset{K}{\ast}} (f_k^{*n_k}), \tag{11.3}$$

where "$*$" denotes the convolution.[3] In practice, it is difficult to find a closed-form expression of the aggregate P&L distribution, although it can be easily approximated by simulations when the individual P&L distributions $f_k, k = 1, \ldots, K$, are known. The procedure is as follows. We perform S successive draws of individual P&L, indexed by $s, s = 1, \ldots, S$. In the first step $s = 1$, we draw independently n_1 individual P&L values in f_1, then n_2 individual P&L values in f_2, and so on, up to the final draw of n_K individual P&L values in f_K. Next, we add up all individual P&L values simulated in step $s = 1$, and denote this sum by $X^s = X^1$. Next, we

---

[3] For two density functions f and g, $f * g(y) = \int f(y - z)g(z)\, dz$.

repeat the draws in the second step $s = 2$, and we end up computing $X^s = X^2$. We continue the simulations until a set of individual P&L aggregates $X^s, s = 1, \ldots, S$, is generated. The sample density of $X^s, s = 1, \ldots, S$, provides an approximation of density f. At this point, a histogram or kernel-smoothed density estimator can be used to illustrate the approximation of f graphically. Given the approximated density, the VaR and expected shortfall are easily inferred.

The individual P&L distributions can be evaluated under the following simplifying assumptions: (1) independence of prepayment and time-to-default, (2) independence of recovery rate and time-to-default, and (3) the possibility to approximate the unknown n distributions by their historical counterparts. Nevertheless, the determination of f_k requires precise information concerning

- the distribution of the potential default date, say $p_{1,h,k}, h = 1, \ldots, H$,

- the distribution of the potential prepayment date, say $p_{2,h,k}, h = 1, \ldots, H-1$,

- the distribution g_k of the recovery rate.

Note that the probabilities $p_{1,h,k} = P$ (a default at h), $h = 1, \ldots, H$, do not sum up to one. Indeed $1 - \sum_{h=1}^{H} p_{1,h,k}$ is the probability of zero potential default during the lifetime of a contract. The same remark applies to the probabilities of potential prepayment.

Recall that the recovery rate was assumed to depend on the contract category, but not on the amount to be recovered, which varies with time-to-default. This assumption has to be changed if one wishes to take into account the fact that the effort needed to recover funds decreases with c_h. This means that the lender puts less effort into recovering an unpaid balance of a small amount.

The individual P&L distribution f_k admits a point mass at $B_{0,k}(mh + c_h), h = 1, \ldots, H$, and is continuous between the points given earlier in the text. More precisely, the discrete component is

$$P_k[X = B_{0,k}(mh + c_h)] = P_k[\text{prepayment at } h, \text{default after } h + 1]$$

$$= p_{2,h,k} \sum_{l \geqslant h+1} p_{1,l,k}, \quad \text{for } h < H;$$

$$P_k[X = B_{0,k}mH] = P_k[\text{no prepayment, no default}]$$

$$= \left(1 - \sum_{l=1}^{H-1} p_{2,l,k}\right)\left(1 - \sum_{l=1}^{H} p_{1,l,k}\right).$$

The continuous component is derived by distinguishing the dates of default:

$$P_k[X \in (x, x + dx)]$$

$$= \sum_{h=1}^{H} P_k[X \in (x, x + dx), \text{ default at } h]$$

$$= \sum_{h=1}^{H} P_k[B_{0,k}(mh + \alpha_h c_h) \in (x, x + dx), \text{ default at } h]$$

$$= \sum_{h=1}^{H} \{P_k[\text{potential default at } h, \text{ potential prepayment after } h],$$

$$P_k[B_{0,k}(mh + \alpha_h c_h) \in (x, x + dx)]\}$$

$$= \sum_{h=1}^{H} \left\{ p_{1,h,k} \sum_{l=h}^{H-1} p_{2,l,k} \frac{1}{B_{0,k}c_h} g_k \left(\frac{x - B_{0,k}mh}{B_{0,k}c_h} \right) \mathbf{1}_{0<((x-B_{0,k}mh)/B_{0,k}c_h)<1} \right\} dx.$$

The continuous component is a mixture of distributions. The number of components in the mixture increases with maturity.

11.2.2   The P&L Distribution for a Credit Portfolio When the Horizon Is Shorter Than the Maturity

Let us propose the following method for evaluation of the P&L distribution when the horizon of VaR is shorter than the maturities of loans in the portfolio. To eliminate most of the incompleteness due to individual heterogeneity, we first define homogeneous categories of credit contracts (with identical initial balance, maturity, interest rate, and contractual monthly payment), and of individuals with almost the same attitude towards default and prepayment. These categories are indexed by k, $k = 1, \ldots, K$. The categories are then partitioned with respect to the dates when the credit contracts were signed, yielding the so-called generations of loans. This leads to a set of cohorts doubly indexed by k and τ, where k is the category index and τ is the date of signature on a credit contract. If the number of contracts in each cohort is sufficiently large (greater than 200–300), most of the incompleteness will be eliminated by computing the arithmetic averages in each group of homogeneous contracts. The averaging will produce aggregate data on default rates, prepayment rates, and recovery rates per cohort. It will also allow for constructing the time series of aggregates that can be used to predict future risks. This approach entails some uncertainty due to unobservable temporal factors (see Section 11.3.2 for discussion on default correlation). To simplify the presentation, we focus on default and disregard prepayments.

11.2.2.1   Default Monitoring

Let us consider a time unit of one semester (equal to six months). For each cohort, we observe the default and recovery rates in all semesters between the beginning of a credit agreement and the current date. Let us denote by $D_k(\tau; h)$, $R_k(\tau; h)$ the default and recovery rates for cohort k, τ at month $\tau + h$; h denotes the age of the contract, that is, the time elapsed since the contract was signed. For each cohort and default or recovery rate, we get a two-way contingency table. The entries in the table can be indexed either by the generation and the current date, or by the generation and

Table 11.1. Default rate by generation and current date.

	Current date					
Generation	97.1	97.2	98.1	98.2	99.1	99.2
97.1	$D(97.1; 1)$	$D(97.1; 2)$	$D(97.1; 3)$	$D(97.1; 4)$		
97.2		$D(97.2; 1)$	$D(97.2; 2)$	$D(97.2; 3)$	$D(97.2; 4)$	
98.1			$D(98.1; 1)$	$D(98.1; 2)$	$D(98.1; 3)$	$D(98.1; 4)$
98.2				$D(98.2; 1)$	$D(98.2; 2)$	$D(98.2; 3)$
99.1					$D(99.1; 1)$	$D(99.1; 2)$
99.2						$D(99.2; 1)$

Table 11.2. Default rate by generation and age.

	Age			
Generation	1	2	3	4
97.1	$D(97.1; 1)$	$D(97.1; 2)$	$D(97.1; 3)$	$D(97.1; 4)$
97.2	$D(97.2; 1)$	$D(97.2; 2)$	$D(97.2; 3)$	$D(97.2; 4)$
98.1	$D(98.1; 1)$	$D(98.1; 2)$	$D(98.1; 3)$	$D(98.1; 4)$
98.2	$D(98.2; 1)$	$D(98.2; 2)$	$D(98.2; 3)$	
99.1	$D(99.1; 1)$	$D(99.1; 2)$		
99.2	$D(99.2; 1)$			

Table 11.3. Default rate by age and current date.

	Current date					
Age	97.1	97.2	98.1	98.2	99.1	99.2
1	$D(97.1; 1)$	$D(97.2; 1)$	$D(98.1; 1)$	$D(98.2; 1)$	$D(99.1; 1)$	$D(99.2; 1)$
2		$D(97.1; 2)$	$D(97.2; 2)$	$D(98.1; 2)$	$D(98.2; 2)$	$D(99.1; 2)$
3			$D(97.1; 3)$	$D(97.2; 3)$	$D(98.1; 3)$	$D(98.2; 3)$
4				$D(97.1; 4)$	$D(97.2; 4)$	$D(98.1; 4)$

the age, or else by the current date and the age. To illustrate these alternative settings, we display in Tables 11.1–11.3 the data on loans with maturity two years. Given that age is counted in semesters, the maximal age of a loan is 4. Only the year and the semester that correspond to the beginning of a contract are marked. The category indexes are omitted for clarity. The most recent observation in the sample, dated 99.2, comes from the second semester of 1999. In practice, Tables 11.2 and 11.3 are easier to read and require less computer memory for storage than Table 11.1. Similar tables can be built for the recovery rates as well.

11.2.2.2 Dynamics of Default Rates

Let us now introduce a dynamic model for aggregate default rates. Formally, we use the logistic representation for aggregate default rates. Among various conceivable specifications, we focus on a model including the autoregressive effects of lagged default, macroeconomic factors, and unobserved heterogeneity.

Due to the presence of the autoregressive component, we need to distinguish between the specification for loans whose age is one semester, and the common specification for loans of higher ages.

Let us consider the specification for loans that are one semester old. Since no information on past default history of the cohort, prior to the sampling period, is available, it has to be approximated by using the basic score for credit granting. Let us denote by $S_{k,\tau}$ and $\sigma^2_{S,k,\tau}$ the average basic score and its dispersion for cohorts k and τ, respectively. For age $h = 1$, the logistic model is

$$l[D_k(\tau; 1)] = a_1 + b_1 l(S_{k,\tau}) + c_1 \sigma^2_{S,k,\tau} + d_1' Z_{\tau+1} + \alpha_1 l[D_k(\tau - 1; 1)] + \varepsilon_k(\tau; 1), \tag{11.4}$$

where the components of Z are macroeconomic variables, $\varepsilon_k(\tau; 1)$ is an error term, and $l(x) = \log[x/(1 - x)]$ denotes the logit transformation.

For ages higher than one, we can introduce an additional autoregressive effect associated with the same cohort plus an effect of the previous generation:

$$l[D_k(\tau; h)] = a_h + b_h l(S_{k,\tau}) + c_h \sigma^2_{S,k,\tau} + d_h' Z_{\tau+h} + \alpha_h l[D_k(\tau - 1; h)]$$
$$+ \beta_h l[D_k(\tau, h - 1)] + \varepsilon_k(\tau, h), \quad h \geqslant 2. \tag{11.5}$$

The joint model in (11.4), (11.5) is completed by specifying the distribution of the error terms $\varepsilon_k(\tau, h)$, k, τ, h varying. We assume independence between the cohorts and the possibility of correlation between ages. More precisely, we assume the following.

Assumption. $[\varepsilon_k(\tau, h), \ h = 1, \ldots, H]$, τ, k varying, are independent, normally distributed, with zero mean and a variance–covariance matrix Σ.

Let us denote by $\hat{a}_h, \hat{b}_h, \ldots, \hat{\beta}_h$ and $\hat{\Sigma}$, the OLS estimators of the age-dependent parameters of the model and by $\hat{\varepsilon}_k(\tau, h)$ the associated residuals.

In model (11.4), (11.5), the individual heterogeneity is assumed to be captured entirely by the individual scores, which act as summary statistics. Therefore, the regression coefficients do not depend on the category. This ensures that a sufficiently large number of observations is available for estimation of the parameters. For example, for estimation of a_1 this number is equal to the number of generations times the number of categories.

11.2.2.3 The Distribution of Future Default Rates

The dynamic model introduced above can be used to simulate the distribution of future default rates. Two cases have to be distinguished depending on whether macro-economic variables are included in the model or not.

Let us first consider the model without macroeconomic explanatory variables, and a given cohort k, τ observed up to the current date t. The default rates are known up to $\tilde{h} = t - \tau$, and have to be predicted for higher ages. These predictions are obtained along the following lines.

Step 1: simulate the unknown error term $\varepsilon_k(\tau, h)$, $h > \tilde{h}$, by drawing in the conditional normal distribution of $\varepsilon_k(\tau, h)$, $h > \tilde{h}$, given $\varepsilon_k(\tau, h)$, $h \leqslant \tilde{h}$, after replacing the variance–covariance matrix Σ by its estimate, and the lagged errors by the associated OLS residuals.

Step 2: if $\varepsilon_k^s(\tau, h)$, $h > \tilde{h}$, denotes a set of simulated error terms, derive simulated future default rates by applying (11.5) recursively, with $\varepsilon_k(\tau, h) = \varepsilon_k^s(\tau, h)$ and using the estimated parameters. The outcomes are values $D_k^s(\tau, h)$, $h > \tilde{h}$.

Step 3: obtain the distribution of future default rates by estimating the sample distribution of simulated default rates from replications $s = 1, \ldots, S$.

When some macroeconomic variables are included in the model, the future default rates cannot be simulated unless the predictions of the future values of these macroeconomic variables are given. For this purpose, an additional model is required in order to represent the dynamics of variables Z. Next, the future values Z_{t+1}^s, Z_{t+2}^s of macroeconomic variables have to be simulated independently of the error, and substituted into equation (11.5) for computation of future default rates. Another, more straightforward, alternative consists of considering various scenarios of future patterns of X. However, since such scenarios are in general deterministic, this approach would eliminate the randomness of future paths. This, in turn, may lead to underestimation of the dispersion of future default rates and of the associated P&L variable.

11.2.2.4 *Improvements*

The methodology discussed so far can be improved in various ways. The approach is illustrated below by a case study of corporate loans in France. In our example, the categories are equivalent to different economic sectors.

(a) The Macroeconomic Covariates.　　It is expected that default depends on some sector-specific macroeconomic covariates. Formally, this means that the regression coefficient d_h may depend on k. The macro variables to be considered are the inflation rate, unemployment rate, index of industrial production, aggregate consumption of households, and gross national product.[4] Of these, the first two are retained in the computations described below.

It is important to accommodate the term structure of default. For this purpose, we distinguish in each year between the default rate of the over-the-counter (OTC) corporate loans issued one year ago, denoted by Y_1, and the default rate of those issued two years ago, denoted by Y_2, and so on. Table 11.4 displays the correlations

---

[4] The last four macroeconomic variables need to be transformed into first-differences of logarithms. The lagged values of any macro variables are used to explain current default.

Table 11.4. Correlations (*p*-values in parentheses) for the period 1987–97.

	Y_1	Y_2	Y_3	Y_4	Unemployment	Inflation
Y_1	1	0.87	0.63	0.39	−0.92	0.76
	(0.00)	(0.00)	(0.04)	(0.22)	(0.00)	(0.01)
Y_2	0.84	1	0.88	0.67	−0.83	0.62
	(0.00)	(0.00)	(0.00)	(0.02)	(0.00)	(0.04)
Y_3	0.63	0.88	1	0.92	−0.64	0.40
	(0.04)	(0.00)	(0.00)	(0.00)	(0.03)	(0.21)
Y_4	0.40	0.67	0.92	1	−0.45	0.26
	(0.22)	(0.02)	(0.00)	(0.00)	(0.16)	(0.44)
Unemployment	−0.92	−0.83	−0.64	−0.45	1	−0.84
	(0.00)	(0.00)	(0.03)	(0.16)	(0.00)	(0.00)
Inflation	0.76	0.62	0.41	0.26	−0.84	1
	(0.01)	(0.04)	(0.21)	(0.44)	(0.00)	(0.00)

between Y_1, Y_2, Y_3, Y_4, the inflation rate, and the unemployment rate. The *p*-values are given in parentheses.

We observe that the correlations decrease in absolute values during the lifetime of a credit and become nonsignificant after two years. We also find positive (respectively, negative) dependence between default and inflation rate (respectively, unemployment rate). All correlations are computed for the period 1987–97.

The large values of the correlations in Table 11.4 could be due to nonstationary features, especially cycles, in the unemployment and inflation rates. Therefore, these results need to be interpreted with caution, as they may be contaminated by the spurious regression effects that arise when some regressors and regressands contain cyclical components. A common cycle analysis of the macro series would provide additional insights. In a preliminary assessment, however, the correlations given above contain sufficient information for comparison of relationships between the macro variables of interest and default. These, in turn, allow us to make appropriate choices of input variables for default-rate predictions. Indeed, the data suggest that past values of unemployment and inflation rates may help predict the current value of the default rate.

The number of corporate loans increased greatly at the beginning of the 1990s, and the structure of corporate credit changed as well. To show the structural change, we report in Table 11.5 the correlations between default and the macroeconomic variables in the period 1977–87.

The inflation rate is no longer significant, while the sign of its relationship with the rate of unemployment became positive.

The effects of macroeconomic variables on default rates can depend on the economic sector. Table 11.6 below displays the significant correlations for the main economic sectors.

Table 11.5. Correlation (*p*-values in parentheses) for the period 1977–87.

	Y_1	Y_2	Y_3	Y_4
Unemployment	0.53	0.79	0.67	0.73
	(0.09)	(0.00)	(0.05)	(0.04)
Inflation	−0.17	−0.37	−0.45	−0.54
	(0.61)	(0.28)	(0.21)	(0.17)

Table 11.6. Selected macro variables (correlation in parentheses).

Sector	Macro variables
Retail	Unemployment: $Y_1(-0.92)$, $Y_2(-0.83)$ Inflation: $Y_1(0.76)$, $Y_2(0.62)$
Services	Unemployment: $Y_1(-0.87)$, $Y_2(-0.79)$ Inflation: $Y_1(0.86)$, $Y_2(-0.58)$
Manufacturing	Unemployment: $Y_1(-0.53)$, $Y_2(-0.62)$ Inflation: $Y_1(0.73)$, $Y_2(0.52)$
Printing and publishing	Unemployment: $Y_1(-0.65)$, $Y_2(-0.55)$ Inflation: $Y_1(0.54)$
Public sector	Unemployment: $Y_1(-0.65)$, $Y_2(-0.57)$
Construction	Unemployment: $Y_2(-0.68)$
Transportation	Unemployment: $Y_1(-0.75)$, $Y_2(-0.78)$ Inflation: $Y_1(0.62)$, $Y_2(0.66)$
Agriculture	Unemployment: $Y_2(-0.78)$, $Y_3(-0.62)$ Inflation: $Y_1(0.62)$, $Y_2(0.65)$
Self Employed	Unemployment: $Y_2(-0.54)$ Inflation: $Y_2(0.53)$

The macro variables can help predict credit risk, but should not be viewed as necessary inputs into the model. In particular, the presence of macro variables eliminates the possibility of predicting the risk at horizons greater than 2, unless a dynamic model for predicting their own future values is available. Forecasting and dynamic analysis of macro indicators is not among the primary duties of a risk-management service in a bank. For this reason, a risk model based on unobservable dynamic factors, such as the one presented in Section 11.3.3 on stochastic transitions, is preferable.

(b) Constraint on the Parameters. To make the computation of VaR robust, it is recommended that one imposes some constraints on the regression parameters of model (11.5). In our study, the coefficients of explanatory variables b_h, c_h, d_h, α_h, β_h are assumed to be independent of age h. The constants a_h are considered to be

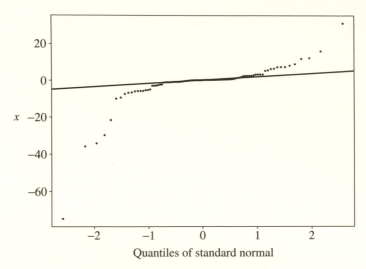

Figure 11.2.   Retail sector, Q–Q plot.

age dependent, and are supposed to capture the variation of default rates during the lifetime of a loan.

(c) Normality of the Error Terms.   The normality assumption concerning the error terms has a strong impact on the computation of VaR. Indeed, the tails of the normal distribution are rather thin, which results in underestimation of the capital requirement (see Remark 11.3). Therefore, it is important to estimate the distribution of residuals in each economic sector, and check if the errors are approximately normal. The empirical results confirm that the error distributions depend on economic sectors. While the normality assumption is not rejected for most sectors, it is clearly violated in the retail sector, since the empirical distribution features skewness and kurtosis much larger than the kurtosis of the Gaussian distribution (which is equal to 3). The Q–Q plot corresponding to the retail sector is provided in Figure 11.2 (the straight line corresponds to a Gaussian distribution). We observe that the tails of the error distribution are much heavier than those of a normal distribution.

To simplify the analysis further, the normality assumption is now imposed on all sectors except retail. Moreover, the structure of dependencies between the retail sector and the other sectors is maintained. Technically the nonnormality of the marginal distribution of errors in the retail sector is accommodated by replacing these errors by well-chosen nonlinear transformations.

(d) Specification of the Recovery Rate.   Finally, it may be insightful to take into account the uncertainty of the recovery rate in a given sector. Instead of using a logistic model, it is preferable to model the recovery rate as a variable with a beta distribution, defined on the interval (0, 1). Next, an autoregressive specification of the recovery rate is obtained by introducing a time-varying, stochastic mean of

the beta distribution, and a constant variance. The associated VaR will intuitively increase with the value of the variance parameter, which may strongly depend on the category of firms. This type of a model for the recovery rate is implemented in the McKinsey methodology, and was suggested by the Basle Committee.

11.3 Corporate Bond Portfolio

Firms can obtain credits directly from banks (OTC) or by issuing bonds tradable on financial markets. In the previous subsection, we considered a portfolio of corporate loans granted by a bank. This portfolio generally consists of a large number of loans, offered to a large number of heterogenous firms. In order to examine the evolution of default rate in each class, the firms are divided into homogeneous classes with respect to risk.

The methodology for corporate bond portfolios is very different. The corporate bond portfolios generally comprise a rather small number of large-size firms. The approach described in the previous subsection is not applicable to the corporate bond portfolios, because it requires the knowledge of histories of observed default rates for a large number of similar firms, which is not available.

11.3.1 *Informational Content of Bond Prices*

Predictions of future failure rates can be obtained indirectly from market prices of bonds at different maturities, along the lines of Section 6.4.2, which assumes the absence of risk premiums on default occurrences.[5] Let us recall how information on future default can be inferred from the spread of interest rates, which is the difference between the rate of a corporate bond and the rate of the Treasury bill (T-bill) with the same maturity.

Let us consider bonds with a fixed coupon and no payment *in fine* (i.e., at the maturity of the contract). We denote by $\gamma_{j,h,t}$ the yield on the bond of corporate j with maturity h, and by $r_{h,t}$ the rate of the T-bill with maturity h evaluated at date t. The following equality is approximately satisfied:

$$\frac{[1+\gamma_{j,h,t}]^h - 1}{\gamma_{j,h,t}[1+\gamma_{j,h,t}]^h} = \frac{\hat{S}_{j,t}(1)}{1+r_{h,t}} + \cdots + \frac{\hat{S}_{j,t}(h)}{(1+r_{h,t})^h}, \quad h = 1, \ldots, H,$$

where $\hat{S}_{j,t}$ denotes the conditional survivor function of corporate j evaluated at date t. This is a recursive system that yields the market values of the survivor function of times to failure. This implied survivor function can be used to analyse the future payoffs for a portfolio of corporate bonds.

Let us consider a portfolio of fixed income securities concerning J different firms. At date t the contractual future payoffs for bonds of firm j are $m_{j,h,t}, h = 1, \ldots, H$,

---

[5] This approach can be extended to include risk premiums (see, for example, Lando 1998; Gourieroux et al. 2006). This extension is beyond the scope of this book.

say. The aggregate cash flow at h for the whole portfolio is then given by

$$\sum_{j=1}^{J} m_{j,h,t} Z_{j,h},$$

$$\text{where } Z_{j,h} = \begin{cases} 1 & \text{if the failure of firm } j \text{ arises after date } t+h+1, \\ 0 & \text{otherwise.} \end{cases}$$

The simulation at date t of the portfolio cash flow is performed by assuming that the default indicators $(Z_{j,h}, \ h = 1, \ldots, H)$ are independent across firms, with the following respective distributions: $P_t[Z_{j,h} = 1] = \hat{S}_{j,t}(h) - \hat{S}_{j,t}(h-1)$. For each simulation we then compute the value of the cash flow at $t+1$ (say) by discounting the sequence of payoffs with the T-bill forward rates. The final outcome is the approximation of the distribution of the future value by the sample distribution of a large number of simulations. This approach has to be used with caution, as it implicitly assumes that the price of default and the probability of default are identical.[6]

11.3.2 Default Correlation

In Section 11.2, we saw the model of default rates for a credit portfolio that included macroeconomic explanatory variables. The macroeconomic variables, especially the business cycle, also play an important role in determining the default rates in a portfolio of corporate bonds. However, as mentioned before, the presence of explanatory macroeconomic variables complicates the prediction of future default rates, since it requires the knowledge of future values of macroeconomic variables, which are not available. To circumvent this difficulty, instead of the observable macroeconomic variables, one can consider unobservable macro factors, which follow their own intrinsic dynamics. Although such a model is technically more difficult to estimate, it has several advantages. In particular, it allows for recovering the number and paths of "unobserved" factors *ex post*, and provides predictions that are more robust with respect to specification errors. A specification error could arise from assuming too few factors or from including a wrong explanatory variable. However, the main advantage of the unobserved factor model is the possibility of examining the so-called *default correlation*. Intuitively, a shock to a macro factor has an impact on the default risk of all firms. When such a shock is not observable, its effect is perceived as risk correlation. The existence of risk correlation (also called *contagion*) needs to be accounted for in risk management, especially in the determination of the mandatory capital reserve. If the default risks of two firms are positively correlated, the capital required to hedge a basket default swap written on two firms (which pays \$1 if both firms are still alive at date $t + H$) will be underestimated if the defaults of the firms are traded separately. The aim of this section is to present some basic results

---

[6] Or equivalently that the risk-neutral distribution is equal to the historical one.

on default correlation. For ease of exposition we consider a "static" unobservable macro factor, that is, a macro factor without serial dependence. In this framework, we discuss default prediction for period $(t, t + 1)$.

11.3.2.1 Stochastic Default Intensity

Let us consider a population of n firms (in a given fixed period of time) and denote by $Y_i, i = 1, \ldots, n$, the indicator of default of firm i:

$$Y_i = \begin{cases} 1 & \text{if default occurs during the fixed period of time,} \\ 0 & \text{otherwise.} \end{cases}$$

Recall that in Chapters 2 and 3 the population of firms was said to be homogeneous if

(A1) the variables $Y_i, i = 1, \ldots, n$, are independent;

(A2) the variables $Y_i, i = 1, \ldots, n$, have identical distributions.

This definition of a homogeneous population is quite restrictive, since it disregards the possibility of dependence between the defaults of several firms. A more general definition of a homogeneous population is as follows.

Definition 11.4. The population of firms $i = 1, \ldots, n$ is homogeneous if the distribution of $Y_1, \ldots, Y_n$ and the distribution of $Y_{\sigma(1)}, \ldots, Y_{\sigma(n)}$ are identical for any permutation σ of the set of firms.

When the condition of invariance by permutation is satisfied, the variables $Y_1, \ldots, Y_n$ are said to be *equidependent* or *exchangeable*. The following property is an important result established in the theory of equidependent variables (see, for example, Gourieroux and Monfort 2002; Frey and McNeil 2003).

Proposition 11.5. *When n is large, the variables $Y_1, \ldots, Y_n$ are equidependent if, and only if, there exists a variable F on $[0, 1]$ such that $Y_1, \ldots, Y_n$ are independent, identically Bernoulli distributed $\mathcal{B}(1, F)$, conditional on F.*

Thus, equidependence requires a stochastic (that is, a random and not deterministic) probability of default F. The randomness of the default probability F modifies the joint distribution of individual firm defaults. Let us give some examples of default distributions when the stochastic intensity is integrated out.

(i) **Marginal distribution of default.** Let us consider the default distribution of one firm. The default indicator for each firm has a Bernoulli distribution $\mathcal{B}(1, p)$ with parameter p:

$$p = P(Y_i = 1) = EP[Y_i = 1 \mid F] = E(F).$$

According to this expression, parameter p is the expectation of the stochastic probability of default.

(ii) Bivariate distribution of default. This is the joint distribution of default indicators for two firms. Let us consider two firms, 1 and 2. We obtain

$$P[Y_1 = 1, \ Y_2 = 1] = E P(Y_1 = 1, \ Y_2 = 1 \mid F)$$

$$= E(P[Y_1 = 1 \mid F]P[Y_2 = 1 \mid F])$$

$$\text{(since } Y_1 \text{ and } Y_2 \text{ are independent, conditional on } F\text{)}$$

$$= E(F^2),$$

and, similarly,

$$P(Y_1 = 1, \ Y_2 = 0) = P(Y_1 = 0, \ Y_2 = 1) = E[F(1 - F)],$$

$$P(Y_1 = 0, \ Y_2 = 0) = E[(1 - F)^2].$$

In particular, the correlation between default indicators, called the *default correlation*, is

$$\rho = \text{Corr}(Y_1, Y_2) = \frac{E(Y_1 Y_2) - E Y_1 E Y_2}{\sqrt{V Y_1}\sqrt{V Y_2}}$$

$$= \frac{P(Y_1 = 1, \ Y_2 = 1) - P(Y_1 = 1)P(Y_2 = 1)}{P(Y_1 = 1)(1 - P[Y_1 = 1])}$$

$$= \frac{E(F^2) - (E(F))^2}{E(F)(1 - E(F))} = \frac{V(F)}{E(F)(1 - E(F))}.$$

Default indicators are correlated whenever $V(F) \neq 0$, that is, if the default probability is stochastic.

11.3.2.2   The Factor Probit Model

In the previous section, we provided the derivation of a dichotomous qualitative model from a Gaussian quantitative model for a latent variable. A similar approach is followed below. Let us consider latent (unobservable) quantitative variables Y_i^*, $i = 1, \ldots, n$, such that

$$Y_i^* = \alpha F + \gamma u_i^*, \quad i = 1, \ldots, n,$$

where $F, u_1^*, \ldots, u_n^*$ are independent standard normal variables, and assume that default is observed when the latent variable Y_i^* is greater than some threshold c (for example $c = 0$):

$$Y_i = 1, \quad \text{if and only if } Y_i^* > c.$$

Conditional on factor F, the dichotomous variables $Y_1, \ldots, Y_n$ are independent with identical Bernoulli distribution and $P[Y_1 = 1 \mid F] = \Phi((\alpha F - c)/\gamma)$. This probability defines a probit model with unobservable variable F.

For an unobservable variable F, the latent variables Y_i^*, $i = 1, \ldots, n$, satisfy the equidependence condition, which in turn implies equidependence of default indicators. We examine this relationship below.

The latent variables are jointly Gaussian with zero mean and variance–covariance matrix such that

$$V Y_i^* = \alpha^2 + \gamma^2, \quad \text{Cov}(Y_i^*, Y_j^*) = \alpha^2, \quad \text{if } i \neq j.$$

Therefore the *latent correlation* is given by

$$\rho^* = \text{Corr}(Y_i^*, Y_j^*) = \frac{\alpha^2}{\alpha^2 + \gamma^2}.$$

The latent correlation is nonnegative and increases with the coefficient α of the factor.

In all probit models, the parameters are identifiable up to a scale factor. Therefore, the identifying restrictions need to be imposed in our model as well. We use the following identifying restriction: $\alpha^2 + \gamma^2 = 1$.

Under this restriction we obtain

$$Y_i^* = \sqrt{\rho^*} F + \sqrt{1 - \rho^*} u_i^*, \quad i = 1, \dots, n.$$

The default distribution for one firm becomes

$$P[Y_i = 1] = P[Y_i^* > c] = \Phi(-c) = p_c \quad \text{(say)}.$$

The joint distribution of default for two firms becomes

$$\begin{aligned}
P[Y_i = 1, \ Y_j = 1] &= P[Y_i^* > c, \ Y_j^* > c] \\
&= P[-Y_i^* < -c, \ -Y_j^* < -c] \\
&= \Psi(-c, -c, \rho^*),
\end{aligned}$$

where $\Psi(-c, -c, \rho^*)$ denotes the bivariate c.d.f. of a pair of Gaussian variables, with zero means, variances equal to one, and correlation ρ^*. Finally, we obtain

$$P[Y_i = 1, \ Y_j = 1] = \Psi[\Phi^{-1}(p_c), \Phi^{-1}(p_c), \rho^*].$$

The joint probability allows us to compute the default correlation. The default correlation is

$$\rho = \text{Corr}(Y_i, Y_j) = \frac{P[Y_i = 1, \ Y_j = 1] - P[Y_i = 1]P[Y_j = 1]}{\sqrt{P[Y_i = 1](1 - P[Y_i = 1])}\sqrt{P[Y_j = 1](1 - P[Y_j = 1])}}.$$

We obtain

$$\rho = \frac{\Psi[\Phi^{-1}(p_c), \Phi^{-1}(p_c), \rho^*] - p_c^2}{p_c(1 - p_c)}. \tag{11.6}$$

From the last expression, we see that the default correlation depends on the latent correlation ρ^* and the average level of risk p_c. The relationship defined by (11.6) is represented graphically in Figure 11.3. This graph displays the joint evolution of latent and default correlations for different values of the marginal probability of default for two firms in the same class of risk.

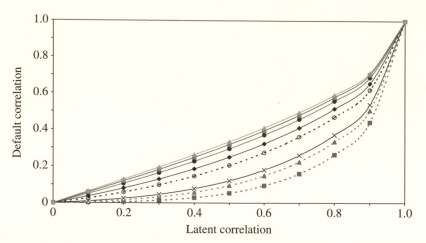

Figure 11.3. Relationship between latent correlation and default correlation (for different levels of default probability). Key for the lines, reading from top to bottom: $p_c = 0.5$, $p_c = 0.3$, $p_c = 0.3$, $p_c = 0.1$, $p_c = 0.05$, $p_c = 0.01$, $p_c = 0.005$, $p_c = 0.001$.

For any value of marginal probability of default p_c, the default correlation is a convex increasing function of the latent correlation, and takes the value 0 at 0 (respectively, 1 at 1). In particular, the default correlation is always smaller than the latent correlation and the difference between the two correlations can be quite large. For example, in the class of risk of firms with marginal probability of default equal to $p_c = 1\%$, latent correlation $\rho^* = 20\% = 0.2$ (respectively, $\rho^* = 0.1$) implies a ten times smaller observed default correlation $\rho = 2.4\%$ (respectively, $\rho = 0.95\%$).

11.3.2.3 The Basle II Proposal

Proposal II of the Basle Committee on Banking Supervision (2004) recommends a factor probit based evaluation of default risk for firms in each class of risk determined by the marginal default probability p_c. The same document of the Basle Committee also defines the latent correlation as the following function of the marginal probability of default:

$$\rho_c^* = 0.12\left[\frac{1 - \exp(-50p_c)}{1 - \exp(-50)}\right] + 0.24\left[1 - \frac{1 - \exp(-50p_c)}{1 - \exp(-50)}\right]. \tag{11.7}$$

We display ρ_c^* as a function of p_c in Figure 11.4. The associated latent correlation ρ_c^* is a decreasing function of marginal probability of default p_c.

Under the additional restriction (11.7) the default correlation becomes a function of the marginal probability of default only (see Figure 11.5).

Formula (11.7) was established by consensus of the Basle Committee members in order to impose a worldwide consistent capital charge requirement. However, it does not seem to have been determined by empirical investigation. The evidence based on financial data and revealed in several recent papers (see, for example,

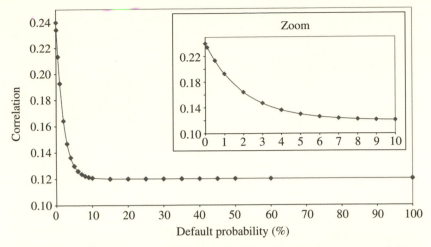

Figure 11.4. Basle II latent correlation as a function of marginal probability of default.

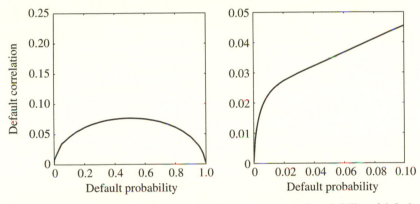

Figure 11.5. Default correlation as a function of the marginal probability of default.

Foulcher et al. 2006; Rosch 2005) does not confirm the adequacy of the functional form chosen by the Basle Committee.

As an illustration, we report in Table 11.7 the estimated latent correlations by economic sector and three classes of risk, from the lowest risk class 1 to the highest risk class 3.

The estimated correlations (in %) are much lower than the values computed using the Basle Committee formula. This difference suggests that the capital charge should be significantly lower than the one required by the Basle Committee. Moreover, the latent correlations do not necessarily decrease with the marginal probability of default, as observed from the diagonal elements for economic sectors. Also, Table 11.7 provides latent correlations for two firms in the same economic sector but in different risk classes. These correlations are sometimes larger than the latent correlations for two firms in the same class of risk, but most of them are a similar

Table 11.7. Latent correlations by economic sector and risk category (%).

		1	2	3
Retail trade	1	0.80	0.63	0.63
	2	0.63	1.50	0.34
	3	0.63	0.34	0.93
Wholesale trade	1	0.22	0.21	0.24
	2	0.21	0.60	0.50
	3	0.24	0.50	1.32
Manufacturing industry	1	0.31	0.31	0.30
	2	0.31	0.60	0.52
	3	0.30	0.52	0.62
Transport	1	0.60	0.30	0.82
	2	0.30	1.30	0.70
	3	0.82	0.70	1.50
Construction	1	1.33	1.30	0.80
	2	1.30	1.90	1.21
	3	0.80	1.21	1.02
Hotels and restaurants	1	2.35	0.50	1.64
	2	0.50	3.90	2.91
	3	1.64	2.91	3.80

size. This finding is important because, according to the Basle Committee proposal, latent correlations of default for two firms in different risk classes are set equal to zero. In conclusion, the appropriate specification for default correlations has not yet been determined.

11.3.3 Stochastic Transition Model

The *stochastic transition models* (also called *migration models*) are natural extensions of the transition models presented in Chapter 8 that include the default correlations discussed in the previous section. By considering default correlation, we examined the dependence between risk histories of firms formed by sequences $Y_{i,t}$, $t = 1, \ldots, T$, where the observed qualitative variable $Y_{i,t}$ takes only two values: 0 if firm i is still alive at time t, and 1 if firm i has defaulted before or at time t. The stochastic intensity model and the factor probit model can be extended to a more detailed classification of firms. Instead of distinguishing between the firms that have defaulted and those that have not, we can rank the firms with respect to their creditworthiness. In practice, the ranking of firms into $k = 1, \ldots, K$ risk categories is carried out systematically by rating agencies such as Standard & Poor's and Moody's. The rating agencies rank firms into eight or more credit quality categories, the lowest category being default. For example, the most concise Standard & Poor's credit risk ranking is as follows: AAA, AA, A, BBB, BB, B, CCC, D (for default).

In the first part of this section, we introduce a simple model to define the migration correlations, which measure the probability of joint upgrades or downgrades of firms in a given rating class. In the second part of the section, we show the ordered factor probit model with dynamic factors.

11.3.3.1 Migration Correlation

The rating histories of firms are formed by their credit quality ratings at different points in time. These are denoted by $(Y_{i,t})$, $t = 1, \ldots, T$, for n firms indexed by $i = 1, \ldots, n$. If, instead of qualitative indicators of rating categories AAA through D, we use quantitative indicators $k = 1, \ldots, 8$, a firm's history may for example be formed by the following sequence: 111223 (which stands for three AAA ratings, followed by two consecutive AA, and then an A). We wish to relax the assumptions of Chapter 8, which imposed independence and a homogeneous Markov chain structure of individual firm histories. In particular, those assumptions imply identical transition matrix P for all times and firms. Therefore, below we rely on the following assumptions.

Assumption (A1). The individual histories $(Y_{i,t}, t = 1, \ldots, T, i = 1, \ldots, n)$ are independent, conditional on some factor process (F_t).

Assumption (A2). Conditional on the factor process (F_t), the individual histories are identically distributed and form Markov chains with transition matrices $P_{t,t+1} = P(F_{t+1})$ for period $[t, t+1]$, which depend on the factor.

Assumption (A3). The factor values $F_t, t = 1, \ldots, T$, are independent and identically distributed.

The factor can be multivariate. From now on, for ease of exposition, we assume that the factor is equal to the transition probability matrix itself, $F_t = P_{t-1,t}$. Recall that the entries in the first row of the $P_{t-1,t}$ matrix are the probabilities that firm i remains in class AAA (denoted 1), moves from AAA to AA, and so on. The entries in the second row of the $P_{t-1,t}$ matrix are the probabilities that firm i migrates from AA to AAA, remains in AA, and so on. In the proposed setup, all transition probabilities become random variables and form one multivariate factor F_t of dimension K by K.

As in Section 11.3.2 we also assume that the factor is unobservable. Under Assumptions (A1)–(A3) it is possible to show the following (see Gagliardini and Gourieroux 2005a).

(i) Any individual history $(Y_{i,t}, t = 1, \ldots, T)$ is a homogeneous Markov chain. Its transition matrix is a (K, K) matrix $Q^{(1)}$ with elements

$$
\begin{aligned}
q_{j,k}^{(1)} &= P[Y_{i,t} = j \mid Y_{i,t-1} = k] \\
&= E\{P[Y_{i,t} = j \mid Y_{i,t-1} = k, \ F_t] \mid Y_{i,t-1} = k\} \\
&= E[p_{j,k}(F_t)], \quad \forall j, k.
\end{aligned}
$$

Therefore,

$$Q^{(1)} = E(P_{t,t+1}). \tag{11.8}$$

(ii) Similarly, any pair of individual histories $(Y_{i,t}, Y_{j,t}), t = 1, \dots, T$, is also a homogeneous Markov chain. Its transition matrix is a (K^2, K^2) matrix $Q^{(2)}$.

The elements in $Q^{(2)}$ are probabilities of joint transitions for two firms. We have

$$
\begin{aligned}
q^{(2)}_{(j_1, j_2),(k_1, k_2)} &= P[Y_{i,t} = j_1, \ Y_{j,t} = j_2 \mid Y_{i,t-1} = k_1, \ Y_{j,t-1} = k_2] \\
&= E\{P[Y_{i,t} = j_1, \ Y_{j,t} = j_2 \mid Y_{i,t-1} = k_1, \ Y_{j,t-1} = k_2, \ F_t] \\
&\qquad\qquad\qquad\qquad\qquad\qquad\qquad \mid Y_{i,t-1} = k_1, \ Y_{j,t-1} = k_2\} \\
&= E[p_{j_1, k_1}(F_t) p_{j_2, k_2}(F_t)], \quad \forall j, k.
\end{aligned}
$$

Thus,

$$Q^{(2)} = E(P_{t,t+1} \otimes P_{t,t+1}), \tag{11.9}$$

where $P_{t,t+1} \otimes P_{t,t+1}$ stands for the tensor product of $P_{t,t+1}$ with itself. The transition probabilities $p_{j,k}$ are influenced by common factors. Therefore, in general,

$$q^{(2)}_{(j_1, j_2),(k_1, k_2)} \neq q^{(1)}_{j_1, k_1} q^{(1)}_{j_2, k_2}.$$

This reflects the so-called *migration dependence*. Migration correlations can be defined in a way similar to default correlations. The *migration correlation* for a joint transition $(j_1, k_1), (j_2, k_2)$ is

$$\rho^2_{(j_1, j_2),(k_1, k_2)} = \frac{q^{(2)}_{(j_1, j_2),(k_1, k_2)} - q^{(1)}_{j_1, k_1} q^{(1)}_{j_2, k_2}}{\sqrt{q^{(1)}_{j_1, k_1}(1 - q^{(1)}_{j_1, k_1})}\sqrt{q^{(1)}_{j_2, k_2}(1 - q^{(1)}_{j_2, k_2})}}. \tag{11.10}$$

The number of migration correlations is quite large. Some correlations are systematically computed and reported by the rating agencies. These are

(i) the upgrade correlations, $\rho^2_{(k_1-1, k_1),(k_2-1, k_2)}$, $\forall k_1, k_2$;

(ii) the downgrade correlations, $\rho^2_{(k_1+1, k_1),(k_2+1, k_2)}$, $\forall k_1, k_2$;

(iii) the default correlations, when the firms are initially in different risk classes, $\rho^2_{(K, k_1),(K, k_2)}$, $\forall k_1, k_2$.

Tables 11.8–11.10 are examples of migration correlation tables.

11.3.3.2 Dynamic Factor Probit Model

The assumption of serially independent factors which underlies the definition and computation of migration correlations is not supported by the available data (see, for example, Gagliardini and Gourieroux 2005a,b; Feng et al. 2004). The main reason (but not the only one) is the influence of the business cycle. To account for both cross-sectional dependence and serial dependence in a unified framework, we

Table 11.8. Upgrade correlations.

	7	6	5	4	3	2	1	0
7	—	—	—	—	—	—	—	—
6	—	0.0018	0.0013	0.0005	0.0000	0.0000	−0.0006	—
5	—	0.0013	0.0023	0.0017	0.0012	−0.0001	−0.0010	—
4	—	0.0005	0.0017	0.0017	0.0014	0.0001	−0.0010	—
3	—	0.0000	0.0012	0.0014	0.0016	0.0002	−0.0006	—
2	—	0.0000	−0.0001	0.0001	0.0002	0.0008	0.0004	—
1	—	−0.0006	−0.0010	−0.0010	−0.0006	0.0004	0.0020	—
0	—	—	—	—	—	—	—	—

Table 11.9. Downgrade correlations.

	7	6	5	4	3	2	1	0
7	0.0021	0.0013	0.0011	0.0008	0.0006	0.0000	−0.0004	—
6	0.0013	0.0011	0.0010	0.0011	0.0009	0.0007	0.0003	—
5	0.0011	0.0010	0.0016	0.0019	0.0017	0.0016	0.0003	—
4	0.0008	0.0011	0.0019	0.0027	0.0024	0.0026	0.0010	—
3	0.0006	0.0009	0.0017	0.0024	0.0024	0.0025	0.0011	—
2	0.0000	0.0007	0.0016	0.0026	0.0025	0.0034	0.0011	—
1	−0.004	0.0003	0.0003	0.0010	0.0011	0.0011	0.0031	—
0	—	—	—	—	—	—	—	—

Table 11.10. Default correlations for two firms in the wholesale sector; the row and column numbers denote the initial rating classes of the two firms.

	7	6	5	4	3	2	1	0
7	0.0004	0.0002	0.0002	0.0000	0.0000	0.0000	0.0000	—
6	0.0002	0.0004	0.0002	0.0002	0.0002	0.0000	0.0000	—
5	0.0002	0.0002	0.0003	0.0001	0.0002	−0.0001	0.0003	—
4	0.0000	0.0002	0.0001	0.0003	0.0002	0.0002	0.0005	—
3	0.0000	0.0002	0.0002	0.0002	0.0006	−0.0003	0.0009	—
2	0.0000	0.0000	−0.0001	0.0002	−0.0003	0.0006	0.0000	—
1	0.0000	0.0000	0.0003	0.0005	0.0009	0.0000	0.0031	—
0	—	—	—	—	—	—	—	—

extend the factor probit model introduced in Section 11.3.2. The observed ratings are obtained by discretizing the latent quantitative scores:

$$Y_{i,t} = k \quad \text{if and only if } a_{k-1} < S_{i,t} < a_k, \tag{11.11}$$

where $a_1 < \cdots < a_{K-1}$ are unknown deterministic thresholds.

For one given firm, the current value of the score at time t is determined by the previous rating at $t - 1$:

$$S_{i,t} = \alpha_l + \beta_l' F_t + \sigma_l \epsilon_{i,t} \quad \text{if } Y_{i,t-1} = l, \tag{11.12}$$

where F_t denotes the common factor and the $\epsilon_{i,t}$ are the idiosyncratic errors, assumed to be independent and standard normal, conditional on factor process (F_t). The expected value of score α_l, its sensitivity with respect to the factor β_l, and its volatility σ_l depend on the previous rating.

The model is completed by specifying the factor dynamics. The factor process is assumed to be the Gaussian vector autoregressive (VAR) process of order 1:

$$F_t = A F_{t-1} + \eta_t, \tag{11.13}$$

where (η_t) is a Gaussian multivariate white noise. Under the factor specification given above, it is easy to compute the transition probabilities conditional on the factor path. We get

$$
\begin{aligned}
p_{k,l,t-1,t} &= P[Y_{i,t} = k \mid Y_{i,t-1} = l, \ (F_t)] \\
&= P[a_{k-1} < S_{i,t} < a_k \mid Y_{i,t-1} = l, \ (F_t)] \\
&= P[a_{k-1} < \alpha_l + \beta_l' F_t + \sigma_l \epsilon_{i,t} < a_k \mid Y_{i,t-1} = l, \ F_t] \\
&= \Phi\left(\frac{a_k - \alpha_l - \beta_l' F_t}{\sigma_l}\right) - \Phi\left(\frac{a_{k-1} - \alpha_l - \beta_l' F_t}{\sigma_l}\right).
\end{aligned}
$$

This expression determines the selection probabilities in an ordered probit model (see Chapter 9) with unobserved explanatory variables F_t. The dynamic factor probit model involves the following parameters:

(i) the thresholds a_k, $k = 1, \ldots, K - 1$, which determine the ratings;

(ii) the parameters defining the score dynamics of firms, α_l, β_l, σ_l;

(iii) the parameter A, which characterizes the factor dynamics.

The estimation of the dynamic factor model from migration data is rather easy whenever the homogeneous classes of risk contain a sufficient number of firms. Indeed, a large cross-sectional dimension contributes to the consistency of the unobserved factor estimators. In particular, the model can be linearized, and next estimated in the linear form by the Kalman filter method (see Gagliardini and Gourieroux 2005a; Feng et al. 2004). However, the parameter estimates in the linear representation are not equally accurate:

(i) The estimated parameters α_l, β_l, σ_l, a_k converge at speed $\sqrt{nT}$, where n is the cross-sectional dimension and T the time-series dimension.

(ii) The estimated macroparameter A converges at a slow rate $\sqrt{T}$, which depends on the time-series dimension only.

(iii) The predicted factor values $\hat{F}_t$ converge at rate $\sqrt{n}$, which depends on the cross-sectional dimension only.

Once the dynamic factor model is estimated, it can be used for credit risk analysis for any type of corporate bond portfolio at any horizon. Indeed, it is easy to simulate the ratings at $t + h$, say, given the ratings at time t. The simulation of future ratings is performed as follows.

Step 1. Simulate the future values of $F : F^s_{t+1}, \ldots, F^s_{t+h}$ given the current one (or its estimator $\hat{F}_t$) and the autoregressive formula of the factor.

Step 2. Draw the errors independently: $\epsilon^s_{i,t+1}, \ldots, \epsilon^s_{i,t+h}, i = 1, \ldots, n$.

Step 3. Compute the simulated scores recursively: $S : S^s_{i,t+1}, \ldots, S^s_{i,t+h}, i = 1, \ldots, n$.

Step 4. Find the associated ratings, $Y^s_{i,t+h}, i = 1, \ldots, n$, by discretization.

This approach can be used, for example, to analyze how migration correlations and capital requirements depend on the horizon and on the initial structure of ratings in the credit portfolio.

11.4 Concluding Remarks

The Basle Committee established a set of guidelines in order to coordinate the efforts of banks and financial institutions towards risk management and control. The VaR is the mandatory rule for determining the capital requirement for a portfolio at risk in a fixed holding period, discussed in the first part of the chapter. A more recent risk measure is CreditVaR, which concerns a portfolio of credits, defined as the quantile of the distribution of future portfolio value (P&L distribution). An important issue in this context is determination of the P&L distribution, which should account for (i) the heterogeneity of individual contracts, (ii) the dynamics of individual risks, (iii) migration correlation, and (iv) the difficulty in pricing a corporate bond in an incomplete market framework. In the second part of the chapter, we gave some hints on the solutions to problems encountered in this area. The work on issues related to risk on credit portfolios is an important domain of ongoing research. Among the references that follow, readers will find several applied papers, which describe the existing problems and some theoretical work providing new modeling methods.

References

Albanese, C. 1997. Credit exposure, diversification risk and coherent VaR. University of Toronto Discussion Paper.

Altman, E. I., and D. L. Kao. 1992. Rating drift in high yield bonds. *Journal of Fixed Income* 2:15–20.

Artzner, P., F. Delbaen, J. Eber, and D. Heath. 1997. Thinking coherently. *Risk* 10:68–71.

Artzner, P., F. Delbaen, J. Eber, and D. Heath. 1999. Coherent measures of risk. *Mathematical Finance* 9:203–28.

Bangia, A., F. Diebold, A. Kronimus, C. Schlagen, and T. Schuermann. 2002. Ratings migration and business cycle, with application to credit portfolio stress testing. *Journal of Banking and Finance* 26:445–74.

Basle Committee on Banking Supervision. 2003. The new Basle capital accord. Third Consultative Document (available at www.bis.org/bcbs/cp3full.pdf).

Basle Committee on Banking Supervision. 2004. Modifications to the capital treatment for expected and unexpected credit losses (available at www.bis.org/publ/bcbs104.pdf).

Bassi, F., P. Embrechts, and M. Kafetzaki. 1997. Risk management and quantile estimation. In *Practical Guide to Heavy Tails* (ed. R. Adler, R. Feldman, and M. Taqqu). Boston, MA: Birkhauser.

Black, F., and J. Cox. 1976. Valuing corporate securities: some effects of bond indenture provisions. *Journal of Finance* 31:351–67.

Brady, B., and R. Bos. 2002. Record default in 2001. The result of poor credit quality and a weak economy. Standard & Poor's Technical Report (February 2002).

Brady, B., D. Vazza, and R. J. Bos. 2003. Ratings performance 2002: default, transition, recovery, and spreads. Standard & Poor's Technical Paper.

Carey, M., and M. Hrycay. 2001. Parameterizing credit risk models with rating data. *Journal of Banking and Finance* 25:197–270.

Carty, L. 1997. Moody's rating migration and credit quality correlation, 1920–96. Moody's Investor Service Technical Report (July 1997).

Credit Suisse Financial Products. 1997. CreditRisk+: technical manual. CSFP (Financial Markets) Discussion Paper.

De Servigny, A., and O. Renault. 2002. Default correlation: empirical evidence. Standard & Poor's Technical Report (September 2002).

Dowd, K. 1998. *Beyond Value at Risks: The New Science of Risk Management*. Wiley.

Duffie, D., and J. Pan. 1997. An overview of Value at Risk. *Journal of Derivatives* 4:7–49.

Embrechts, P., A. McNeil, and D. Straumann. 2002. Correlation and dependency in risk management: properties and pitfalls. In *Risk Management, Value-at-Risk and Beyond* (ed. M. Dempster), 176–223. Cambridge University Press.

Feng, D., C. Gourieroux, and J. Jasiak. 2004. The ordered qualitative model for credit rating transitions. CREF Discussion Paper.

Foulcher, S., C. Gouriéroux, and A. Tiomo. 2004. Term structure of defaults and ratings. *Insurance and Risk Management* 72:207–76.

Foulcher, S., C. Gouriéroux, and A. Tiomo. 2006. Latent variable approach to modelling dependence of credit risks: application to French firms and implications for regulatory capital. *Annales d'Economie et Statistiques*, forthcoming.

Frey, R., and A. McNeil. 2003. Dependent defaults in models of portfolio credit risk. *Journal of Risk* 6:59–62.

Gagliardini, P., and C. Gouriéroux. 2005a. Stochastic migration models. *Journal of Financial Econometrics* 3:188–226.

Gagliardini, P., and C. Gouriéroux. 2005b. Migration correlation: definition and consistent estimation. *Journal of Banking and Finance* 29:865–94.

Gourieroux, C., and J. Jasiak. 2000. *Financial Econometrics*. Princeton University Press.

Gourieroux, C., and J. Jasiak. 2004. Value at Risk. In *Handbook of Financial Econometrics*, forthcoming.

Gourieroux, C., and A. Monfort. 2002. Equidependence in duration models. CREST Discussion Paper.

Gourieroux, C., A. Monfort, and V. Polimenis. 2006. Affine model for credit risk analysis. *Journal of Financial Econometrics* 4:494–530.

Gupton, G., C. Finger, and M. Bhatia. 1997. Creditmetrics: technical document. JPMorgan Technical Report.

Hamilton, D., R. Cantor, and S. Ou. 2002. Default and recovery rates of corporate bond issuers: a statistical review of Moody's ratings performance 1970–2001. Moody's Working Paper.

Jarrow, R., and S. Turnbull. 1992. Drawing the analogy. *Risk Magazine* 5:63–71.

Jarrow, R., and S. Turnbull. 1995. Pricing derivatives on financial securities subject to credit risk. *Journal of Finance* 50:53–85.

Jorion, P. 1997. *Value at Risk: The New Benchmark for Controlling Market Risk*. Chicago, IL: Irwin.

JPMorgan. 1996. *Risk Metrics Technical Document*, 4th edn. New York: JPMorgan.

JPMorgan. 1997. *CreditMetrics Technical Document*. New York: JPMorgan.

Kim, I., K. Ramaswamy, and S. Sundaresan. 1993. Does default risk affect the valuation of corporate bonds? A contingent claims model. *Financial Management* Autumn:117–31.

Lando, D. 1998. On Cox processes and credit risky securities. *Review of Derivatives Research* 2:99–120.

Lando, D., and T. Skodeberg. 2002. Analyzing rating transitions and rating drift with continuous observations. *Journal of Banking and Finance* 26:423–44.

Loffler, G. 2004. An anatomy of rating through the cycle. *Journal of Banking and Finance* 28:695–720.

Lucas, D. 1995. Default correlation and credit analysis. *Journal of Fixed Income* March:76–87.

Merton, R. 1974. On the pricing of corporate debt: the risk structure of interest rates. *Journal of Finance* 29:449–70.

Nagpal, K., and R. Bahar. 1999. An analytical approach for credit risk analysis under correlated default. *CreditMetrics Monitor* April:51–79.

Nickell, P., W. Perraudin, and S. Varotto. 2000. Stability of rating transitions. *Journal of Banking & Finance* 24:203–27.

Rosch, D. 2003. Correlations and business cycles of credit risks: evidence from bankruptcies in Germany. *Financial Markets and Portfolio Management* 17:309–31.

Rosch, D. 2005. An empirical comparison of default risk forecasts from alternative credit rating philosophies. *International Journal of Forecasting* 21:37–51.

Santomero, A., and D. Babbel. 1996. Risk management by insurers: an analysis of the process. Wharton Financial Institutions Center, Discussion Paper 96-16.

Stulz, R. 1998. *Derivatives, Risk Management and Financial Engineering*. Belmont, CA: Southwestern Publishing.

Wang, T. 1998. A characterization of dynamic risk measures. University of British Columbia Discussion Paper (October).

Zhou, C. 1997. A jump diffusion approach to modeling credit risk and valuing defaultable securities. Finance and Economics, Federal Reserve Board Discussion Paper.

Index

42,